UNIVERSITY OF MAINE ICE HOCKEY

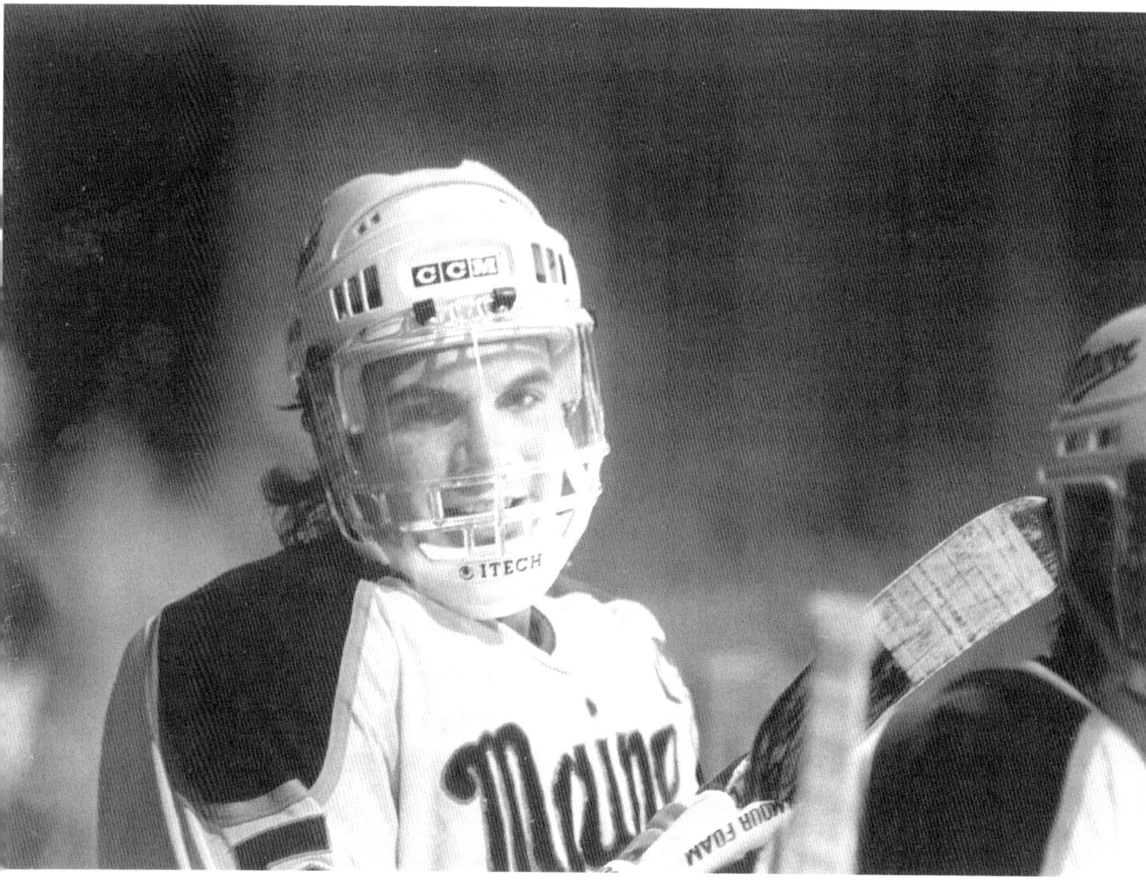

ERIC WEINRICH. Mainer, Olympian, All-American, NHL star, and University of Maine great Eric "Weino" Weinrich is seen here.

On the front cover: **WALSH AND PLAYERS.** Legendary coach Shawn Walsh instructs players Dave Wensley (No. 22) and Bob Corkum (No. 19) during a home game at the Harold Alfond Sports Arena. (Courtesy of the University of Maine.)

On the back cover: **FIRST GAME.** Harold Alfond shakes hands with Maine captain Gary Conn before the first game at Alfond Arena on November 19, 1978, against Arcadia University. Maine won 7-5. (Courtesy of the University of Maine.)

Cover background: **ENTHUSIASTIC FANS AT ALFOND.** Maine fans enjoy their Black Bears at a sold-out Alfond Arena. (Courtesy of the University of Maine.)

UNIVERSITY OF MAINE ICE HOCKEY

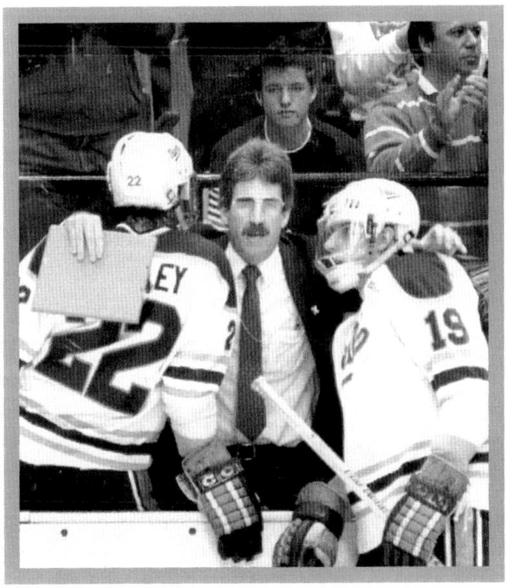

Bob Briggs

ARCADIA PUBLISHING

ISBN 978-0-7385-5515-7

Published by Arcadia Publishing
Charleston SC, Chicago IL, Portsmouth NH, San Francisco CA

Printed in the United States of America

Library of Congress Catalog Card Number: 2007929497

For all general information contact Arcadia Publishing at:
Telephone 843-853-2070
Fax 843-853-0044
E-mail sales@arcadiapublishing.com
For customer service and orders:
Toll-Free 1-888-313-2665

Visit us on the Internet at www.arcadiapublishing.com

To my father, Robert H. Briggs, class of 1950, Beta Theta Pi, and my niece, Ashleigh Marie Briggs, class of 2009.

CONTENTS

ACKNOWLEDGMENTS

I am happy for the opportunity to acknowledge the efforts of all those who contributed to this book. Many thanks to Brent Williamson, assistant athletic director for public relations, for leading me through the proper channels. Thanks Brent for loaning me your *Men's Ice Hockey Media Guide*, which has been a valuable reference.

I am grateful for the tremendous resources that lie on the third floor of the Raymond H. Fogler Library Special Collections. My thanks to Richard Hollinger, Elaine Smith, Jeffery Hollowell, and Brenda Howitson Steeves for their patient assistance.

To Michael Shepherd for his help in research and scanning photographs. A special thanks to Steve Solloway, the premier sports writer in New England, for writing a notable introduction. Also to my brother-in-law Tim Nevins, who is slowly making me computer literate. And to Stephanie Palleschi for editing and proofreading the manuscript.

A special thanks to photographer Michael York, who was behind the camera for the vast majority of the images you are about to view. I count this book as much his as it is mine.

Unless otherwise noted, all images are the property of the University of Maine.

The author can be reached at rcbriggs.1@netzero.net.

INTRODUCTION

The passage of time has blurred the precise motions but not the imagery. Paul Kariya passes the puck to line mate Jim Montgomery, who beats the opposing goalkeeper. Coming in the last period of the last game of the 1993 college hockey season, it was the shot of hope.

The University of Maine now trailed Lake Superior State by one goal, 4-3. Sitting in the press box at the Bradley Center in Milwaukee, I looked at my colleague from the *Portland Press Herald*. Can Maine come back? Mike Lowe shook his head. He didn't think so.

The story of a state's love affair with its university hockey team didn't begin that April evening in the game for the NCAA Division I national championship. But what happened in that final 20 minutes helps explain the state of Maine's fascination and its fanaticism, if you will, with the coaches and the players who are Maine hockey.

Kariya had the puck again. He was just a freshman but had gifts that belied his youth. The day before he was presented with college hockey's most important individual prize, the Hobey Baker Memorial Award. Montgomery, the senior captain, was also a finalist, and both had entered the hotel ballroom together with their coach Shawn Walsh for the presentation. Many in the crowd of hundreds of Maine hockey fans stood on chairs. The cheering became a roar.

Kariya stepped to the microphone. He stepped back. For one of the few times, his unshakable poise was shaken. The crowd went crazy.

On the ice, Montgomery looked to Kariya. With Cal Ingraham, they had played together for just one season but had developed that sense of anticipation of what the other would do. Montgomery took the pass and scored again. Now the score was tied at 4-4. My colleague looked at me.

Maine is going to win, he said.

The success of Maine hockey didn't happen overnight. A brash, young coach named Shawn Walsh arrived in 1984, building on what Jack Semler had started with the first Maine team in 1977. Walsh beat the drums and sounded the trumpets even when Maine lost and the Black Bears did. Walsh wasn't shy, and he was stubbornly optimistic. He was laying the groundwork, he insisted. Watch and see. Mainers did just that.

Once more, Kariya took control of the puck. Minutes had fallen off the scoreboard clock, but there was still time. Days earlier, Walsh had courted the Wisconsin crowd. With their team eliminated in the NCAA regional tournament, he asked them to adopt the Black Bears. As Maine rallied, the Wisconsin Badger fans could not remain quiet. The noise got louder until it was bedlam as Montgomery took another shot.

He scored.

The faces have changed. College teams always renew themselves every few years as players graduate or turn professional. Cancer took Shawn Walsh, but not before his fight to beat the disease won new respect for a coach who had no peer.

The hockey program itself was shaken by the failure to heed NCAA rules. Its integrity and credibility was tested. Walsh was suspended by the university for a year, and there were cries that he be fired. He returned from his suspension a chastened and changed man, and led Maine to another national championship in 1999.

The words of Bob Briggs and the many photographs do their part to keep the story of Maine Black Bears hockey fresh. So do you, the reader, every time you turn the page and remember.

—Steve Solloway, *Portland Press Herald* writer

1

BEGINNINGS

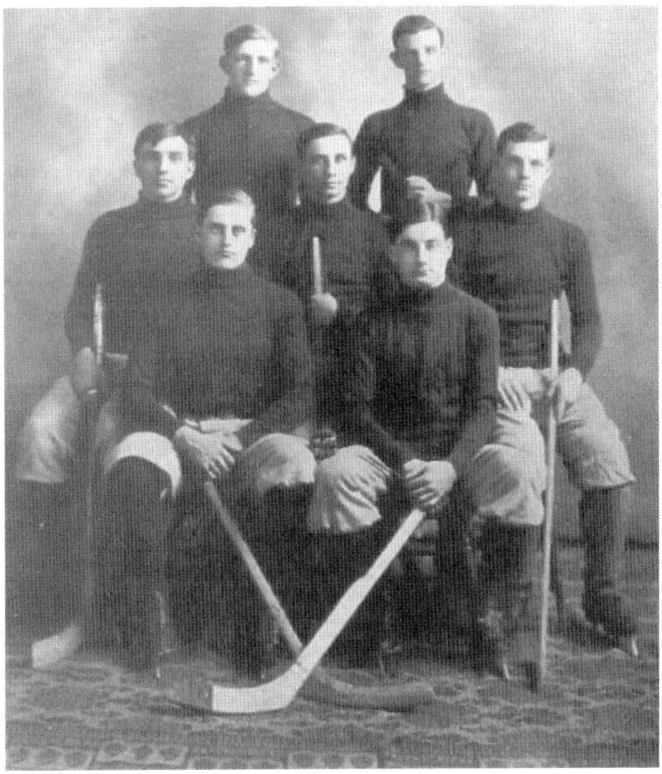

THE 1906 UNIVERSITY OF MAINE MEN'S ICE HOCKEY TEAM. From left to right are (first row) R. Lambe (acting captain) and E. Lambe; (second row) ? Milliken, ? Miner, and ? Hosmer; (third row) ? Chase and ? Bagg. The team played an eclectic schedule against in-state college rivals Bates and Bowdoin, local high school teams, fraternities, and touring professionals. University of Maine (UMaine) was the first Maine college to recognize hockey as an organized team sport.

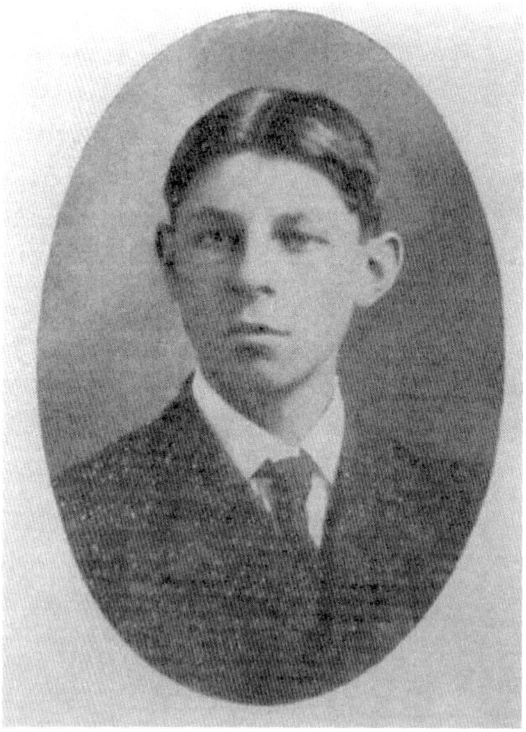

THE LAMBE BROTHERS. The Lambe brothers were the first of many brother tandems to play hockey at UMaine. Multisport athletes Emerson Peavey Lambe (left), and brother Reginald Robert Lambe (below) hailed from Calais, Maine, and studied engineering. Despite efforts to establish hockey as a varsity sport to join baseball and football, the team quickly lost its varsity status and support of the athletic association. An editorial appearing in the *Maine Campus*, however, said that a hockey program "would show the people outside our own state that Maine is not behind in any branch of college activities. If our athletes are to keep pace with our growth, a hockey team must come sooner or later, and the earlier the foundation is laid the better for us in the future."

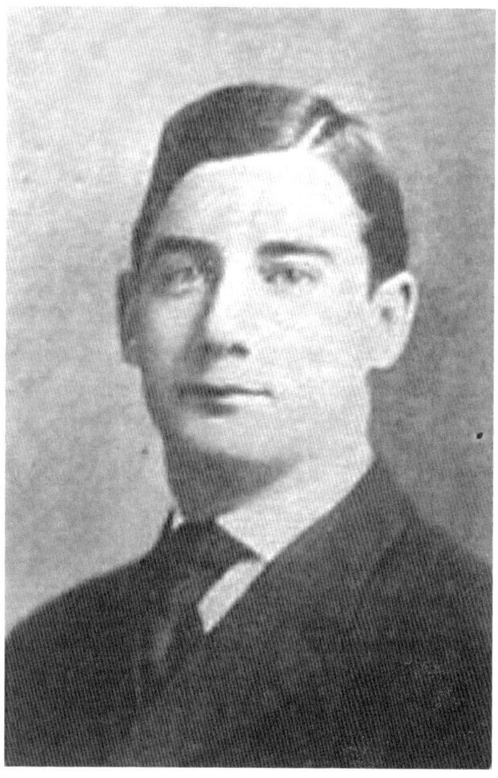

On Washington's Birthday Maine meets Bowdoin in the first intercollegiate hockey game ever played at Maine. The bleachers on the athletic field are to be placed on the ice surrounding the rink to accomodate the spectators. As this is something entirely new in the line of athletics in the state, a good attendance is expected. At least every man in college should see the game. Any game with Bowdoin is sure to arouse a good deal of interest among the student body and all who attend will not go home disappointed. The game will be called at three o'clock.

MAINE TO MEET ARCHRIVAL BOWDOIN. An advertisement in the *Maine Campus* entices students to attend the game against Bowdoin. The game was held at Bowdoin on a portion of the football field that had been flooded for the occasion. Home games at Maine were played on the Stillwater River in front of the campus. Games were contingent, however, on there being sufficient ice.

The first intercollegiate hockey game ever played in Maine was played on the ic hittier field Saturday afternoon, Feb. 16, between Bowdoin and the University of Maine. Bowdoin won by a score of 4 to 1. The game was witnessed by a good sized crowd, and it is fafe to predict that another winter will see the game very popular among the Maine colleges.

The first goal of the game was quickly scored. Maine rushed the puck down the rink to a point directly in front of Bowdoin's goal, where in a scrimmage, in which several men were mixed up, R. Lamb, the Maine center, succeeded in sending the rubber disk between the goal posts. The next 15 minutes passed with no scoring on either side. The puck remained in the vicinity of the Bowdoin goal the greater part of the time, but the Maine men were unable to put it between the posts. The puck was sent up and down the rink, and then Dresser, the Bowdoin center, made a pretty shot from about the middle of the field, sending the puck directly between the Maine goal posts. This ended the scoring for the first half, although several times both sides came near accomplishing the trick.

The second half Bowdoin made a decided change in its work, and played a far better game than in the first half. Cleaves twice shot the puck through the Maine goal posts, and Abbott scored once. This was all the scoring of the half.

Dresser, Hughes, and Abbott all played excellent games for Bowdoin, and R. Lamb, Milliken and Miner all did good work for Maine. An unpleasant feature of the game was the condition of the ice, which was so soft that the skates cut it badly. The worst place was on the rink in the vicinity of west goal, and it was in front of this goal that the greater part of the playing was done. Bowdoin defended it during the first half and Maine the second. Several times a forward would start toward the goal with a clear field only to lose the puck in the uneven places of the ice. It is safe to say that had the ice been hard both sides would have scored much more. The bad condition of the ice also interfered with the skating and caused many falls, which otherwise would have been avoided.

FIRST INTERCOLLEGIATE GAME FOR MAINE HOCKEY. A reporter for the *Maine Campus* traveled to Brunswick to capture the historic event of the first-ever intercollegiate hockey game played in Maine. "The game was witnessed by a good size crowd, and it is safe to predict that another winter will see the game very popular among the Maine colleges. . . . intercollegiate hockey has probably come into Maine athletics to stay," said the writer. Bowdoin won by a 4-1 count.

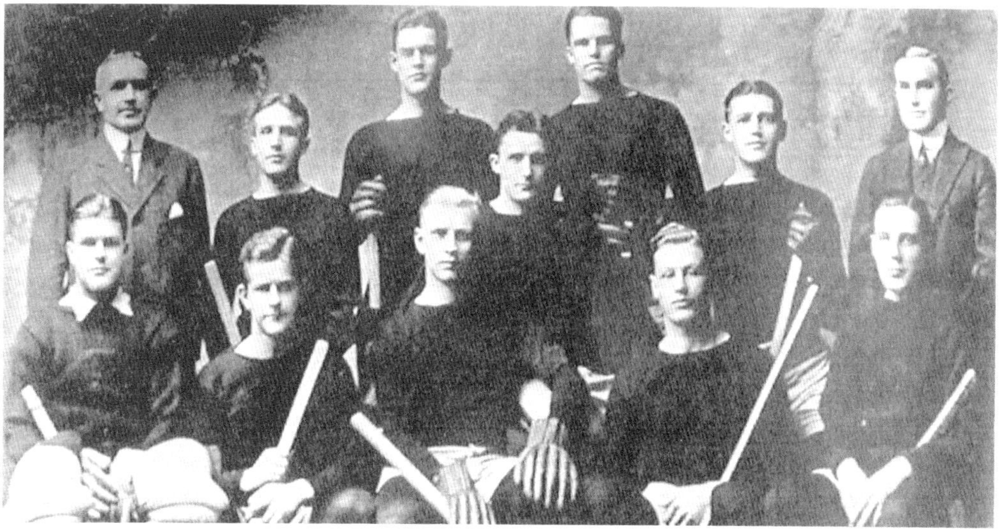

PRINCETON UNIVERSITY MEN'S ICE HOCKEY TEAM, 1911. Seated in the first row, fourth from the left, is Hobey Baker. While the state of Maine seemed an ideal environment to be the genesis for hockey in the United States, it was in the eastern Ivy League schools like Princeton where hockey began to take root. The modern game in North America was developed at McGill University in Montreal in 1875, with official rules being posted in the *Montreal Gazette* in 1877. Hockey began to gain momentum in the United States in the 1890s. In 1893, organized matches between Yale, Princeton, John Hopkins, Harvard, and Brown took place and leagues were formed. In the 1920s, teams and leagues were formed in the Midwest as the game's popularity began to spread. In 1948, the NCAA took over governing the sport and eventually broke college hockey into three divisions.

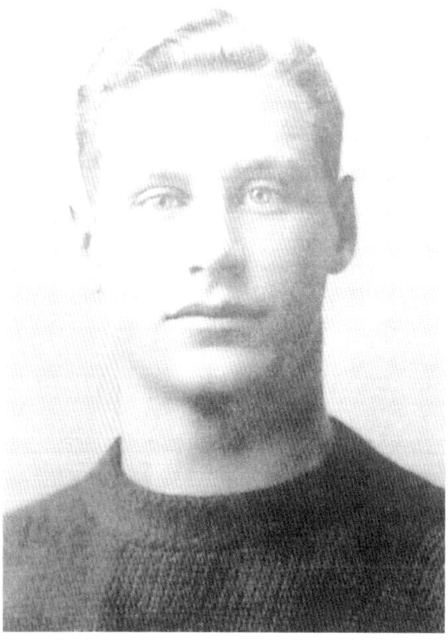

HOCKEY PIONEER HOBEY BAKER. Hobey Baker was a three-sport athlete at Princeton who led the Princeton hockey team to two national titles. He is considered the greatest hockey player of his era. Baker enlisted in the U.S. Army as a pilot in 1917 and was killed in a tragic air accident returning from the war. The award given to the top college hockey player in the nation bears his name.

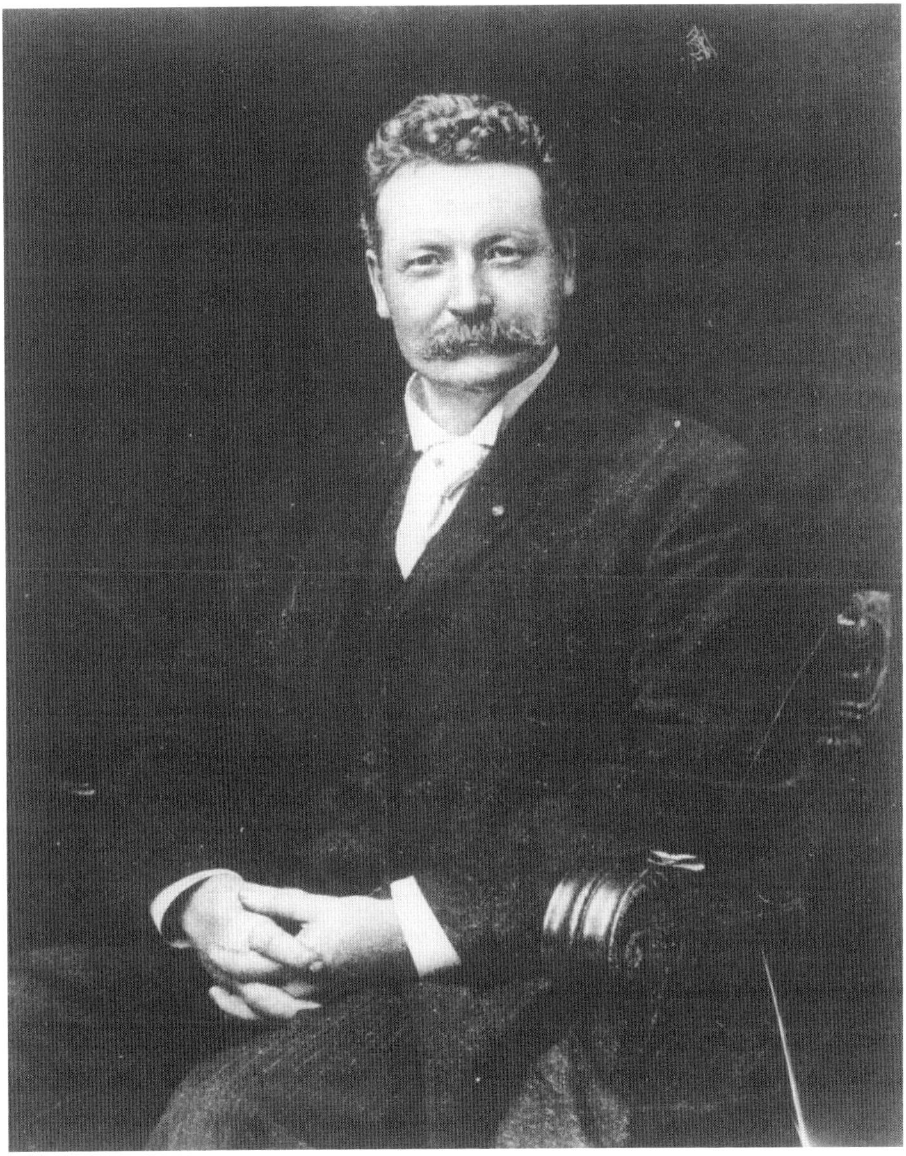

UMaine President George Emory Fellows. A hopeful beginning for hockey being established as a varsity sport was lost in part to a lack of competition. After displaying some interest, Colby backed out of the formation of a league with Bates and Bowdoin. Perhaps the greater obstacle, however, was the stance on athletics in general taken by UMaine president George Fellows. He was quoted in a 1908 issue of the *Illustrated Outdoor News* as saying, "Whenever the alumni or friends of a college or university are disposed to furnish means of corruption, or, to use a milder term, for assisting young men through college where the well known purpose of these young men is to be a star in athletics, deplorable conditions will exist." Besides, baseball and football were firmly entrenched at the university with substantial gate receipts helping to defray their costs. And who wanted to watch a game played outside in the blistery cold?

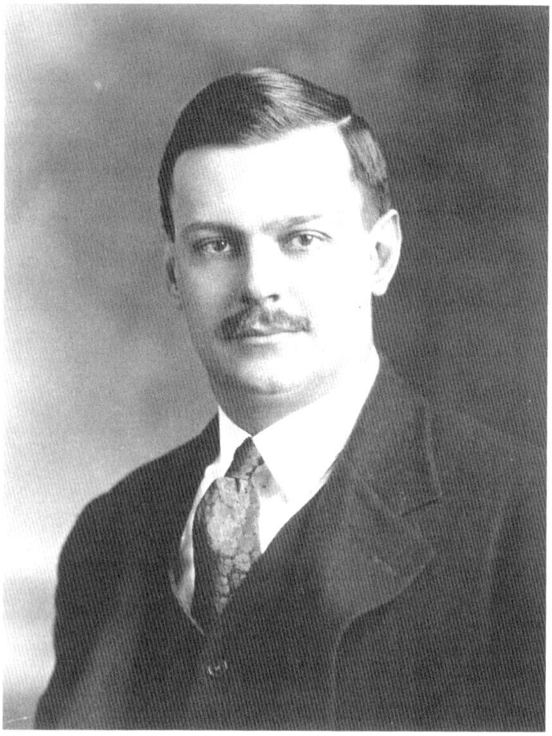

UMaine President Clarence Cook Little. Clarence Cook Little had a much different philosophy about athletics and the benefits of competing. In the early 1920s, athletics enjoyed a renaissance at the university. Little believed that a college education must challenge the body as well as the mind. He opened the campaign for the building of the Memorial Gymnasium and Armory and was an advocate for women's athletics. In 1922, hockey made another appearance as a varsity sport at UMaine although it was listed as a "minor sport." One of Little's hires was James T. " Cuddy" Murphy to coach the team.

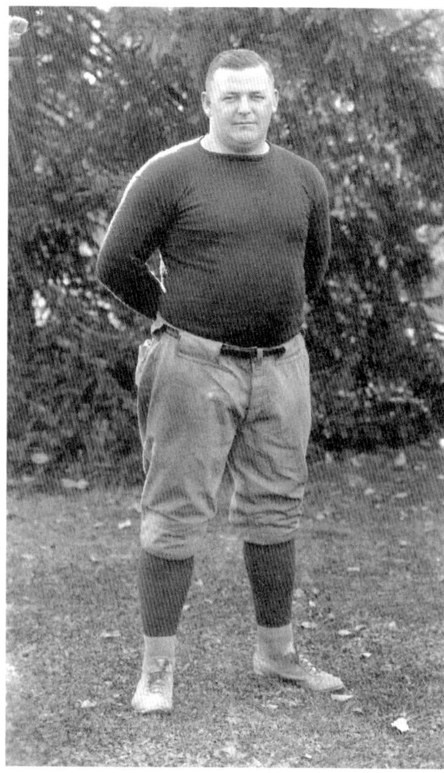

All-Year Coach James T. Murphy. Murphy was hired as an "all year coach" and he did just that. He was the assistant football coach in the fall, assistant baseball coach in the spring, and head hockey coach in the winter. Murphy was himself an accomplished athlete. An All-American at Dartmouth, he set records in the shot, hammer, and discuss. He played professional baseball for the Boston Red Sox and professional football for the Canton Bulldogs under the legendary Jim Thorpe. He later became the athletic director at Dartmouth College.

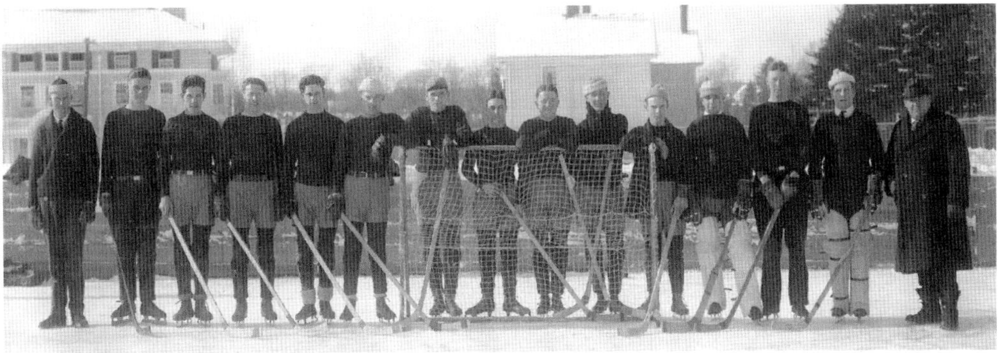

THE 1922–1923 UMAINE MEN'S ICE HOCKEY TEAM. Members of the team included C. J. Austin, D. T. Stearns, W. R. Elliot, R. D. Mackay, C. N. Stover, R. B. Stone, J. H. Foster, C. L. Baxter, R. G. Coakley, and coach J. T. Murphy. The Black Bears posted a 2-3 record with wins over in-state rivals Colby and Bates. Home games were played on an outdoor rink where the Corbett Hall and the Memorial Gymnasium parking lot now exist.

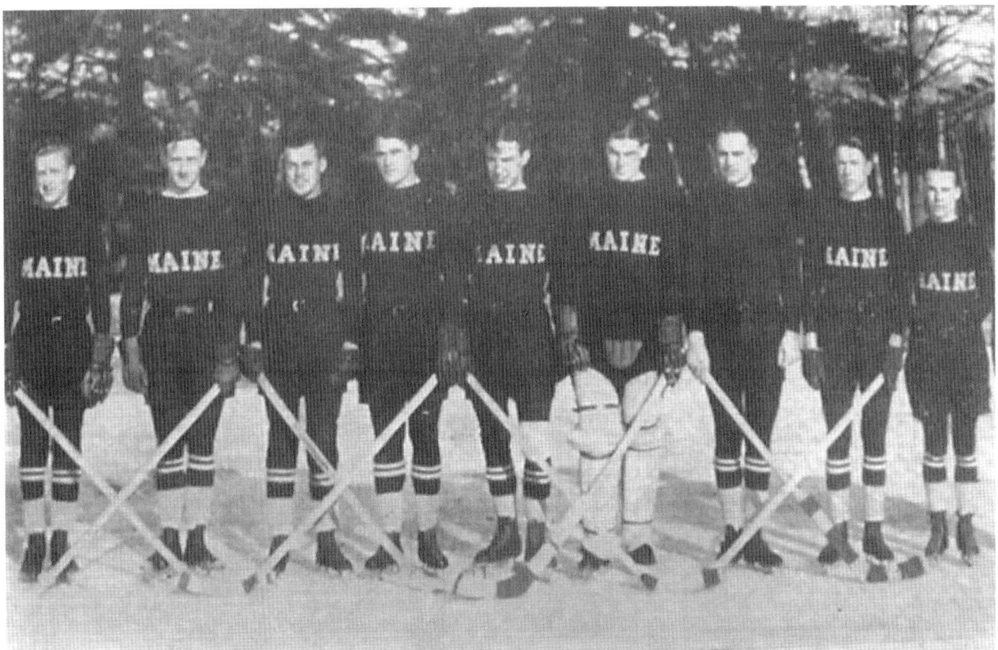

THE 1923–1924 UMAINE MEN'S ICE HOCKEY TEAM. The team upgraded its schedule to include 12 games and new competitors, including Boston University. While the team finished at 4-8, it posted big wins over Bowdoin and Boston University and showed promise under first-year coach Stanley Wallace. Despite the improved schedule and enthusiastic response from the student body, the athletic board recommended that hockey be discontinued after the season. The board promised, however, that varsity hockey would be restored as soon as an indoor facility could be built. It would be a long, cold wait until a facility was finally built in 1976.

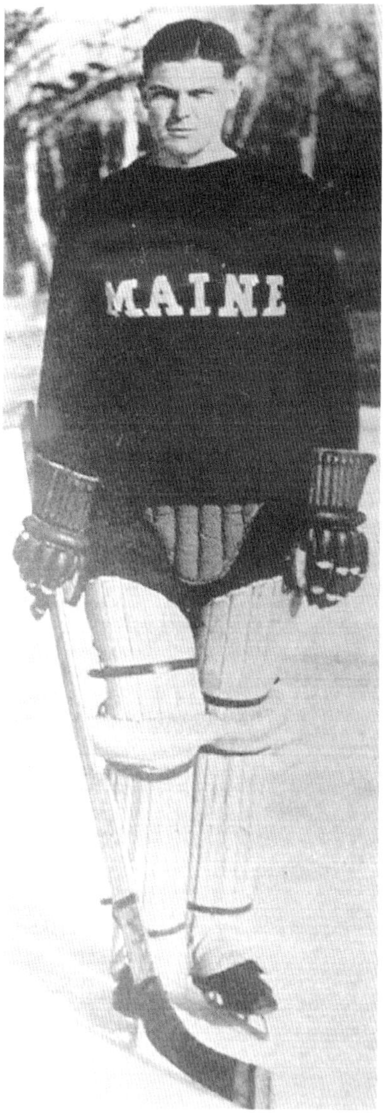

CAPTAIN CHARLES BAXTER IN THE HOCKEY GEAR OF THE DAY. Administrators also saw hockey as a dangerous sport. Its hard checking action, pucks traveling in excess of 100 miles per hour, and games played on a hard, unyielding surface all led to serious injury. The game could only be played outside and under sometimes dangerous weather conditions to both players and fans alike. Protective equipment for hockey players, such as goalie pads, goalie masks, and helmets, while invented in the 1920s, were not in general use. Although leather hockey gloves had been in use since the early 1900s, they were heavy and often used as a weapon. Skates were sometimes merely a steel blade clamped on a boot or shoe. In 1913, a hockey skirt was developed to add some protection, which was minimal at best. Most hockey sticks were custom made from a single piece of wood, usually hickory, with short handles and small rounded blades. Goalies protected themselves with the wicket keepers' pads used by cricket players.

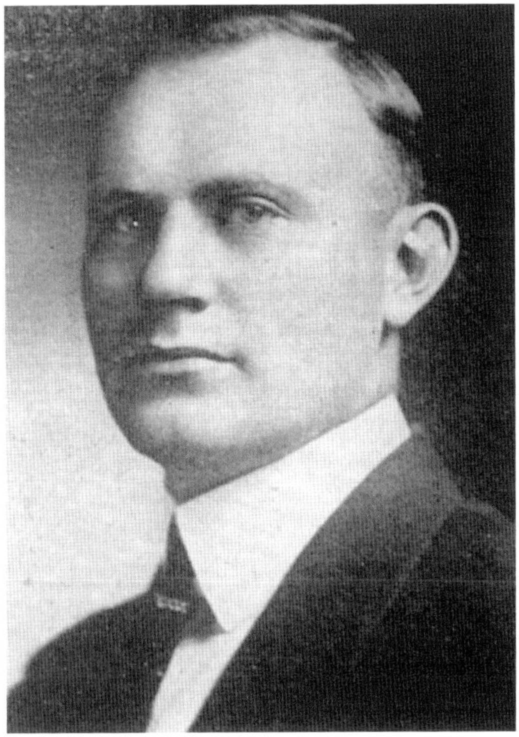

TEACHER AND COACH STANLEY WALLACE. Stanley Wallace came to the university in 1921 after graduating from Arnold College, where he excelled in basketball, baseball, and track. His appearance as men's ice hockey coach in 1923–1924 would be his last, and there would be a 54-year gap between Wallace and the next hockey coach, Jack Semler. Wallace is credited with establishing and sustaining an extensive intramural program at the university that included ice hockey.

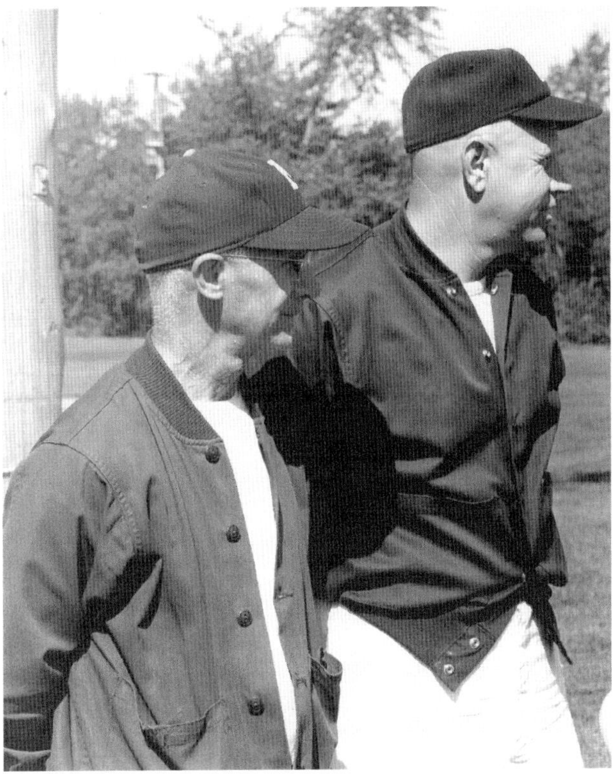

WALLACE AND HEAD FOOTBALL COACH HAROLD WOODBURY IN 1958. Although he advocated a return for men's hockey as a varsity sport, Wallace never saw it happen in his long tenure at the university (1921–1959). His work in establishing hockey as an intramural sport, however, kept the dream alive. At UMaine, Wallace served as coach, physical education instructor, and sports trainer. The Olympic-size pool located inside the Memorial Gymnasium was named in his honor.

NEW SKATING RINK FOR WOMEN ONLY

—M—

"For Women Only," the Girls' Athletic Association is having made a skating rink, 80 by 180 feet, on the stream back of the power house. This - ll be for the girls only unless the Intermural Association decides to cooperate with the Girls' A. A. in the cost of building and upkeep. In this case both men and women will have opportunity to use the rink and definite days will be set aside for the men's hockey team.

EQUAL TIME FOR WOMEN. Stanley Wallace and Pres. Clarence Cook Little were both advocates for women's athletics. A varsity basketball team and a field hockey team were both established in the 1920s. This notice appeared in a 1924 *Maine Campus* for the completion of a women's ice rink. The university, however, later decided to eliminate intercollegiate women's sports, and from 1931 to the early 1970s there was no varsity competition for females.

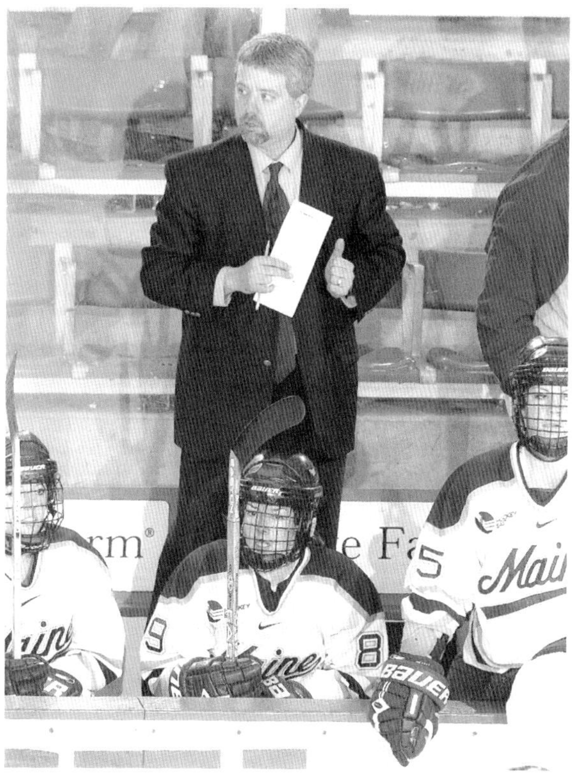

COACH RICK FILIGHERA. In 1997, a women's varsity ice hockey team was formed and played its home games at the Alfond Arena. The team had a successful season at 12 wins, 6 losses, and 2 ties.

LYRICS TO THE MAINE "STEIN SONG." Although varsity sports programs in the late 1920s were being cut back, it did not curtail the increasing popularity of the UMaine sports fight song, also known as the "University of Maine Stein Song." Lyrics to the song and composition were provided by two UMaine graduates, Lincoln Colcord and Adelbert W. Sprague. It was crooner Rudy Vallee (below), however, who popularized it as host of the *Fleischman Radio Hour.* It became the only college fight song to ever reach No. 1 on the pop charts, which it did in 1930. However, its obvious reference to drinking led to protests from temperance groups who said it was in violation of the Volstead Act and the ethics of a reputable college.

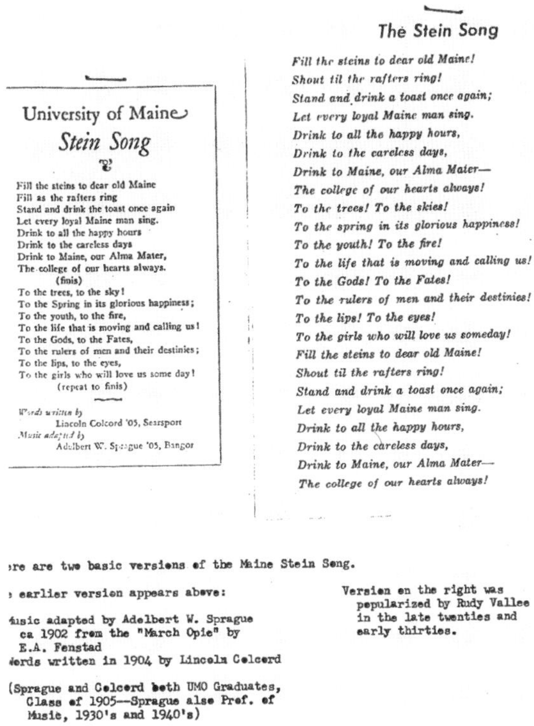
University of Maine
Stein Song

Fill the steins to dear old Maine
Fill as the rafters ring
Stand and drink the toast once again
Let every loyal Maine man sing.
Drink to all the happy hours
Drink to the careless days
Drink to Maine, our Alma Mater,
The college of our hearts always.
(finis)
To the trees, to the sky!
To the Spring in its glorious happiness;
To the youth, to the fire,
To the life that is moving and calling us!
To the Gods, to the Fates,
To the rulers of men and their destinies;
To the lips, to the eyes,
To the girls who will love us some day!
(repeat to finis)

Words written by
Lincoln Colcord '05, Searsport
Music adapted by
Adelbert W. Sprague '05, Bangor

The Stein Song

Fill the steins to dear old Maine!
Shout til the rafters ring!
Stand and drink a toast once again;
Let every loyal Maine man sing.
Drink to all the happy hours,
Drink to the careless days,
Drink to Maine, our Alma Mater—
The college of our hearts always!
To the trees! To the skies!
To the spring in its glorious happiness!
To the youth! To the fire!
To the life that is moving and calling us!
To the Gods! To the Fates!
To the rulers of men and their destinies!
To the lips! To the eyes!
To the girls who will love us someday!
Fill the steins to dear old Maine!
Shout til the rafters ring!
Stand and drink a toast once again;
Let every loyal Maine man sing.
Drink to all the happy hours,
Drink to the careless days,
Drink to Maine, our Alma Mater—
The college of our hearts always!

re are twe basic versiens ef the Maine Stein Seng.

earlier versien appears abeve:

usic adapted by Adelbert W. Sprague
ca 1902 frem the "March Opie" by
E.A. Fenstad
erds written in 1904 by Lincela Celcerd

(Sprague and Celcerd beth UMO Graduates,
Class ef 1905—Sprague alse Pref. ef
Music, 1930's and 1940's)

Versien en the right was
pepularized by Rudy Vallee
in the late twenties and
early thirties.

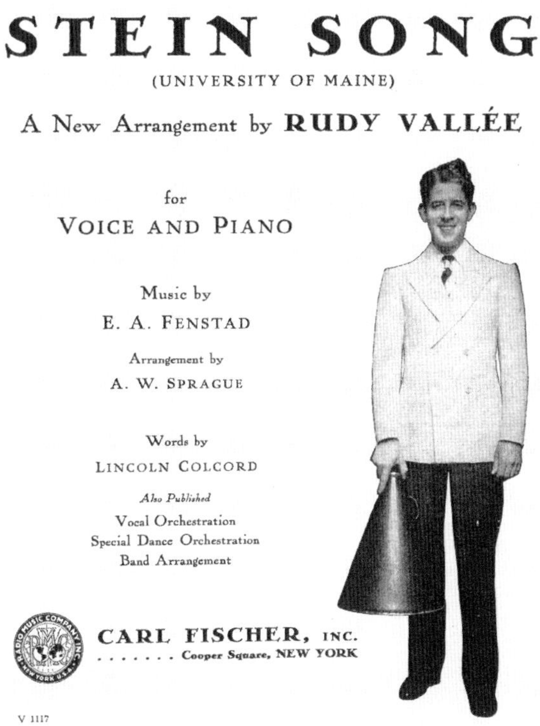

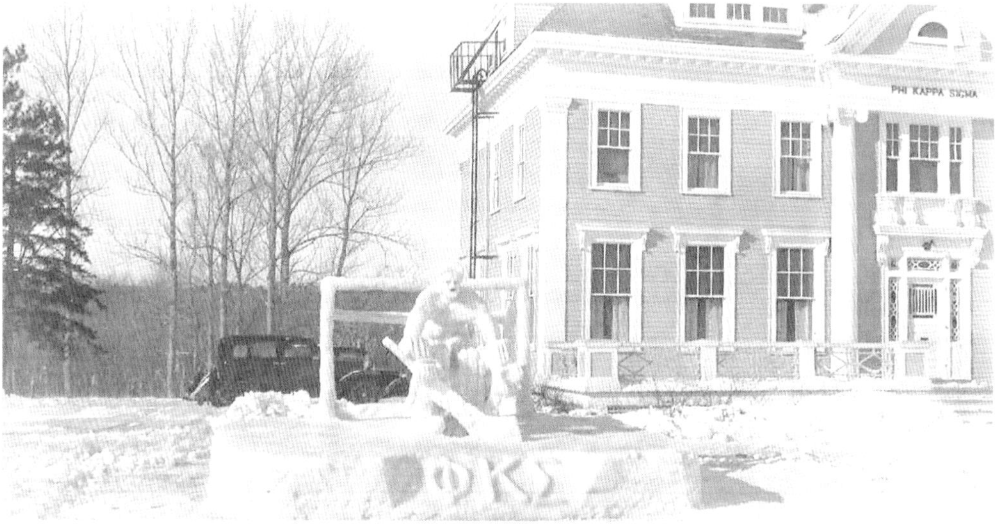

UMaine Hockey Alive But Not Well. Frozen monuments are one of the few reminders that hockey was alive at the university for the next 52 years. From time to time there were attempts to form clubs that would play local teams. The intramural program offered heated rivalries between fraternities such as Phi Kappa Sigma, seen above. For the decades of the 1930s, 1940s, 1950s, and 1960s, hockey at the university would be the domain of intramural programs, winter carnival activities, and fraternity battles.

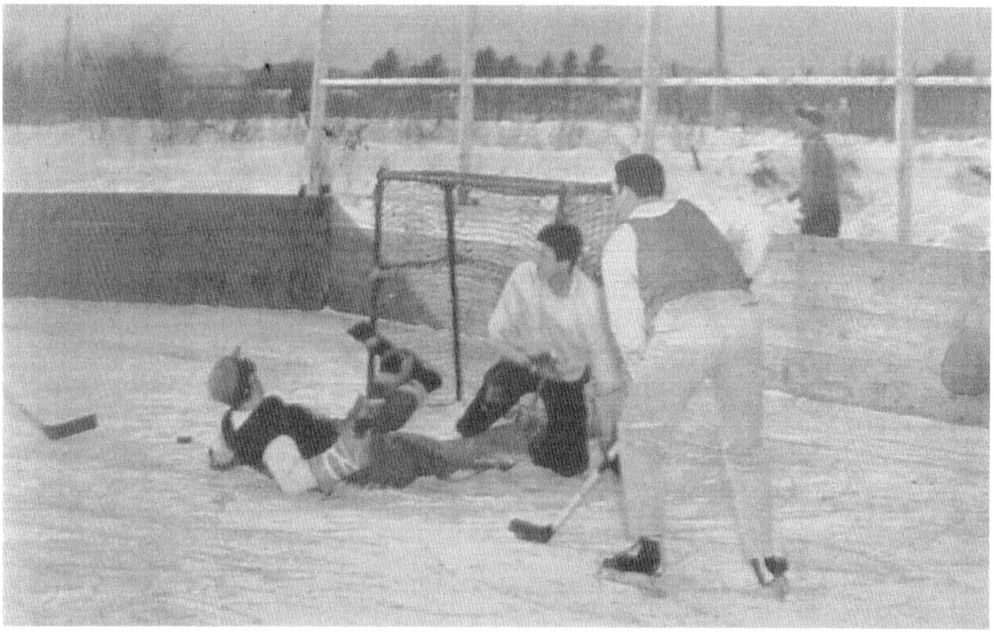

Scoring Fast And Furious. The 1950 *Prism* offers this image of a fraternity game played on the Stillwater River, just across from the ski jump that was located on the other bank. The event was part of winter carnival activities taking place at the university. The caption read in part "score 12-9, where are the goalies?"

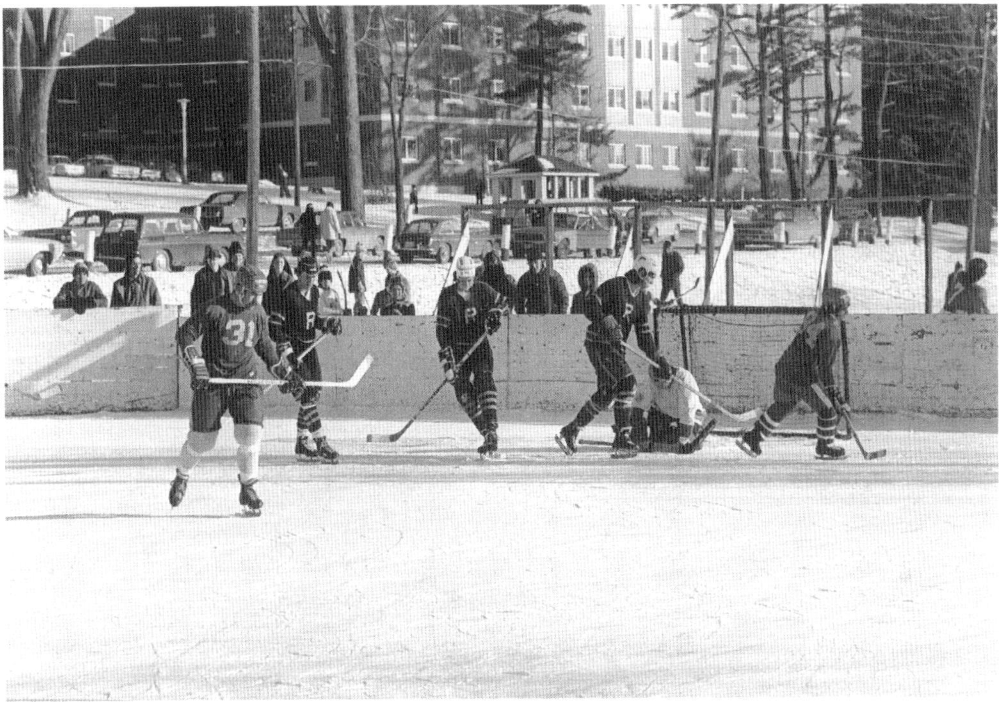

UMaine Hockey Club in Action. In the early 1970s, a fresh move to form a club sport, just under varsity level, was born. There were rumblings about an indoor rink being built next to the field house, and a UMaine hockey club to supplement the intramural hockey program was needed. UMaine student Glen Bushel and Dr. Fred Bibilbert helped found the club. The athletic department helped by furnishing goalie equipment, pucks, and nets and maintaining the ice. Once again, the program would rise or fall on the establishment of a new indoor arena.

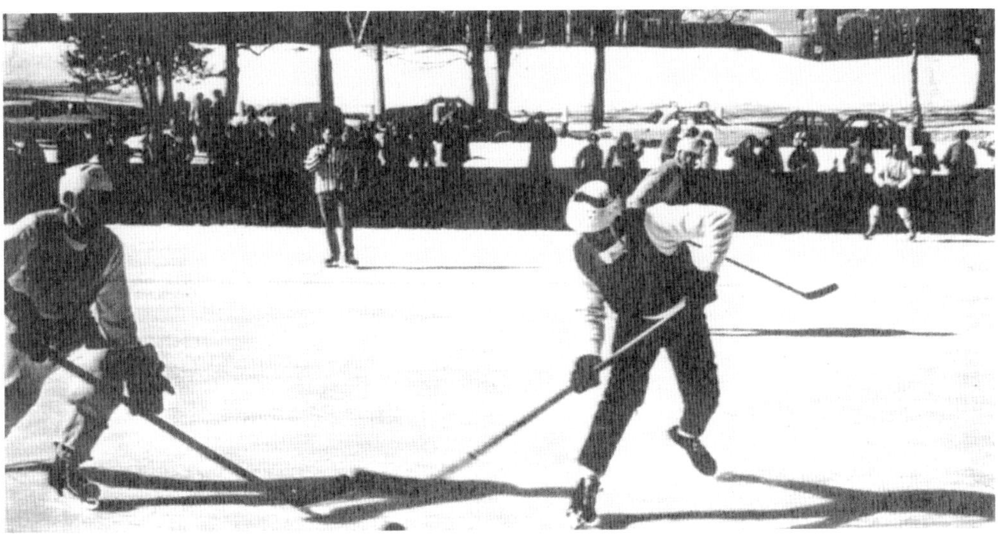

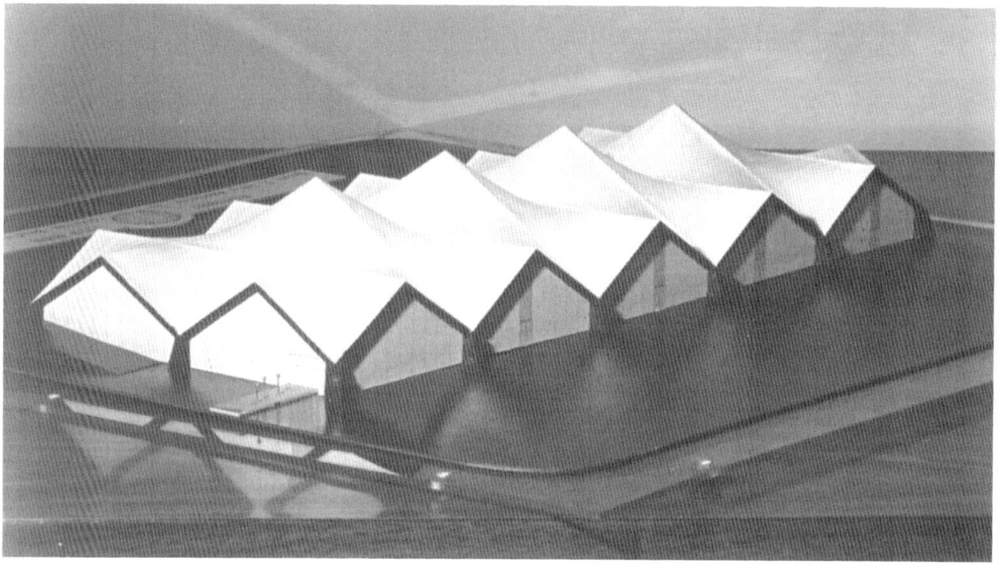

Artists Conception of the New Ice Hockey Facility at UMaine. Ever since it was first envisioned to establish hockey as a varsity sport at UMaine, there have been various moves to build a suitable arena. "As a result of a recent action of the executive committee of the Athletic Association in appropriating money to build a rink, hockey has at last gained a foothold here at the university," wrote the *Maine Campus* in 1906. The *Maine Campus* wrote again in 1923 that "work on the new rink is being rushed . . . one of the largest in the state. It is to be illuminated by a complex system of lights that will make it as bright as day." Although administrators vowed that hockey would be restored as soon as an indoor facility could be constructed, it would take the generosity of a Maine man, Harold Alfond, to finally get the puck rolling.

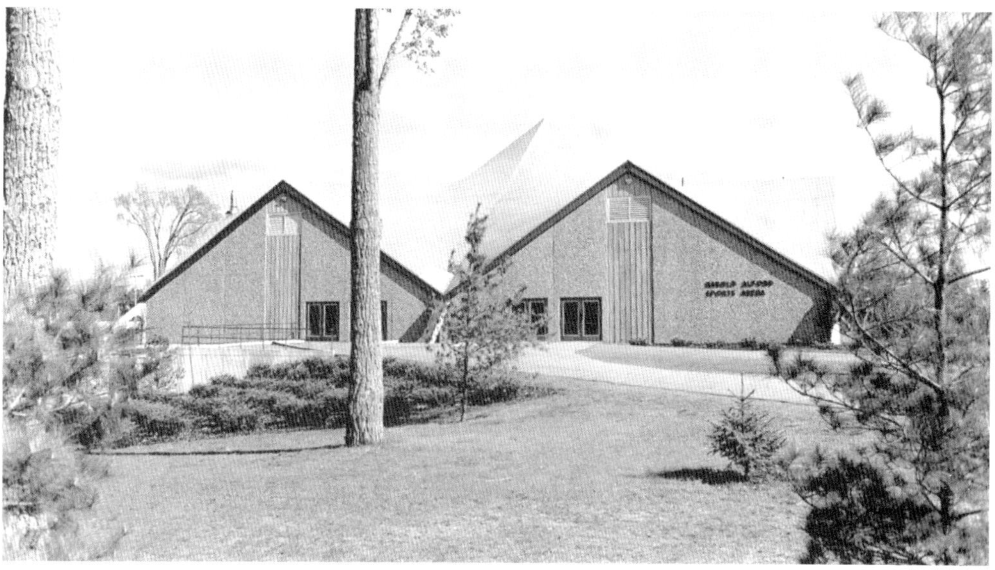

From Dream to Reality. This image shows the completed facility as it looked in the fall of 1978. Many changes to the building and the program lie ahead.

2

A HOME FOR HOCKEY

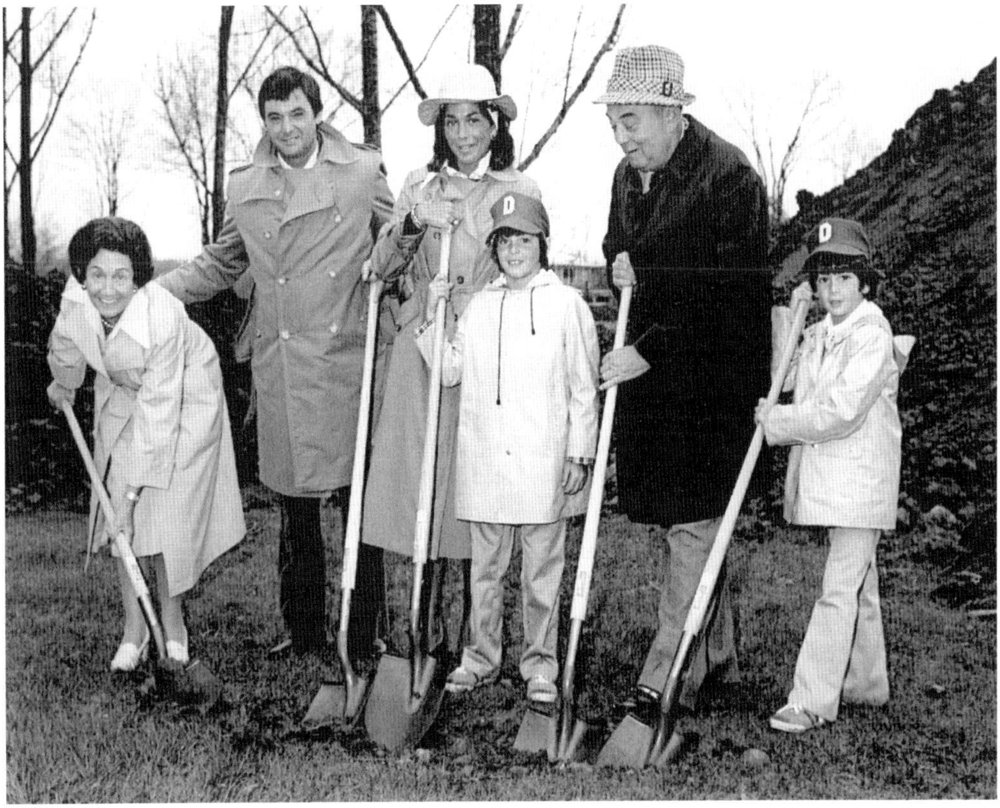

GROUNDBREAKING CEREMONY FOR THE NEW HAROLD ALFOND SPORTS ARENA. An outstanding high school athlete and lifelong sports enthusiast, Harold Alfond enabled the dream to become a reality with a large bequest that would bring hockey back to UMaine to stay. In 1956, Alfond founded the Dexter Shoe Company and from its home base in Dexter, Maine, began selling to big box stores like Sears and J. C. Penney. Alfond later developed his own line of shoes and is credited as being the first to open factory shoe outlets, selling shoes with slight defects at a discounted cost. In 1978, he joined a group of businessmen to purchase the Boston Red Sox and remains a limited partner in the franchise. A noted philanthropist, Alfond has given more than $100 million to charitable causes since 1950, and since 1968 more than $6.5 million to UMaine. Alfond was married to the late Dorothy "Bibby" Alfond and has four children, Ted, Susan, Bill, and Peter.

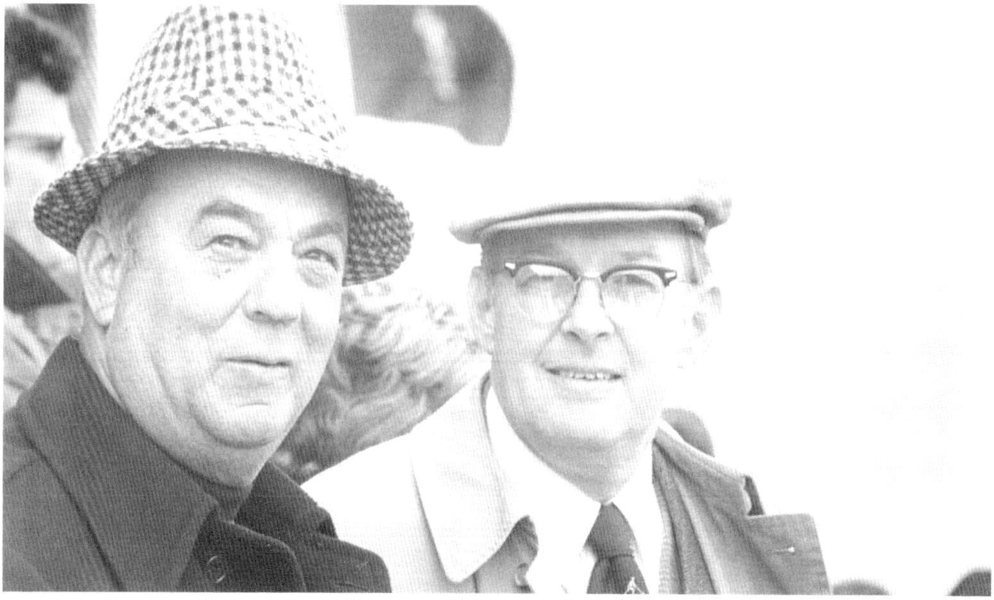

HAROLD ALFOND AT A UMAINE FOOTBALL GAME. Harold Alfond was not alone in picking up the tab. The building of a new hockey facility was truly a team effort with over 2,000 donors investing in the cause. He is seen here with UMaine president Howard Neville.

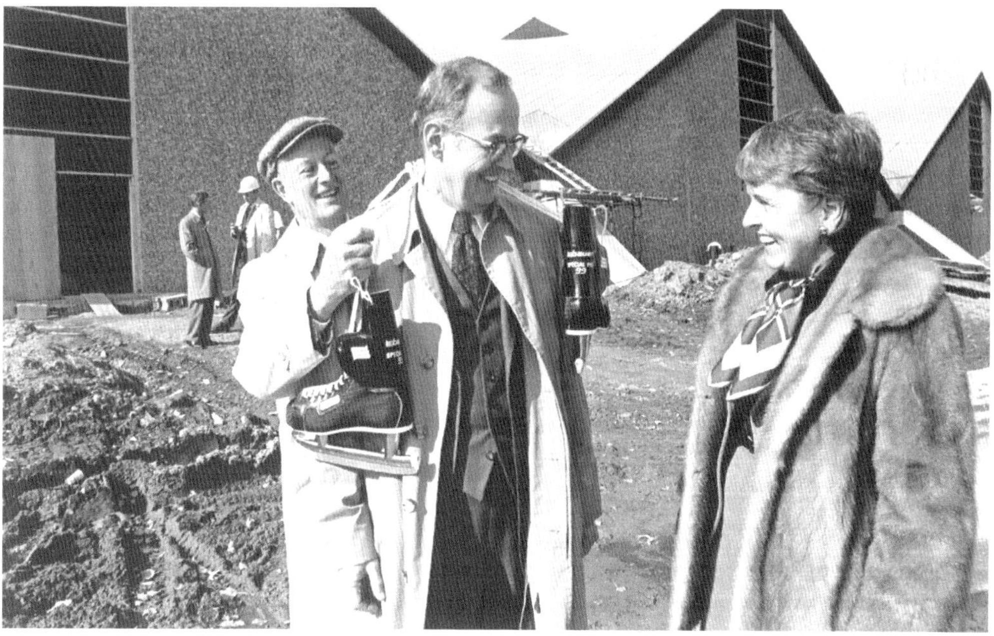

PRES. HOWARD NEVILLE ADMIRES NEW CONSTRUCTION. Working behind the scenes at the administrative level were UMaine president Howard Neville and athletic director Harold Westerman. Neville garnered support inside and outside the university, spearheading the Second Century Fund Campaign to raise money for the arena and calling the new facility "an important part of the overall learning experience that is our university."

ATHLETIC DEPARTMENT HEAD HAROLD WESTERMAN. It was Westerman's job to get the program off the ground. He put together a coaching staff for the initial season and began to recruit players. Getting tips from high school coaches and other contacts, Westerman had 80 prospects who reported to tryouts in September 1977. He got Maine to play in the East Coast Athletic Conference Division II East League. From a large pool of applicants he chose Jack Semler to be UMaine's head coach.

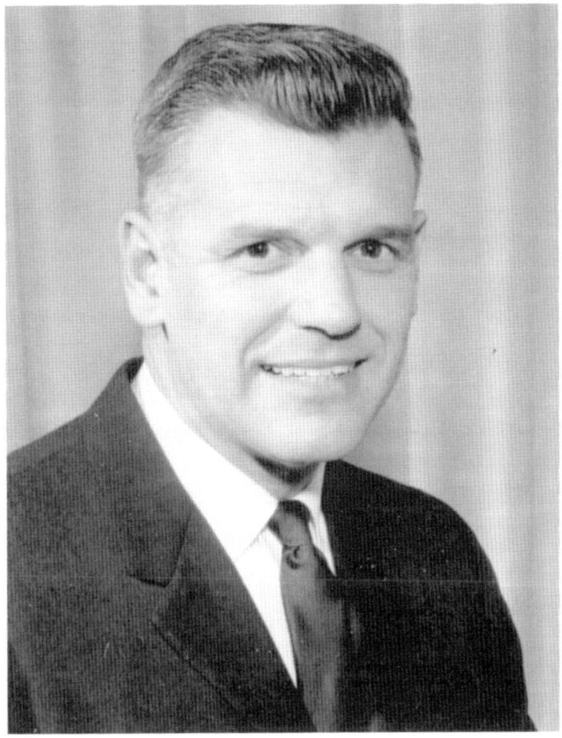

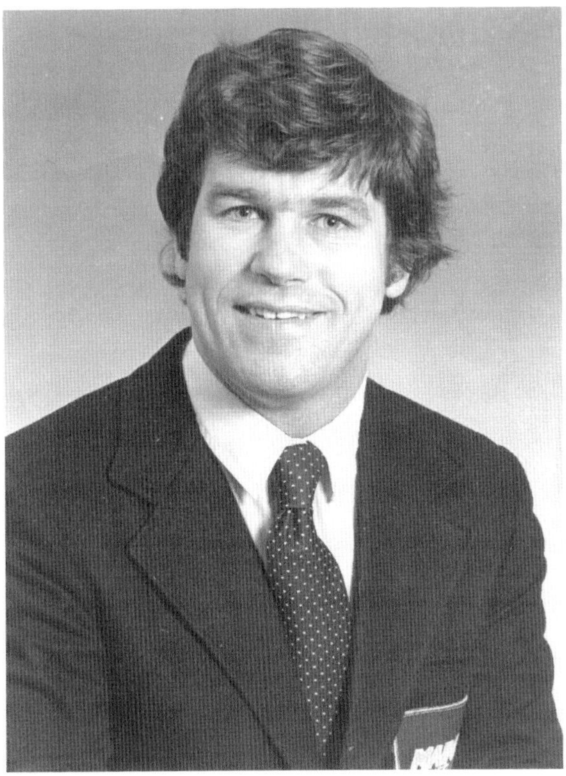

JACK SEMLER, FIRST COACH OF THE MODERN ERA. Athletic director Westerman said of the appointment, "He has a rare combination of abilities that will be of great benefit to all the skating programs within Maine's new arena. He is a skilled, dedicated, and conscientious leader and is anxious to build our hockey program within the framework of UMaine's academic and athletic policies."

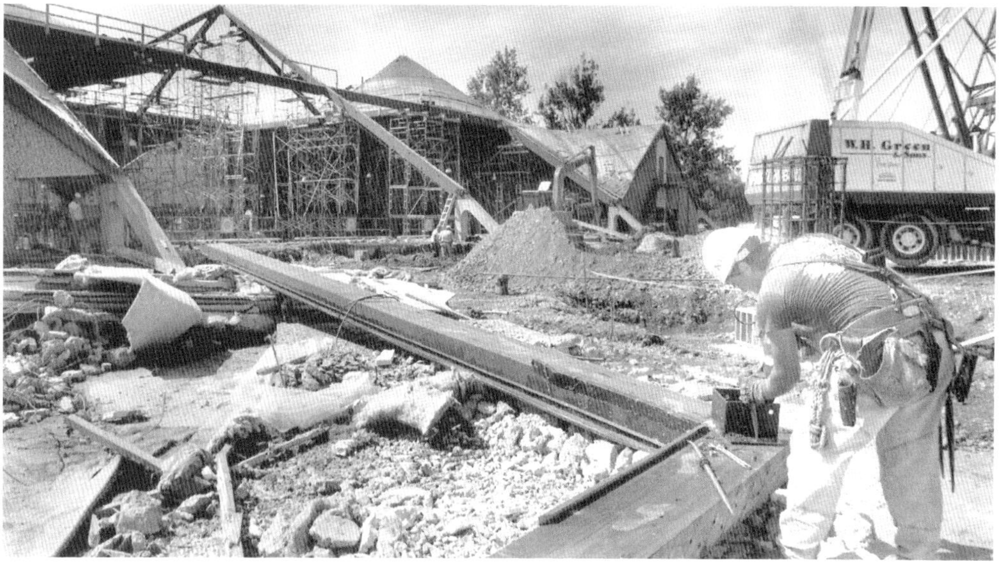

CONTRACTORS HARD AT WORK ON THE HAROLD ALFOND SPORTS ARENA. Actual construction began in May 1976 and was completed eight months later, mostly on schedule and on budget. Originally the facility was built exclusively for hockey and would accommodate 2,828 fans. Later the success of the program would necessitate a greater seating capacity. The price tag for the new facility would exceed $1.6 million.

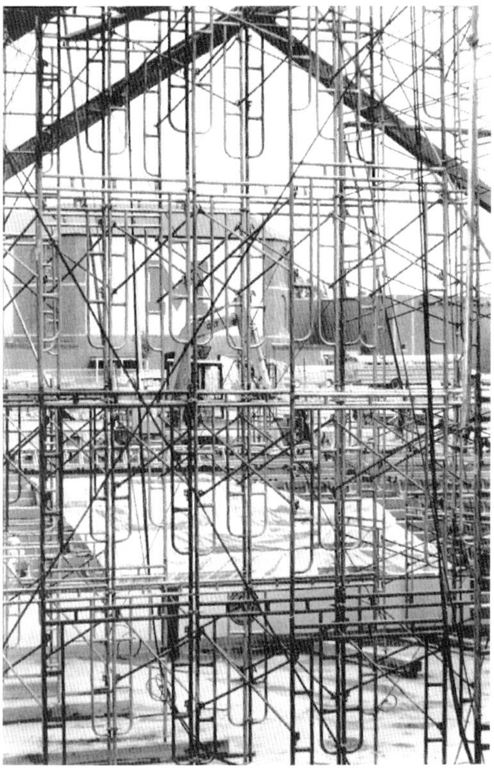

BIRDS-EYE VIEW OF THE MEMORIAL GYMNASIUM AND FIELD HOUSE. Through the skeleton of the new facility can be seen the Memorial Gymnasium and Field House that has served the university's athletes and students since 1926. The versatile building has hosted varsity track events, men's and women's basketball, wrestling, and a host of intramural activities. The facility was constructed entirely by contributions from faculty, alumni, and other interested parties in honor of those who perished in the Spanish-American War and World War I.

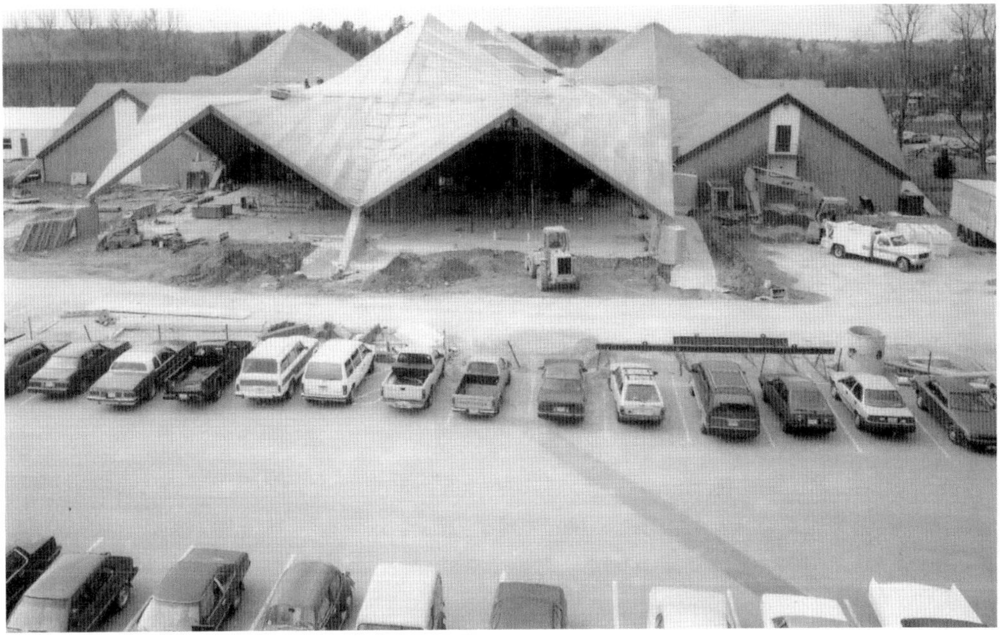

Needed: More Parking Space. The unique pavilion-style roofing can be seen in this photograph. Increased parking would be needed when seating capacity would grow to over 5,200.

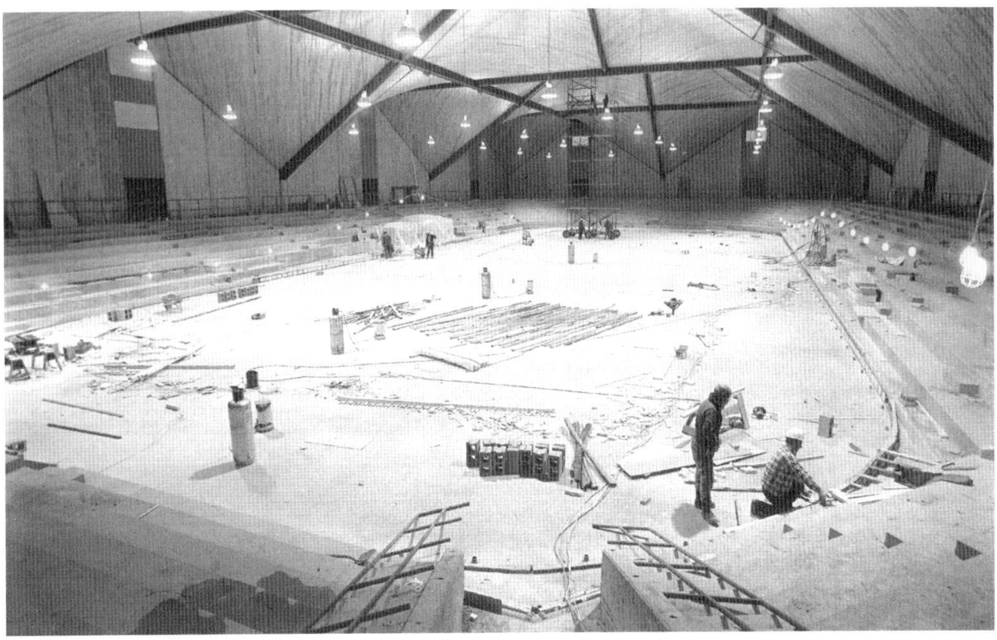

An Inside View of the Alfond Arena. Workers begin to lay surface for the ice rink. In 1991, changes would be made to the surface to allow basketball games to be played. It takes a crew of 25 about four hours to tear down the hockey rink, lay down insulation over the ice, and assemble the 4-by-8-foot panels that make up the basketball floor.

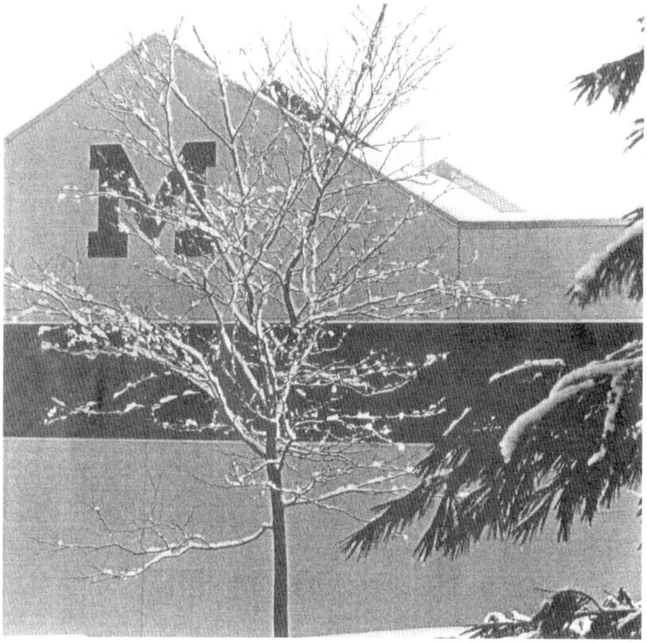

The Alfond Arena as It Looked in the Winter of 1977. Its unique, multiangular roof design was also used by other sports arenas, including the Pavilion at Villanova University. It was hailed at the time as one of the finest hockey facilities in the nation. Maine was now ready to join in-state rivals Colby and Bowdoin, who had played in indoor facilities for a number of years . The facility was completed in February 1977.

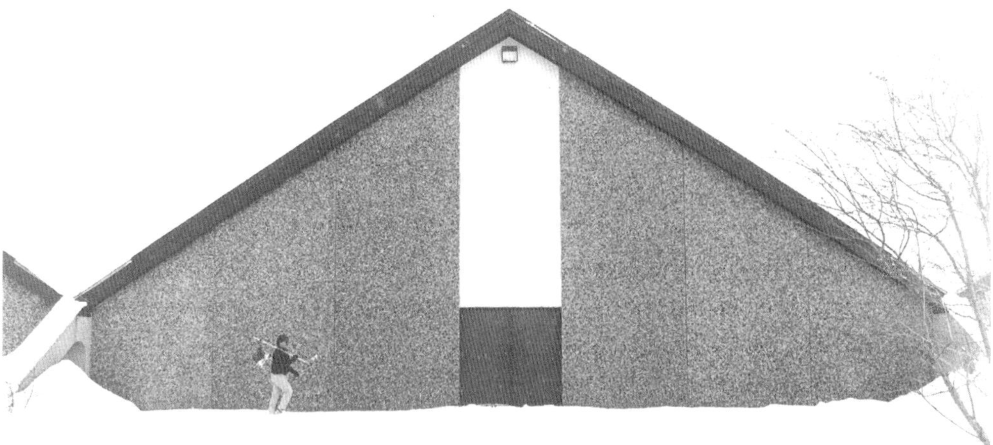

A Cold Walk to Practice. Even having a new indoor facility did not solve all of the players' problems. They still had to trudge through the snow and the endure freezing temps of a cold Maine winter.

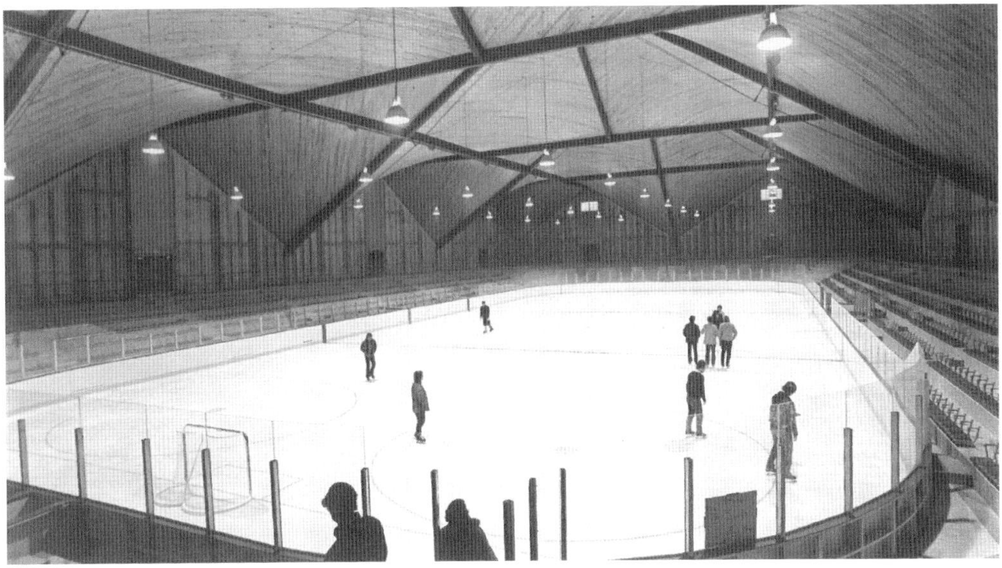

Sunday Skating at Alfond. The arena was not the exclusive domain of the UMaine hockey team. It was open to public skating, high school hockey, and men's leagues. It also played host to traveling ice shows, including Olympian Scott Hamilton's Stars on Ice. Future UMaine hockey great Derek Damon learned to skate at Alfond Arena while growing up in Bangor.

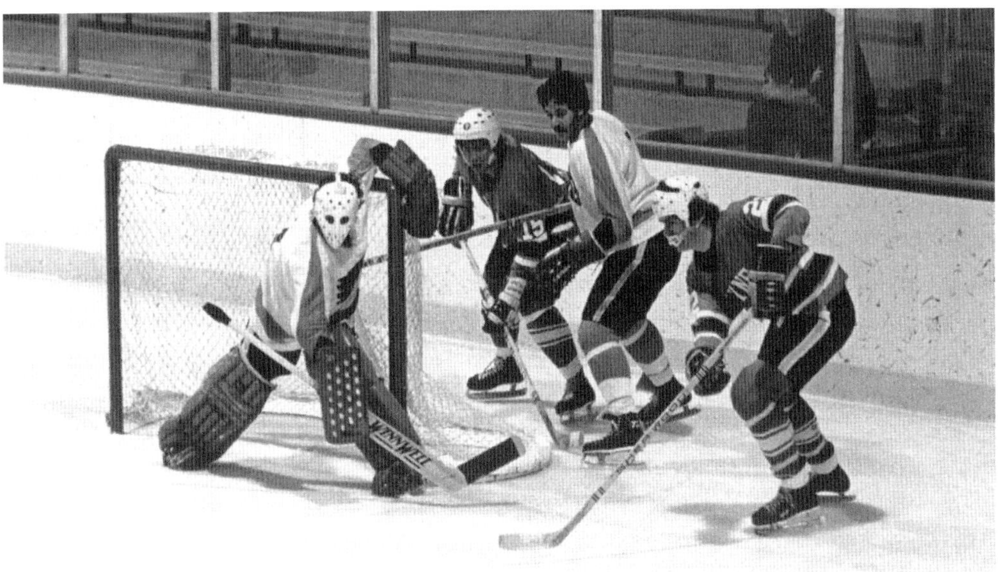

UMaine Hockey Club in Action. The first tenant of the newly constructed facility was the UMaine hockey club, which played a schedule against fraternity teams, prep schools, and high school teams. Fortunately, attendance would increase. The inaugural season the Black Bears had an attendance of 30,450 and an average of 2,175 per game. By the 2005–2006 season, they would average 5,385 per game, and on seven occasions they would lead Hockey East in attendance.

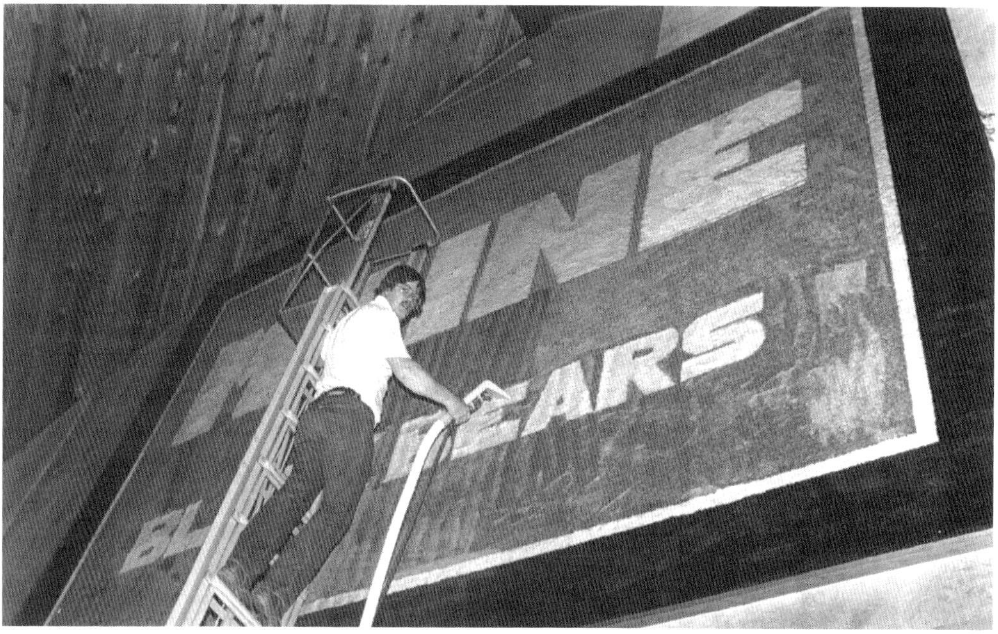

PREPARING FOR THE OPENER. The staff at Alfond Arena had to work overtime to get ready for the season opener, an exhibition game against Arcadia University to be held on November 18, 1977.

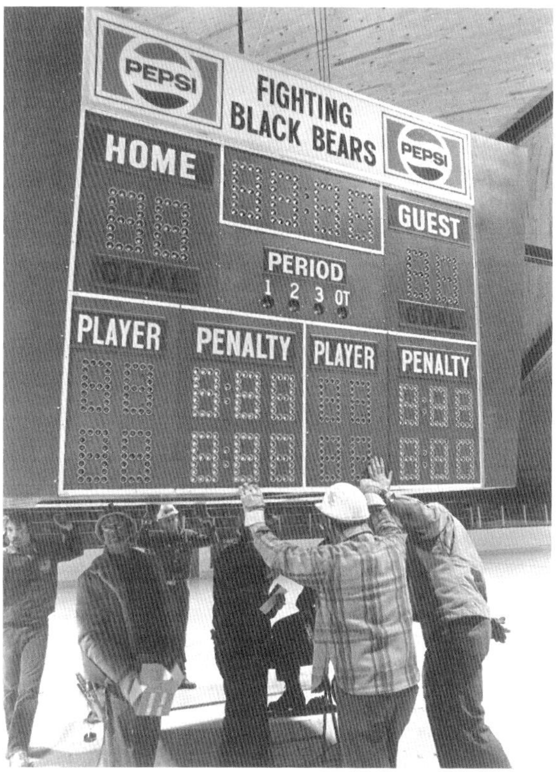

SPONSORS NEEDED. Corporate sponsorship for sports was becoming increasingly popular and controversial at this time. Commercial use of sport sponsorship, however, is nothing new. It can be traced back to the 1896 Olympics when sponsors ran advertisements in the Olympic program. In the early 1900s, tobacco advertisements lined outfield fences in major-league baseball, and in the 1936 Olympics, Jesse Owens became the first athlete to receive an endorsement: a free pair of Adidas sneakers.

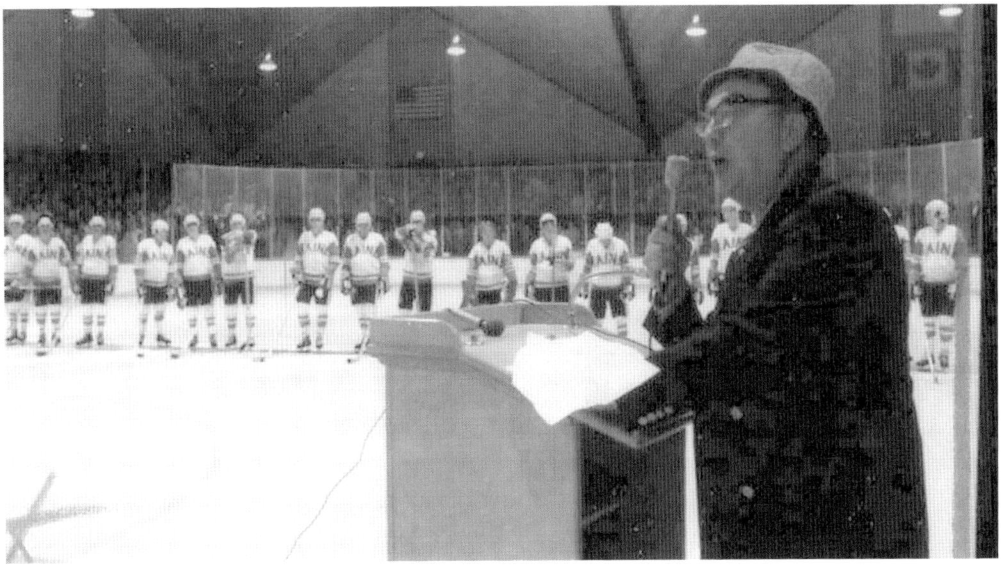

Opening Night at the Alfond Arena. The big night at the Alfond Arena arrived on November 18, 1977, the Black Bears' first game of the modern era. The evening was highlighted by an address from Harold Alfond. Alfond expressed his appreciation for having the facility named in his honor and gave the audience the following charge: "I know that the students and the young people in the years ahead will do everything possible to maintain this arena for the good and betterment of the university and the community."

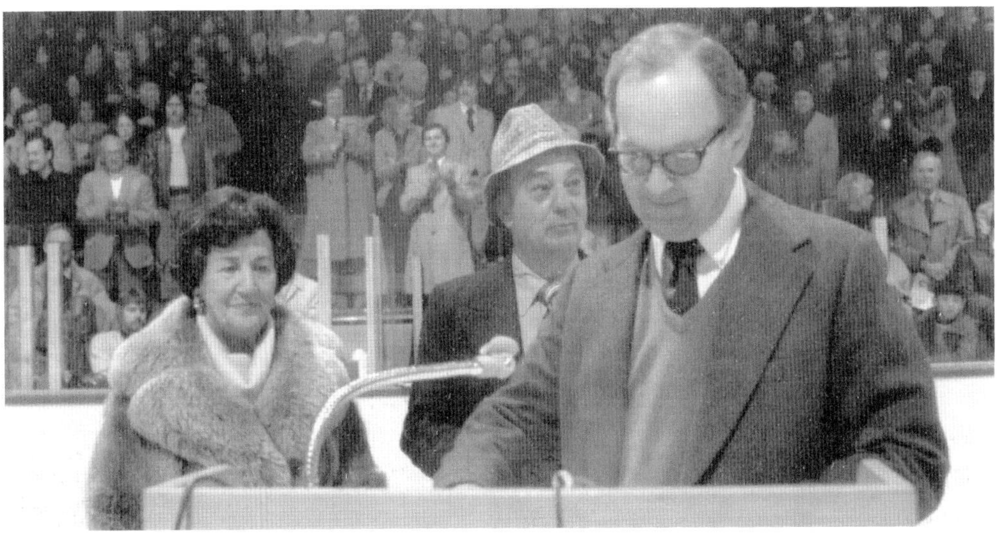

UMaine President Howard R. Neville. Addressing the crowd, UMaine president Howard Neville talked of the synthesis between education, athletics, and citizenship. "Here individuals will test themselves to find their limits and go beyond those limits. At the same time they will learn social value of cooperation, sportsmanship and concern for others." Neville also acknowledged the contribution of others who gave monetarily and of their expertise in the development and construction of the arena.

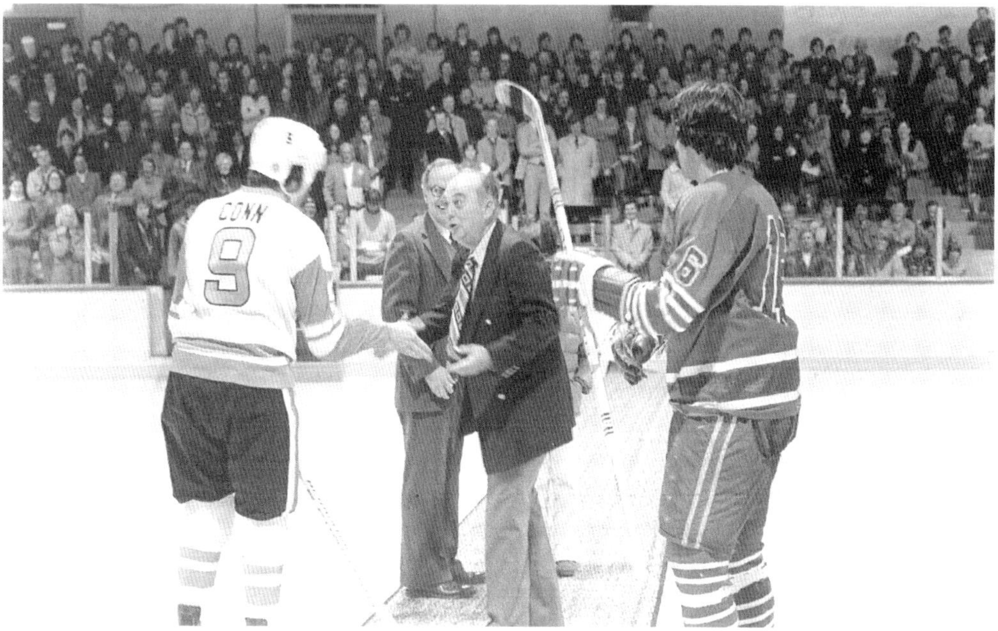

Game Captain Gary Conn and Harold Alfond. Time for the main event, the first varsity hockey played at Maine in 53 years. Pictured is Harold Alfond, who shakes hands with Black Bear captain Gary Conn (No. 9) as Pres. Howard Neville looks on.

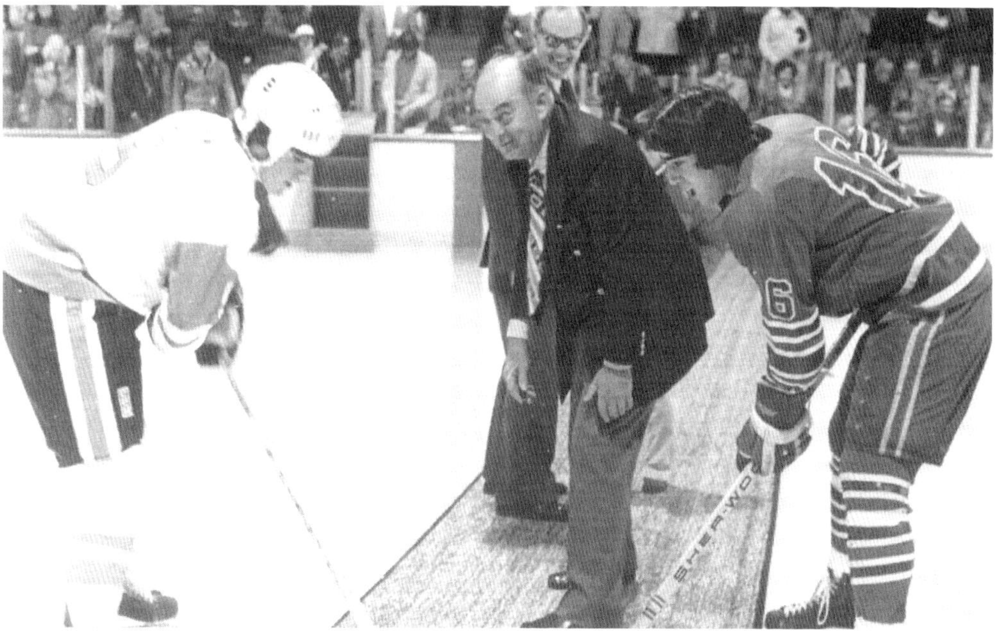

Let the Game Begin. Harold Alfond drops the ceremonial first puck between captain Conn and Arcadia's captain Bill Young. Although just an exhibition game, Maine won 7-5 to the delight of a sold-out crowd. The *Bangor Daily News* quoted one fan as saying of the game and the sport, "Great! . . . Fantastic sport, . . . quick, exciting, full of action. . . . Insanely brutal, but I love it!"

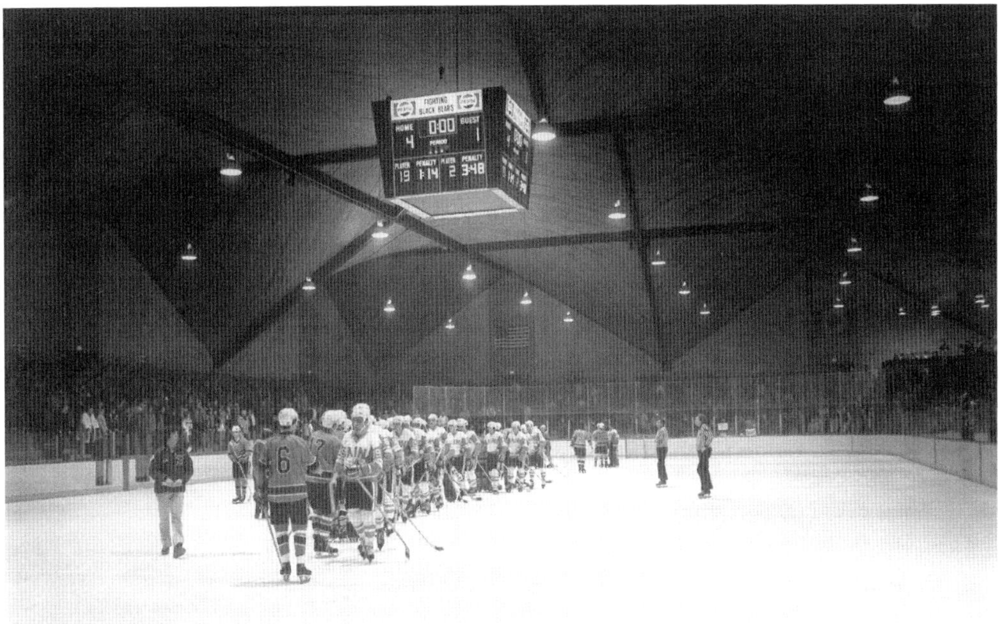

UMaine Skates Off with First Win. After starting the season with three consecutive losses, Maine's first victory was a sweet one at home against longtime in-state rival Colby. The 4-1 victory was their first against Colby since 1922. Since the 1990s, Maine has had one of the best home ice winning percentages in the country. The Black Bears at one time had not lost in 49 straight games at Alfond Arena before losing in overtime to Boston University in 1993.

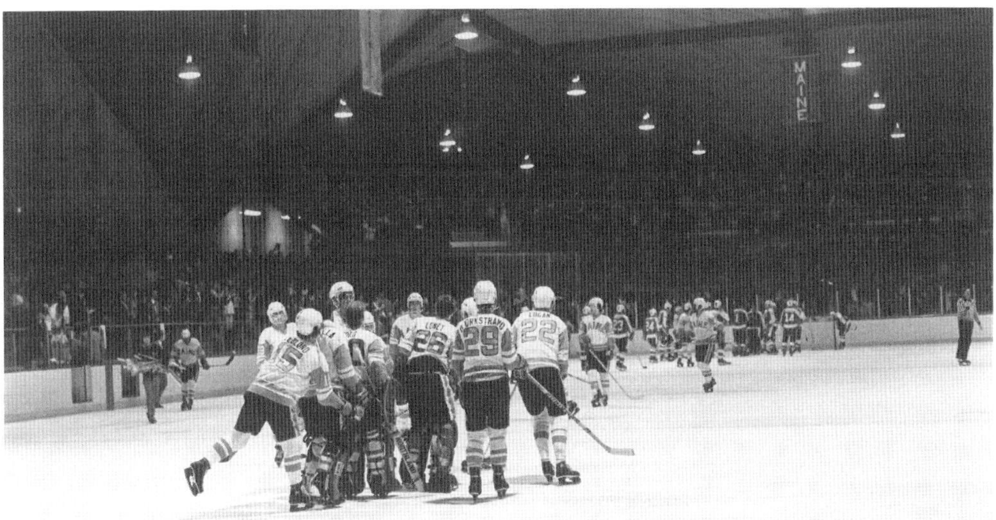

A Time of Transition. The early success of the program created problems of space for seating, media, and locker room areas. The blossoming women's basketball program and the men's team had moved out of the Memorial Gymnasium and were playing home games at the Bangor Auditorium. Both squads were looking to return home. But change was on the horizon, and the financing was coming from a familiar source.

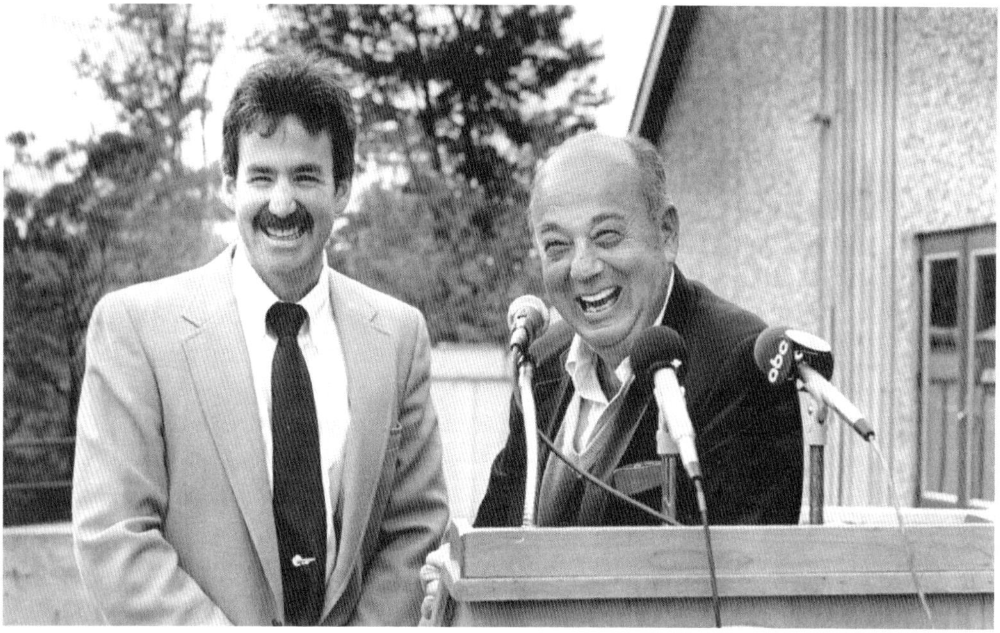

Shawn Walsh and Harold Alfond at Groundbreaking Ceremony. In 1990, the Harold Alfond Sports Center would begin improvements and expansion that would be ongoing for the next 14 years. In 1990, Harold Alfond presented the university with a $2 million gift to increase the arena's seating capacity to 5,200 for hockey. Also added were additional concession areas, restrooms, locker rooms, and media facilities. The arena would also become home to Black Bear basketball teams that had been playing their home games at the Bangor Auditorium. In 1997, the UMaine women's ice hockey team played its first game at Alfond Arena.

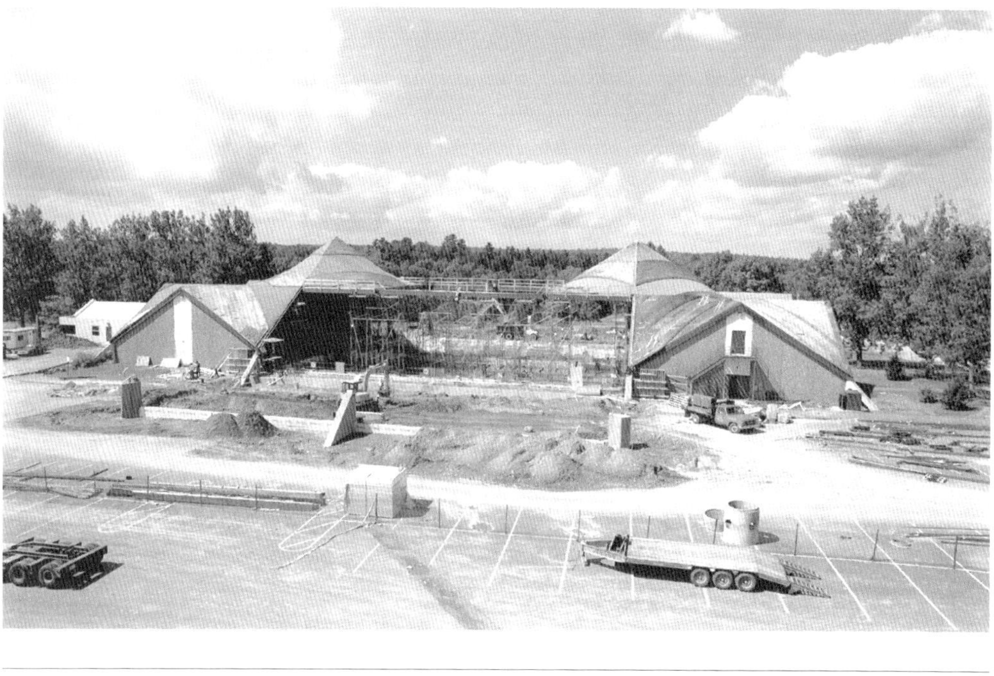

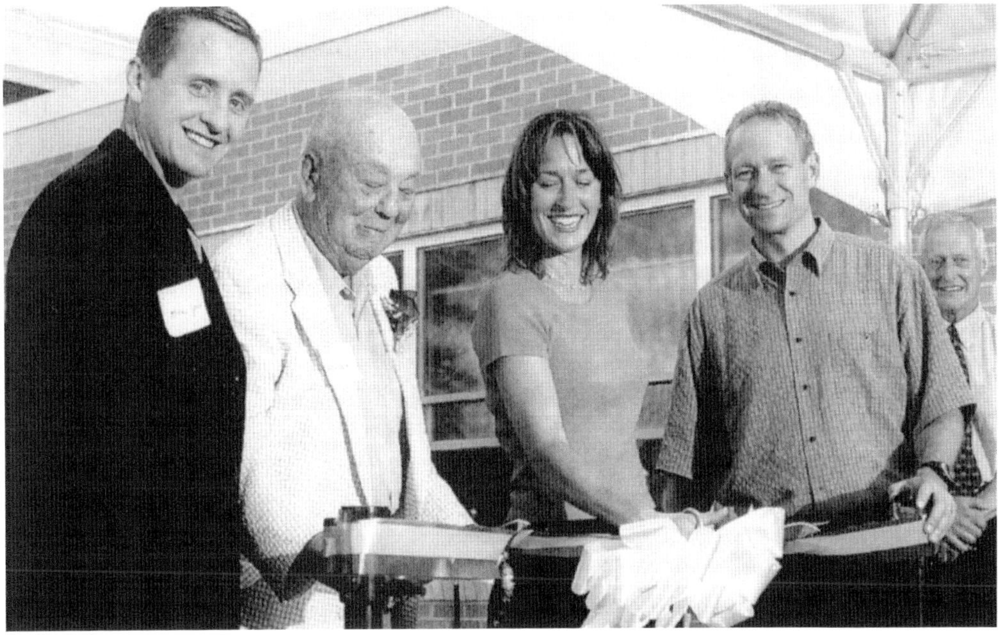

DEDICATION OF THE SHAWN WALSH HOCKEY CENTER. Lynne Walsh, widow of former UMaine coach Shawn Walsh, is flanked by athletic director Blake James, Harold Alfond, coach Tim Whitehead, and Grant Standbrook as she cuts the ribbon at the opening of the Shawn Walsh Hockey Center. The center was ready for the 2005–2006 season.

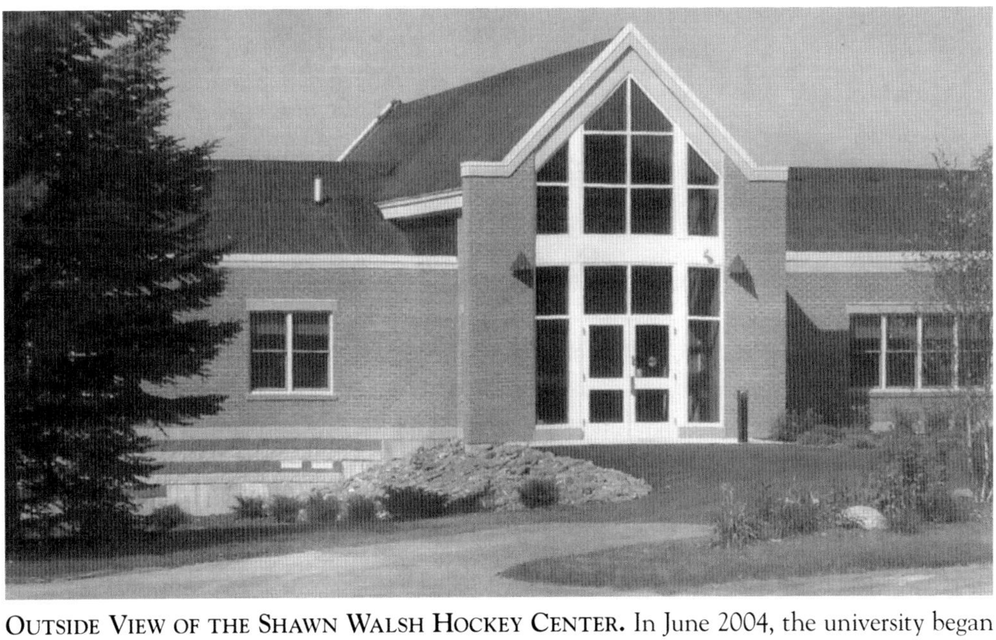

OUTSIDE VIEW OF THE SHAWN WALSH HOCKEY CENTER. In June 2004, the university began construction of the Shawn Walsh Hockey Center in the memory of its legendary coach. The complex includes a state-of-the-art strength and conditioning area, an athletic training room, and the UMaine Hockey Hall of Fame. (Courtesy of Brent Williamson.)

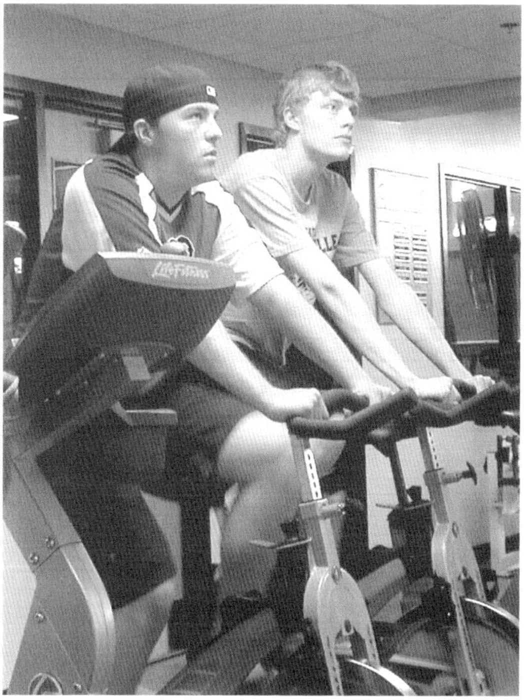

Athletes Using Stationary Bikes. For a complete cardiovascular workout the center has six stationary bikes, a treadmill, and a StairMaster. Fitness and training have become an integral part of the hockey program both to treat and prevent sports-related injuries. The sports medicine team consists of six full-time certified athletic trainers, team physician Dr. Craig W. Curtis, and a wide variety of medical specialists and student athletic trainers.

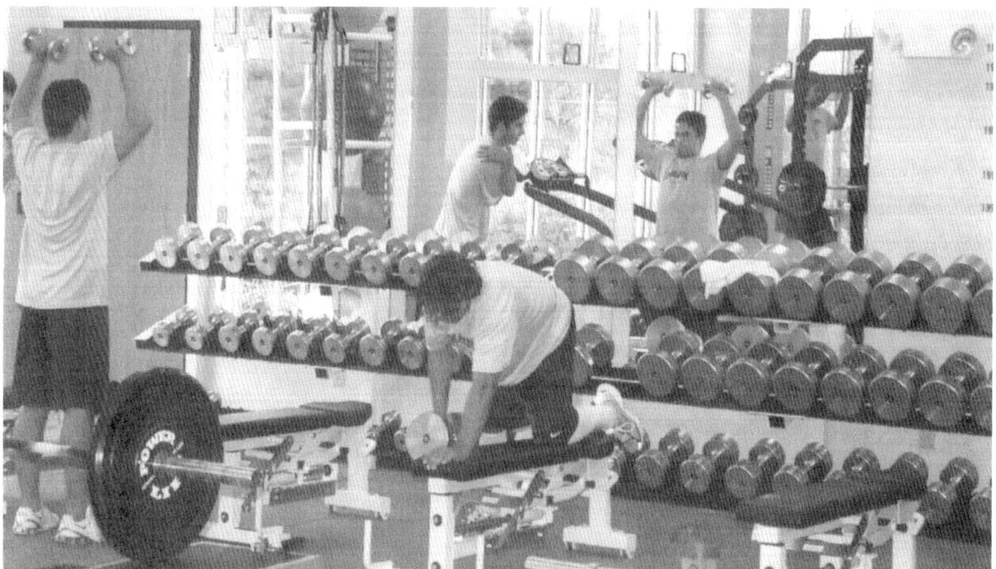

Time to Train. Weight training is an integral part of Black Bear hockey players' conditioning during and after the season. Assistant coach Grant Standbrook is considered an innovator in training methods and techniques, and first initiated weight and resistance training programs in the 1960s, well before they became popular. The Shawn Walsh Hockey Center weight room contains power racks, lifting benches, and Olympic platforms with weights and bars. (Courtesy of Brent Williamson.)

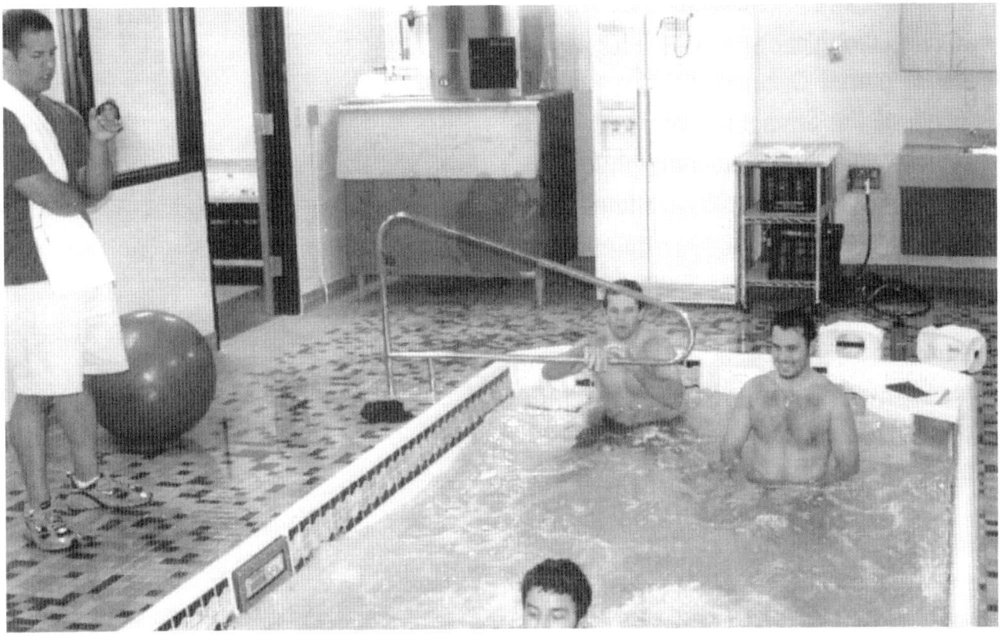

Therapy in the Hydropool. Prevention of injury is the primary focus of the athletic training department. The Shawn Walsh Hockey Center contains two areas for the prevention and treatment of athletic injuries. The therapy room contains a treatment table and taping stations, and in the "hydro" room are whirlpool tubs and a therapy pool, seen above. (Courtesy of Brent Williamson.)

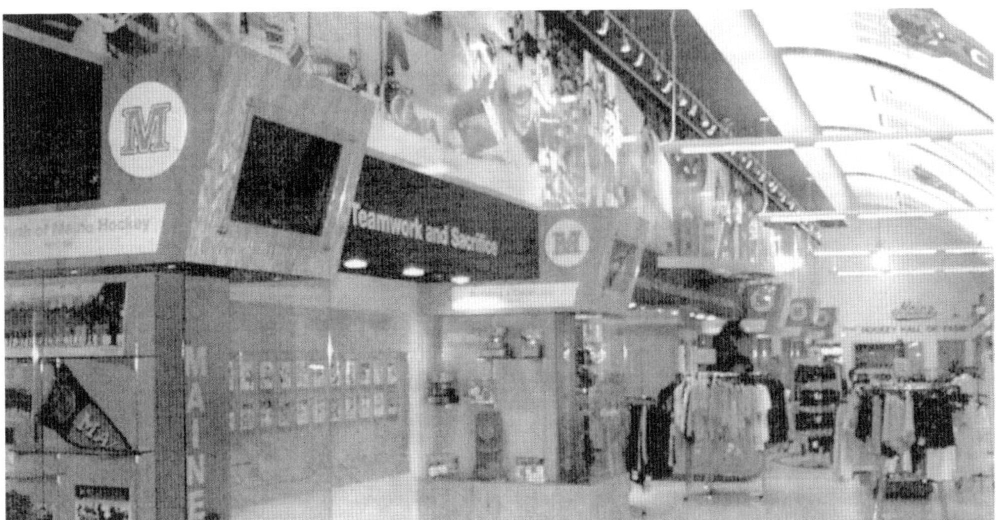

Inside the UMaine Hockey Hall of Fame. Recording the history of hockey at the university is the UMaine Hockey Hall of Fame. The archive contains photographs, trophies, jerseys, and other memorabilia that lay out in chronological order the history of the sport. The display was paid for in part by donations from former UMaine players headed up by Art Demoulas, who played on the 1977–1978 team.

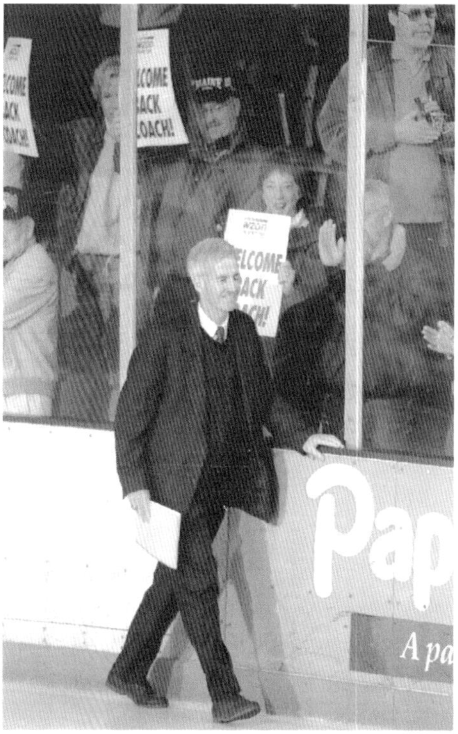

COACH WALSH BACK ON THE ICE. A banner hangs on the wall of the weight training center dedicated to coach Shawn Walsh by the 2001 UMaine football team. It reads, "Press On. Nothing in the world can take the place of Persistence. Talent will not. Nothing is more common than unsuccessful men with talent. Genius will not. Unrewarded genius is almost a proverb. Education alone will not. The world is full of educated derelicts. Persistence and determination alone are omnipotent."

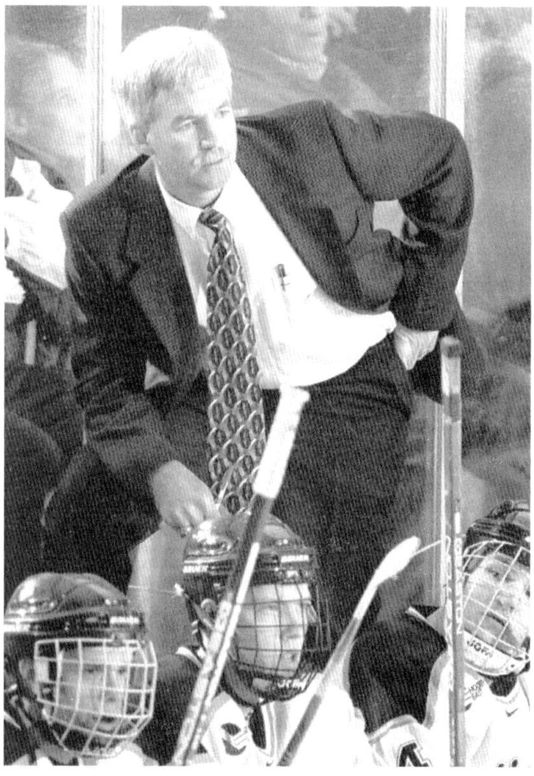

MAINE COACH SHAWN WALSH. In triumph and tragedy, UMaine hockey coach Shawn Walsh was an inspiration to players and fans alike.

3

The Making of a Champion

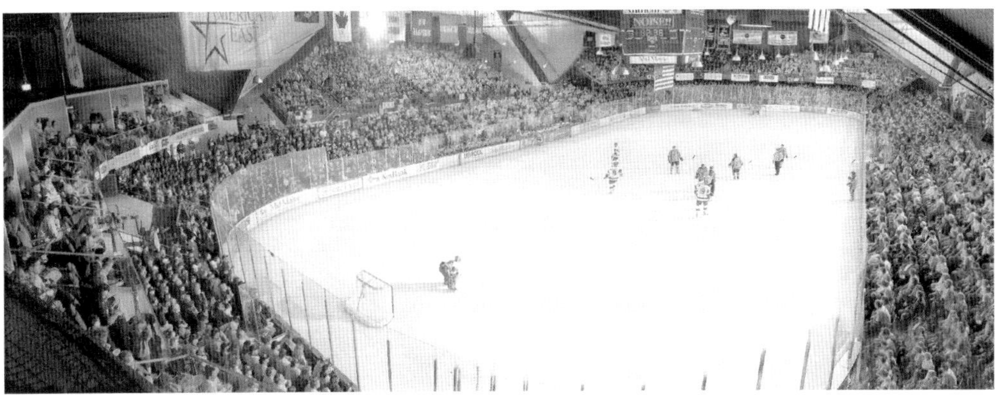

UMaine in Action against Boston University. It was one thing to build one of the elite centers for hockey in the nation but quite another to put an elite team on the ice. In less than a decade, however, the UMaine hockey rose from club status to a Division I schedule, to competing in the prestigious Hockey East conference. The Black Bears would go on to garner six Hockey East crowns, qualify for the NCAA tournament 16 times, and win two national championships. Since 1998, Maine's winning percentage of .696 is the best in the nation. In the long history of varsity sports at UMaine, hockey is the only sport to capture a national title.

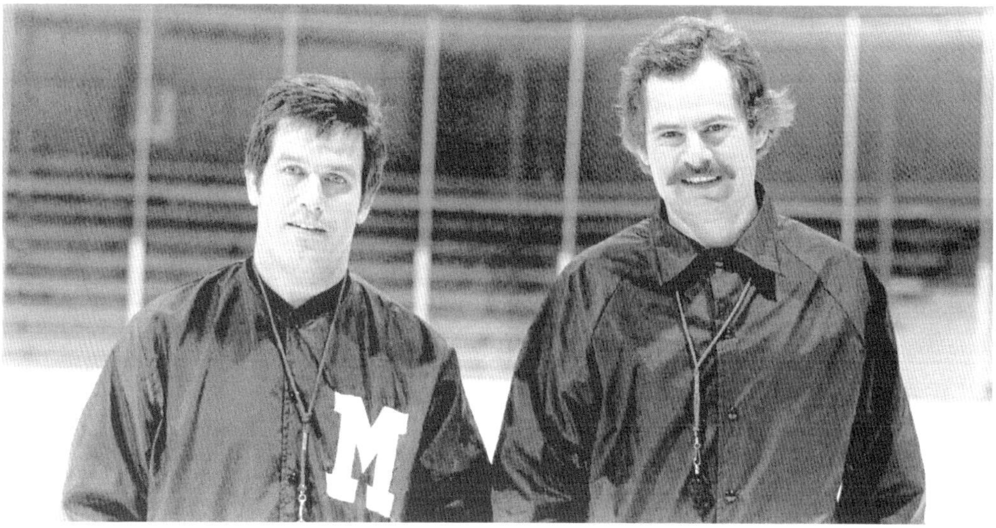

JACK SEMLER AND TED CASTLE BEFORE PRACTICE, 1977. Building a champion starts with coaching. In the modern era, Black Bear hockey has only had three head coaches in its 30-year history. On April 7, 1977, the university named Jack Semler to be the varsity hockey coach, rink coordinator of the Alfond Arena, and lecturer in physical education. Chosen from a pool of 60 applicants, Semler had been the head coach of the Princeton University hockey team for four years and had an outstanding collegiate career at the University of Vermont, where he was captain and Most Valuable Player (MVP) of the hockey team. Semler had also served in the armed forces as a captain in the U.S. Marine Corps from 1968 to 1971.

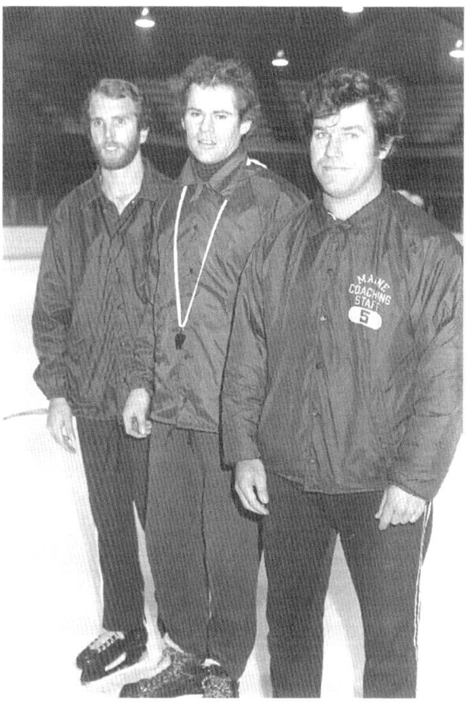

COACH SEMLER WITH ASSISTANTS GARY WRIGHT AND KEN YEATES. In the early years at Alfond Arena, coaching responsibilities included much more than recruiting and training players. Coaches were in charge of organizing events, hosting youth hockey programs, and laying the groundwork for a growing hockey program and rink complex.

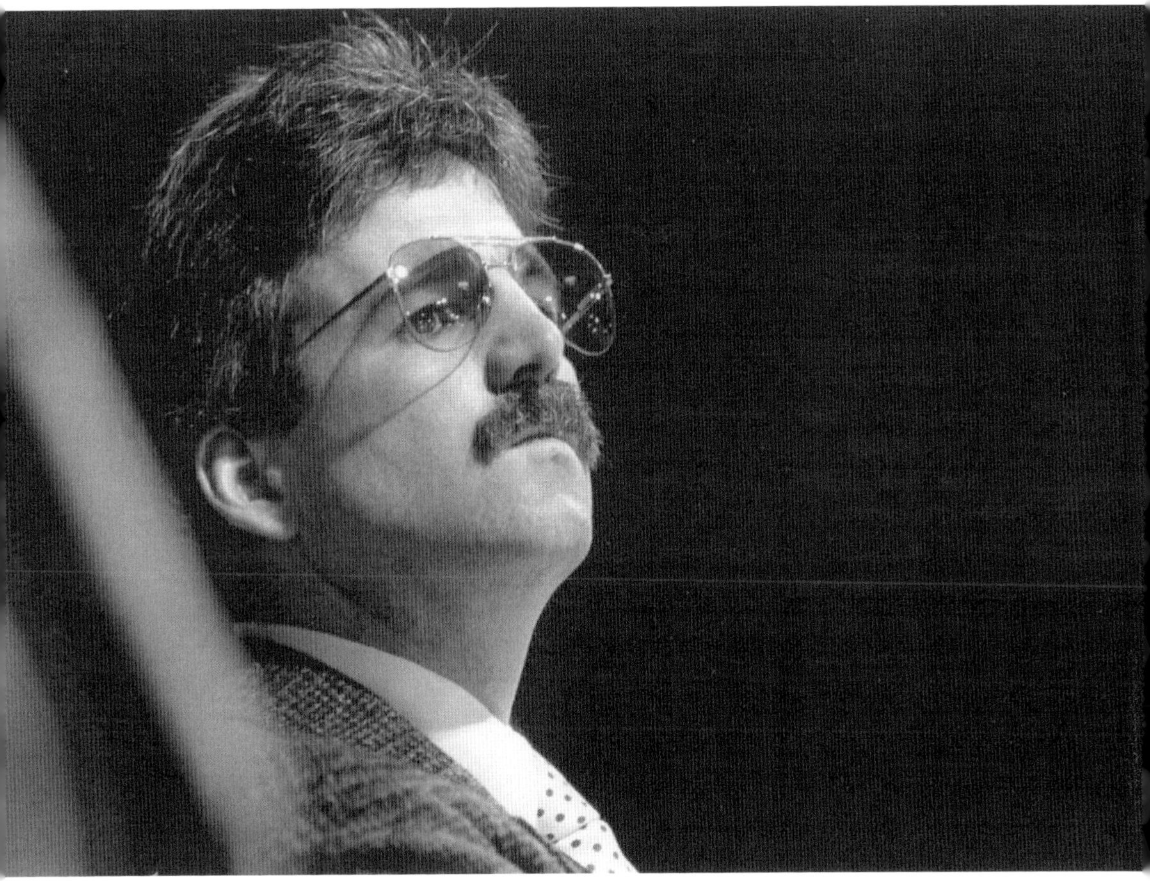

SHAWN WALSH HIRED TO TAKE OVER TEAM. Coach Semler's departure in 1984 left an opening for a little-known former backup college goalie named Shawn Walsh. At 28, Walsh would be the youngest Division I coach in the nation. A former assistant at Michigan State University, Walsh inherited a team that had gone 14-20-0 the previous year. Walsh had the added burden of now playing a Hockey East schedule that included games against powerhouses such as Wisconsin, Minnesota, and Northern Michigan. Success did not come over night, with Walsh struggling through his first year, 1984–1985, with a 12-29-1 record. The following season the Black Bears were not much better at 11-28-1.

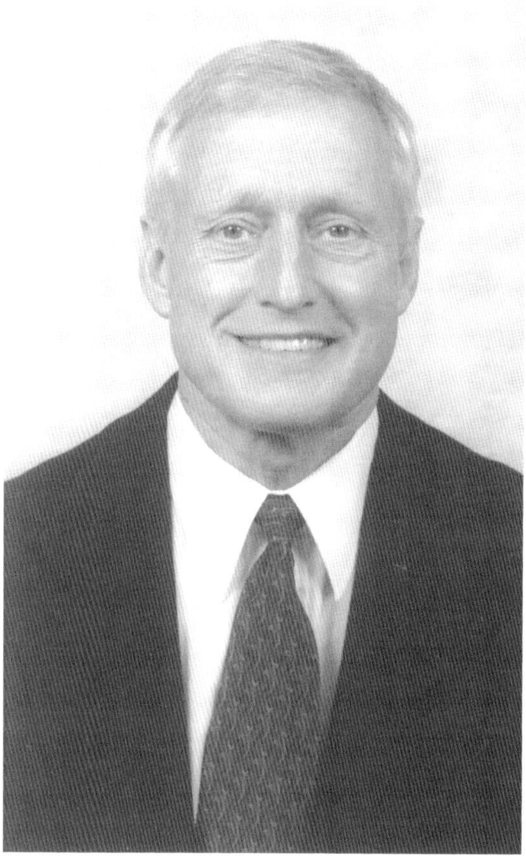

Assistant Coach Grant Standbrook. For most of his 17-year career at UMaine, Shawn Walsh was fortunate to have one of the finest assistant coaches in the country, Grant Standbrook. Standbrook has spent much of his hockey career as a scout and has recruited and coached 51 All-Americans in stints at Maine and Wisconsin. Fifty-six of his players went on to play in the NHL and 29 in the Olympics. Standbrook's eye for talent is obvious, but he said he looks for more than just talent. "You look for the player who is a champion in life, socially, in the classroom, and has overall character," Standbrook said. Standbrook's resume includes being assistant coach on the 1976 Olympic team and the U.S. National Team on two occasions. In 2005, he was the recipient of the Terry Flanagan Award for the recognition of his career accomplishments as an assistant coach.

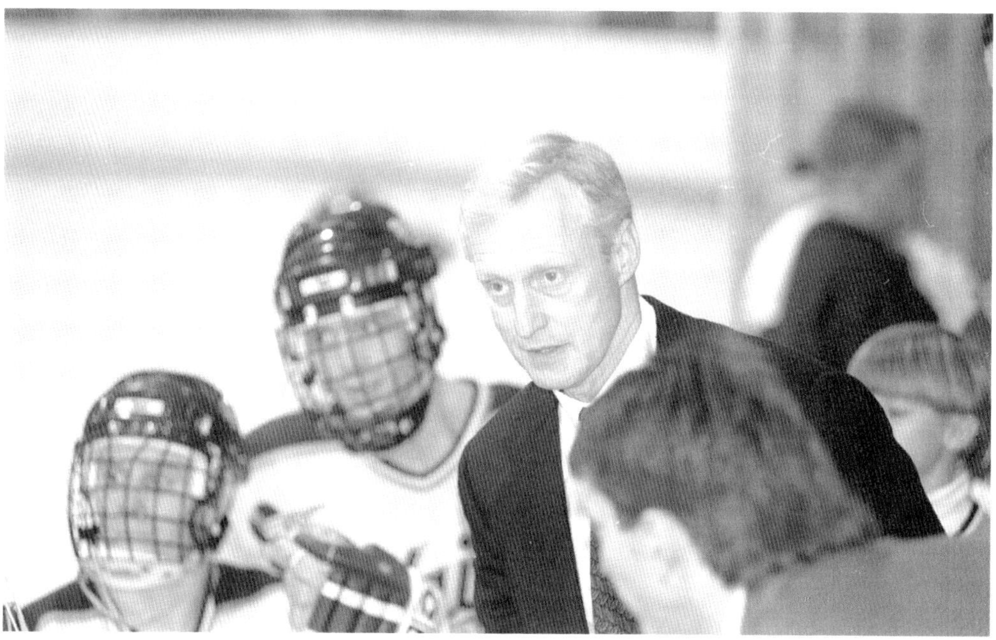

ASSISTANT COACH TIM WHITEHEAD. In 1990, Walsh happened upon the services of Tim Whitehead, who was studying at the university, earning a master's degree in education. Walsh, who also had a master's in education, promoted the concept of the student-athlete, and in Whitehead he had the perfect role model. Whitehead returned to Maine in 2001–2002 after stints as a player in Europe and as a head coach at the University of Massachusetts (UMass), Lowell.

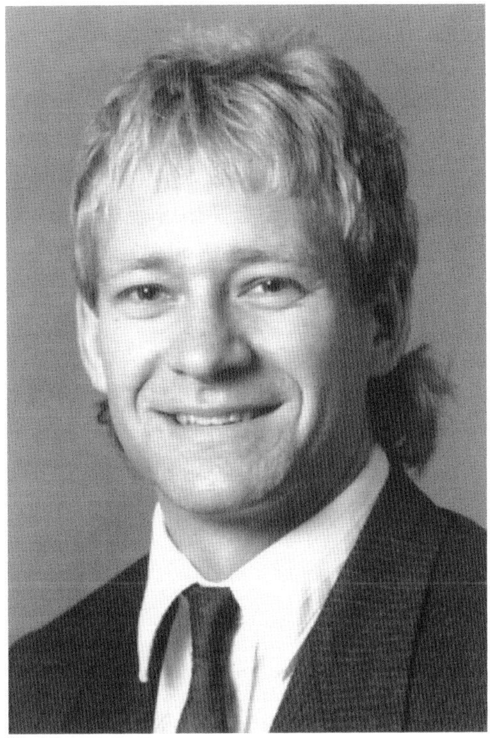

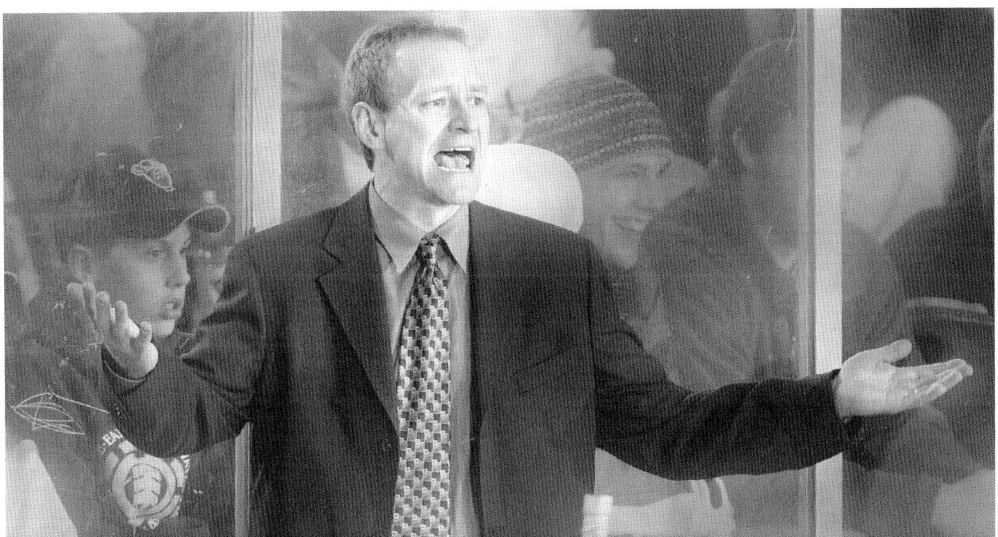

HEAD COACH TIM WHITEHEAD. After the untimely death of coach Walsh in September 2001, Maine looked to one of its own to succeed him. Assistant coach Tim Whitehead was first named interim coach and then on April 8, 2002, was hired as head coach. His resume included two seasons as a professional hockey player in Europe, and assistant coach at Middlebury College. From 1996 to 2001, he had served as head coach at UMass Lowell, leading his team to four Hockey East tournament appearances.

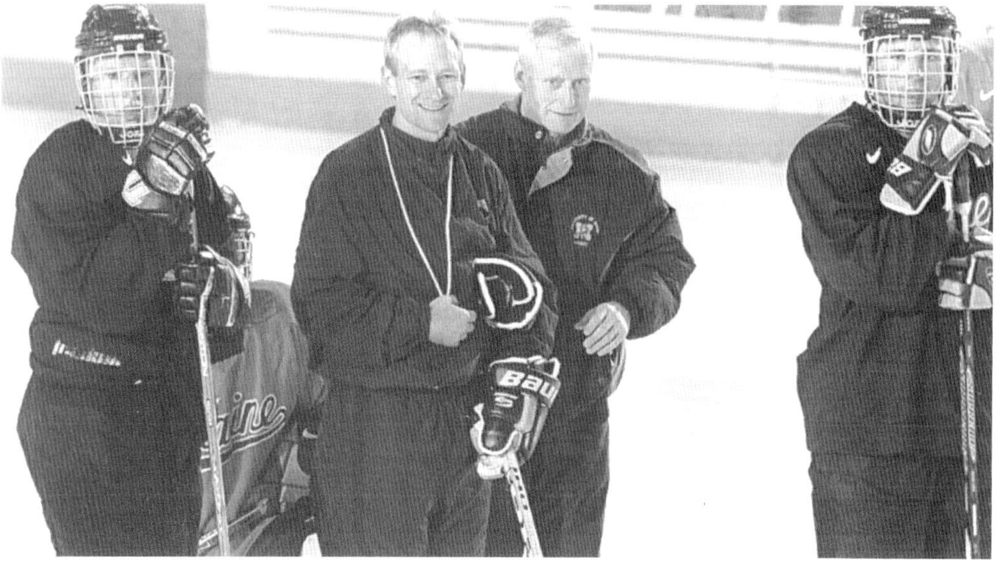

Coach Whitehead and Assistant Grant Standbrook Conduct Practice. Tim Whitehead was fortunate to secure the services of Grant Standbrook, who gave continuity and stability to a team that had not only lost its coach but a good friend and mentor. The team seemed not to miss a beat in 2001 and became a finalist in the NCAA National Championship Series. Whitehead was awarded the Spencer Penrose Award as the national collegiate coach of the year for his accomplishments.

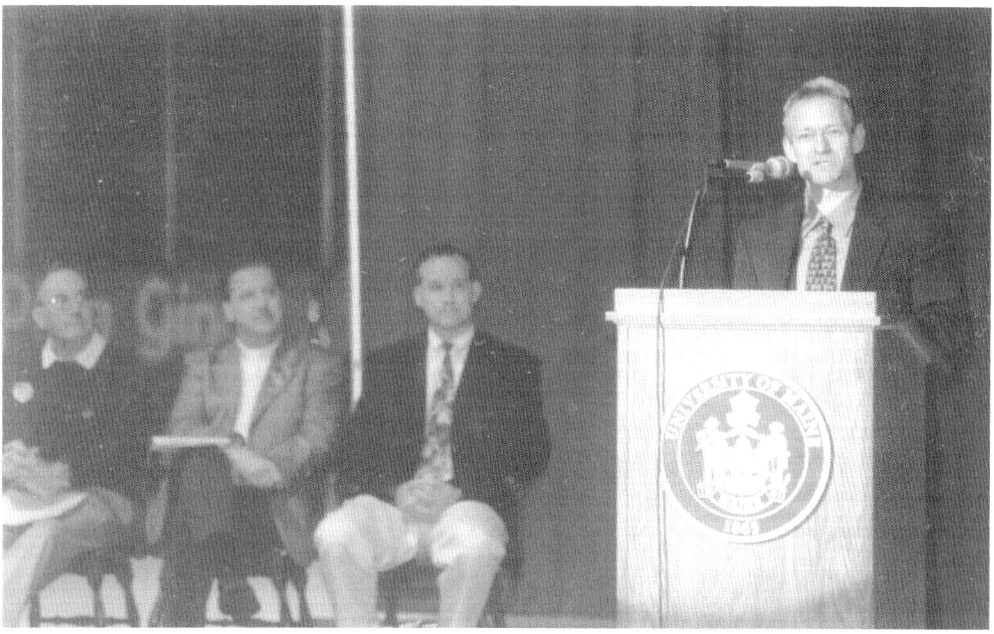

Whitehead Speaks at University. Whitehead learned from Shawn Walsh that being a coach at UMaine meant more than coaching and recruiting. Handling the media and being a good spokesman for the team became essential qualities for being a successful coach.

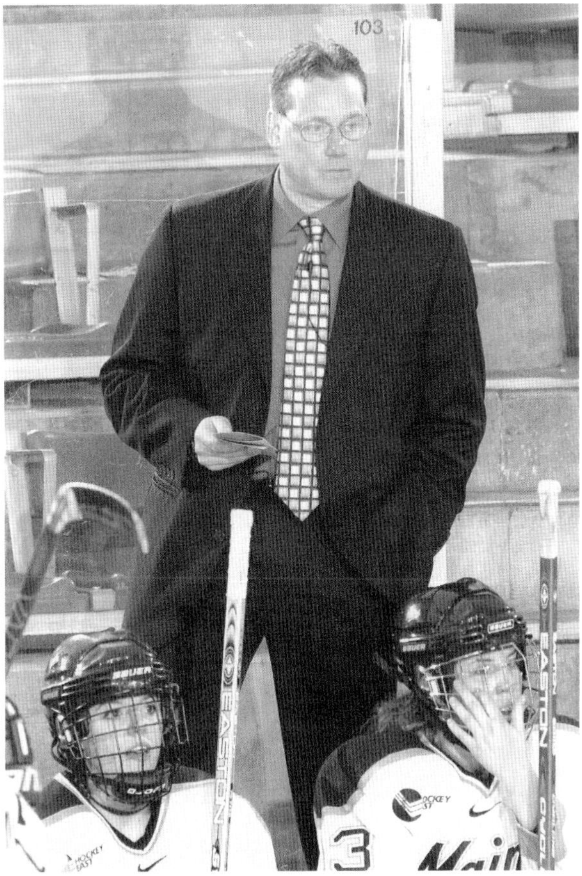

GUY PERRON, FORMER UMAINE PLAYER AND WOMEN'S ICE HOCKEY COACH. In June 2006, Guy Perron joined Whitehead's staff as associate head coach. Perron was no stranger to UMaine hockey. He was a four-year letterman at Maine (1986–1990) and appeared in 136 career games. He captained the team on two occasions and lists in the Black Bears' top 10 in goals, assists, and points scored. He served two stints as an assistant under coach Walsh and for two seasons was the coach of the Black Bears women's hockey team, compiling a 31-24-9 record.

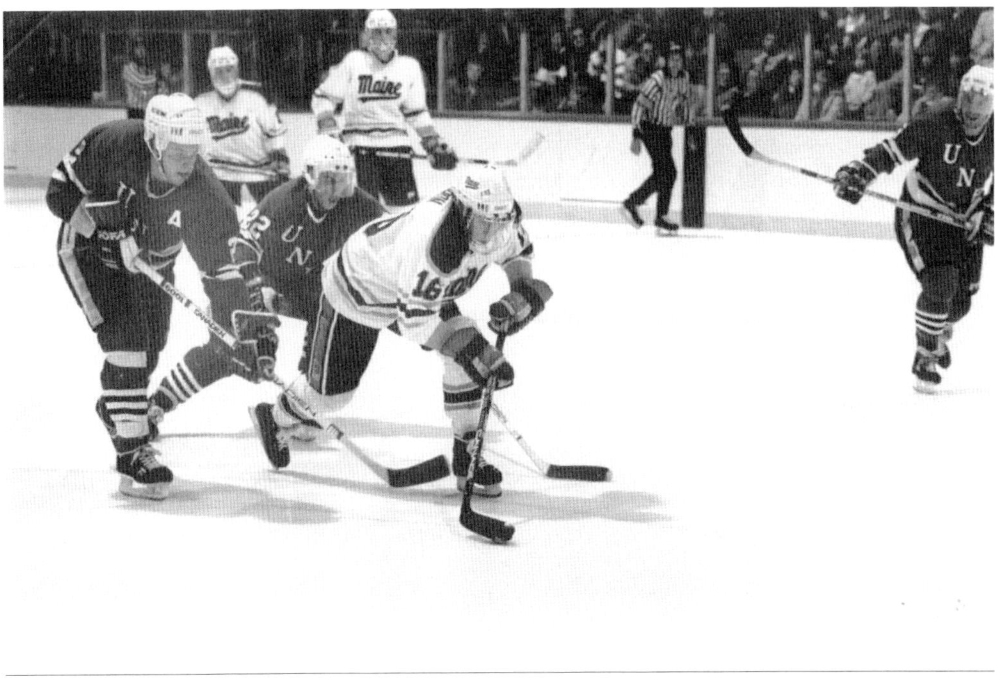

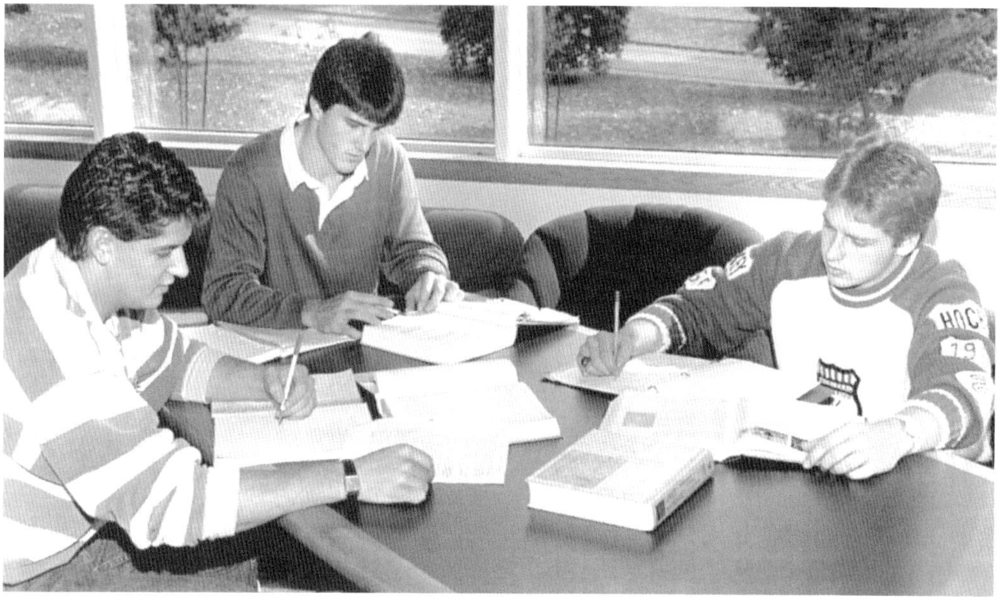

STUDENT-ATHLETES AT WORK. The essential building material of any championship team is of course the players. Coaches and administrators alike set their goals on players not only succeeding on the ice but in the classroom and going on to successful careers after they have turned in their sticks. The university offers a comprehensive academic support program that includes tutoring services, academic progress checks, and exclusive use of the Sezak academic center and career counseling. The athletic department honors Maine's scholar-athletes who attain a 3.0 grade point average or better. In 2004, Maine was awarded the America East Academic Cup after compiling a 3.12 overall average. In Tim Whitehead's tenure, five Black Bear players have been named to the Hockey East All-Academic team.

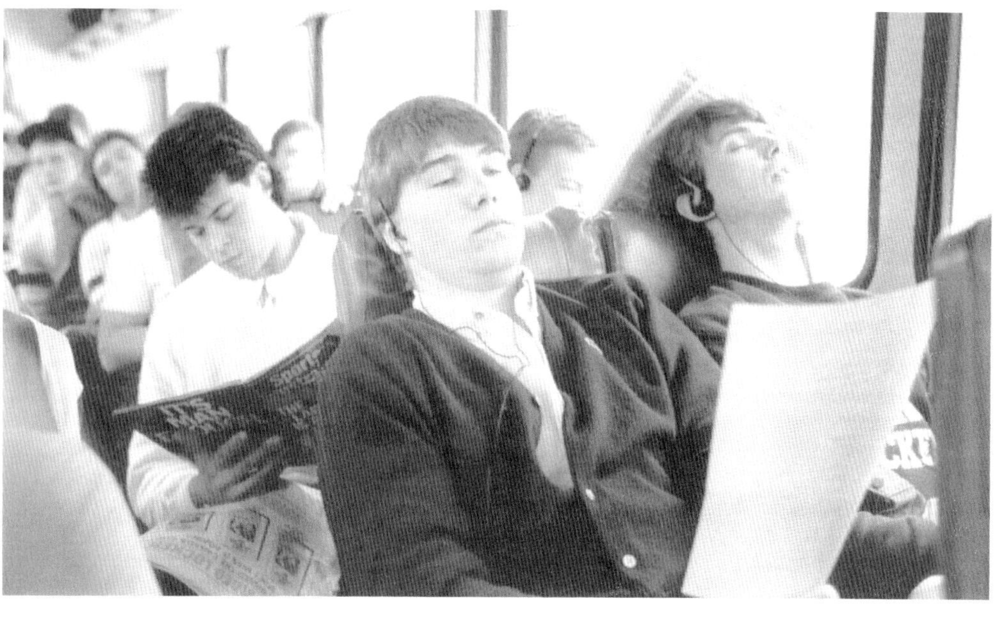

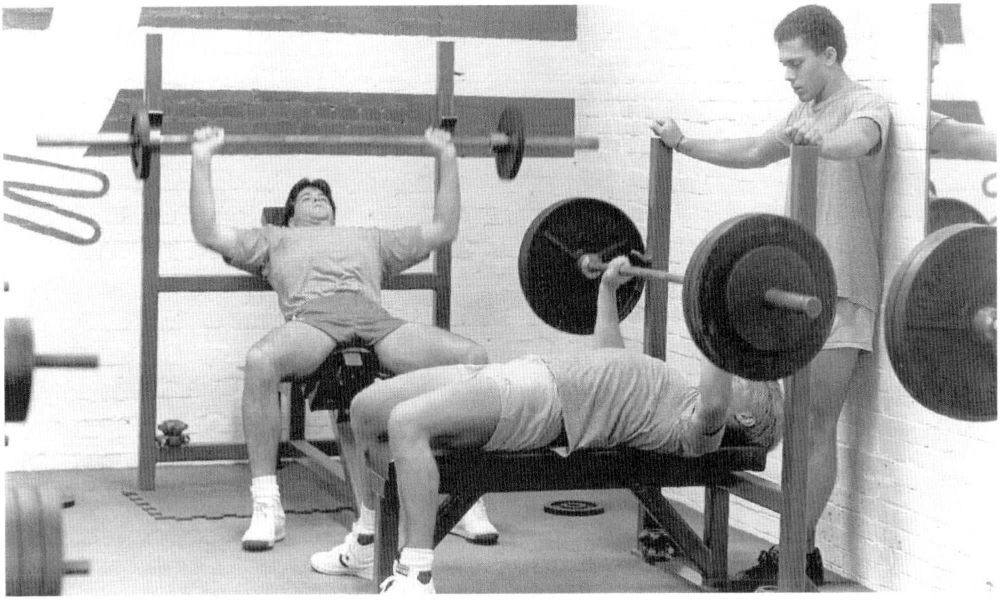

UMaine Hockey Players Lift. Weight training has become an increasing part of the rigorous off-season workout regimen that players must participate in to play championship-caliber hockey. Shown here are players from the 1984–1985 season in the old weight room inside the Memorial Gymnasium. A new weight training facility resides inside the Shawn Walsh Hockey Center, and the Latti Fitness Center also offers weight and aerobic training equipment.

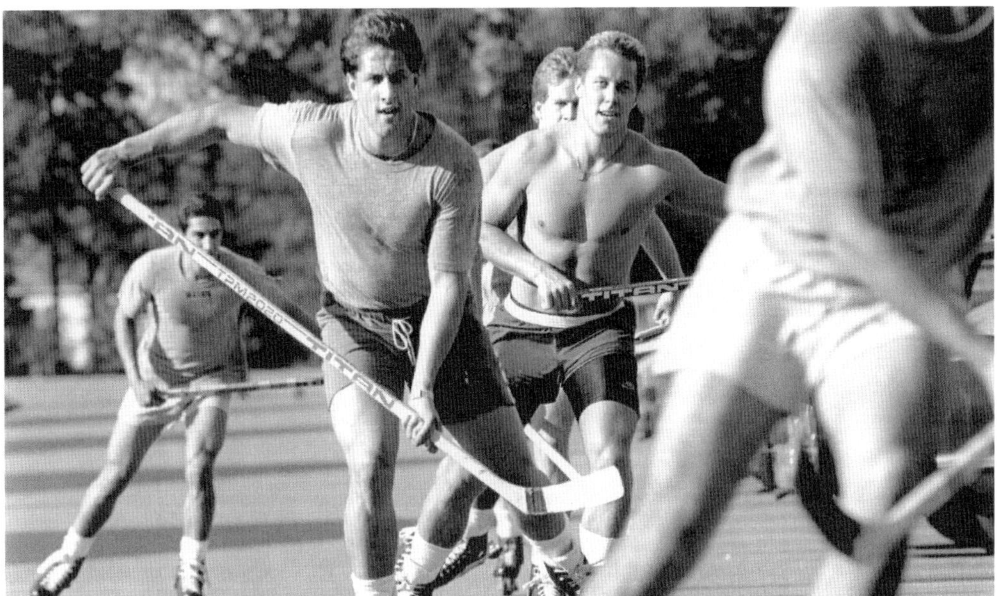

Expensive Equipment Not Needed. The only essentials are a hockey stick, roller blades, and a sunny day.

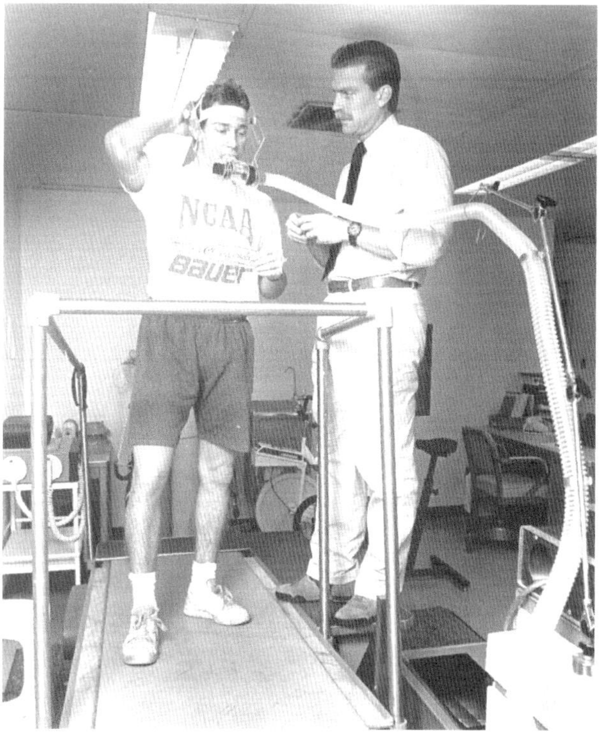

PLAYER EVALUATION, 1984. Sports medicine has come a long way since this 1984 photograph. New facilities located inside the Shawn Walsh Hockey Center include a Hydropool and a therapy room equipped with state-of-the-art equipment for the prevention, treatment, and rehabilitation needs of athletes.

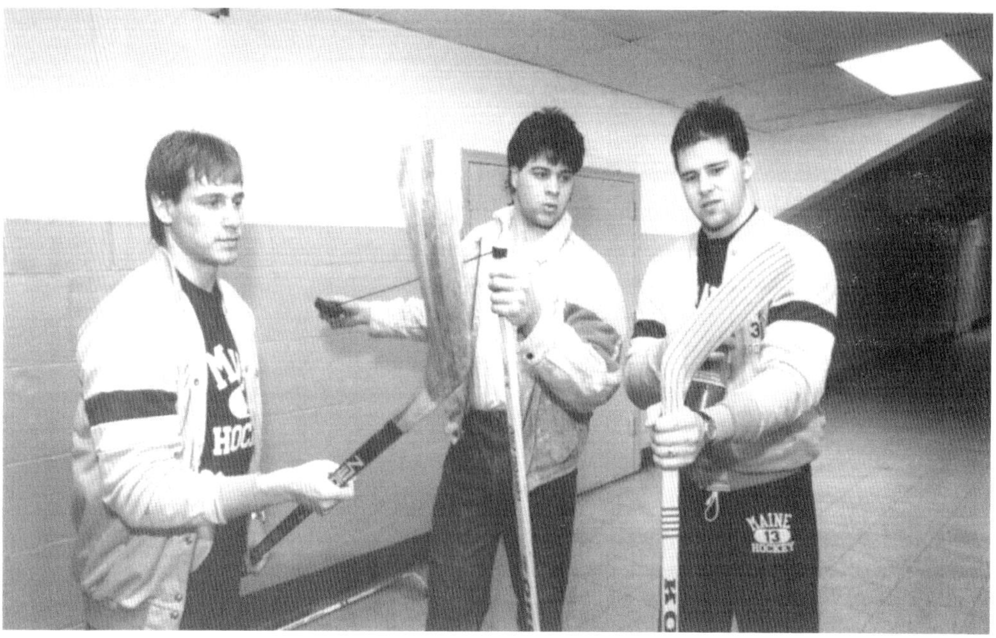

EXAMINING THE TOOLS OF THE TRADE. Players from the mid-1980s check out their sticks. Equipping a player from skates to helmet runs about $1,100 per player. To equip a goalie, the cost jumps to about $3,700. These estimates do not include the extra sticks most players go through, about 15 to 30 per season, at a cost of $110 per stick.

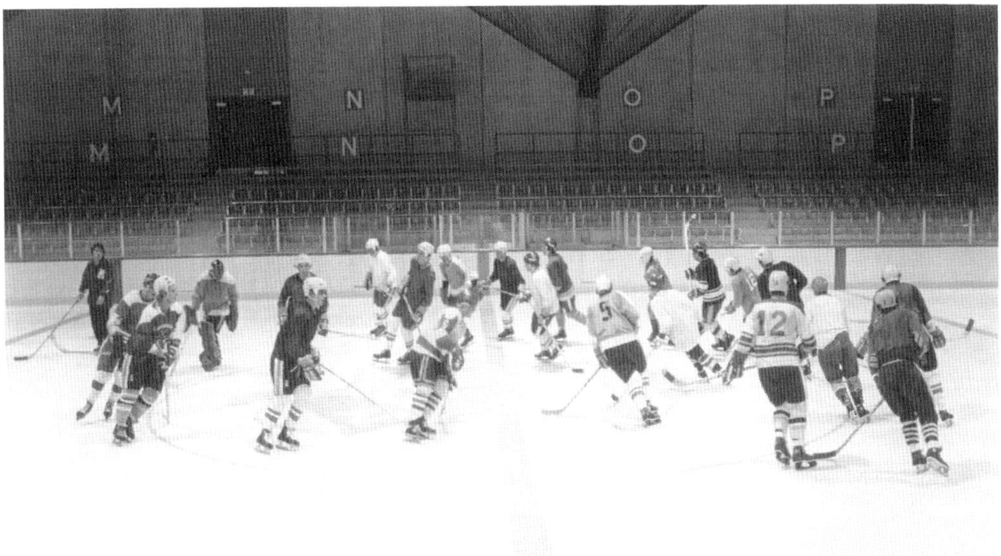

Players Skate before Practice or Tryouts. Recruiting players is the lifeblood of the program. Recruiting wars over elite players led the NCAA to set down strict recruiting guidelines with stiff penalties for violations. UMaine can offer 18 scholarships on a team that has 27 roster spots. The nine open slots are filled by recruited walk-ons and, rarely, a tryout player.

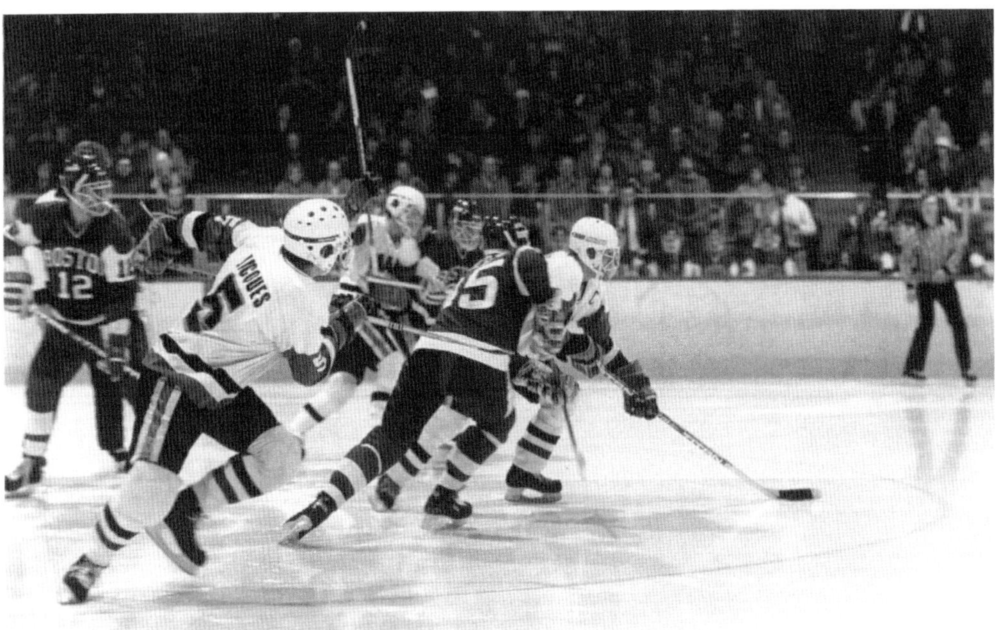

Mike McHugh Leads Breakaway. Mike McHugh, who played at UMaine from 1984 to 1988, was a recruited walk-on. McHugh would earn All-American honors and be drafted with the first pick in the 1988 NHL supplemental draft by the Minnesota North Stars. He became one of 52 African Americans to ever play in the NHL.

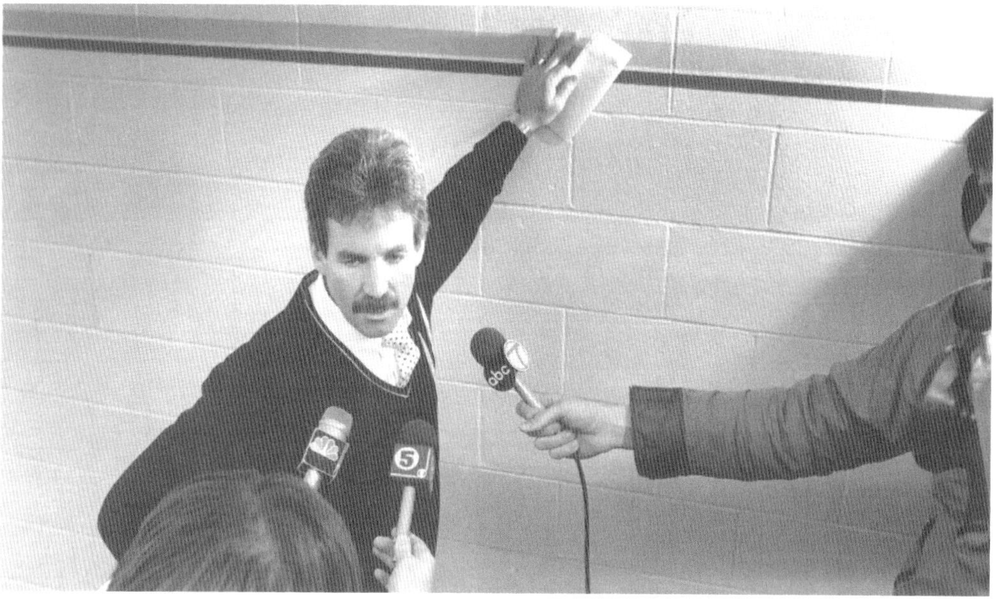

COACH WALSH MEETS THE MEDIA. Maine's rise to prominence as a championship-caliber program created its own set of problems. The media was scrutinizing the program's every move, and there were new levels of accountability. Savvy skills in dealing with the media became essential in being the face and the voice of the program. Coaches Shawn Walsh and Tim Whitehead gained respect as being forthright and accessible to local and national media.

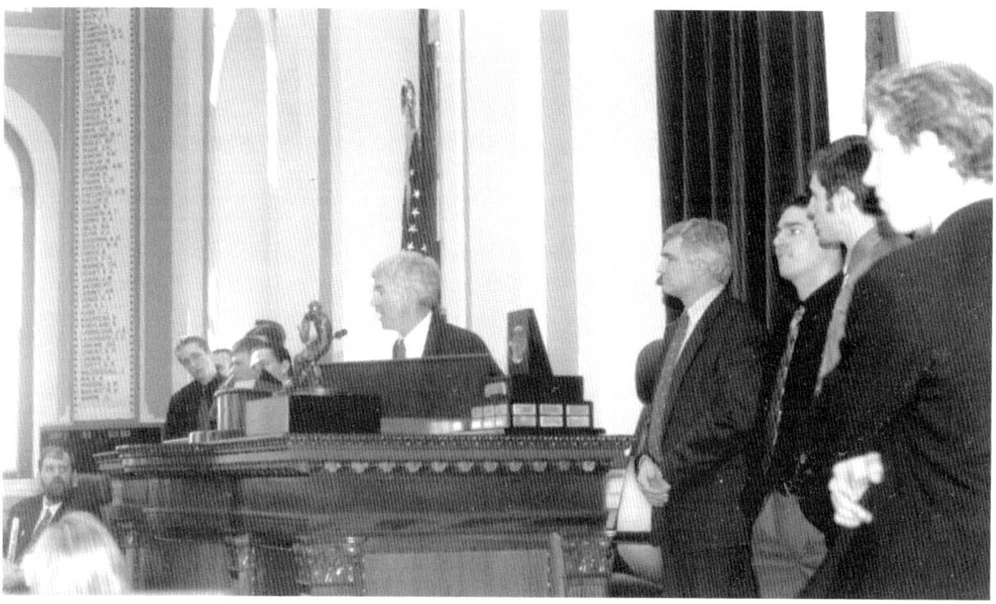

UMAINE CHAMPIONS MEET BEFORE MAINE SENATE, 1999. The reach of the media extends to the athletes as well, as they are expected to be role models and make public appearances. Walsh once compared his vacillating popularity to that of a politician. "In 1993, you could have put my face on a postage stamp, but in '95 some people didn't know which side to spit on."

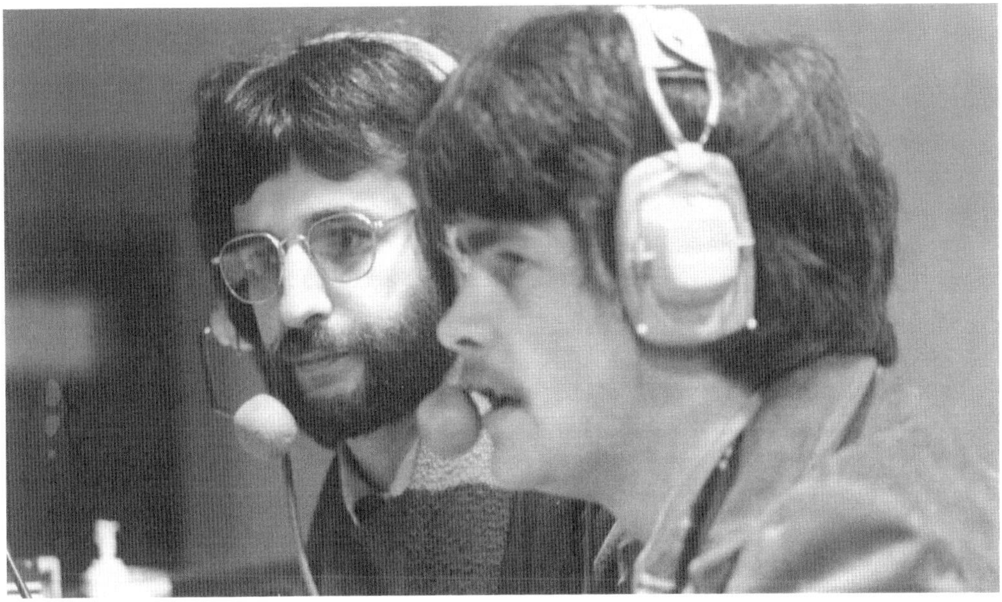

WMEB BROADCASTS AN EARLY UMAINE HOCKEY GAME. Since the early 1960s the campus radio station WMEB has been a voice for UMaine sports. In 1964, the station was officially licensed by the FCC. WMEB has broadcast Maine hockey since the inaugural 1977–1978 season and is a teaching laboratory for journalists and broadcasters. Gary Thorne, one of the most recognizable voices in professional sports, covering major-league baseball, NHL hockey, and the Olympics, got some early training there. Thorne is a 1970 graduate of the UMaine.

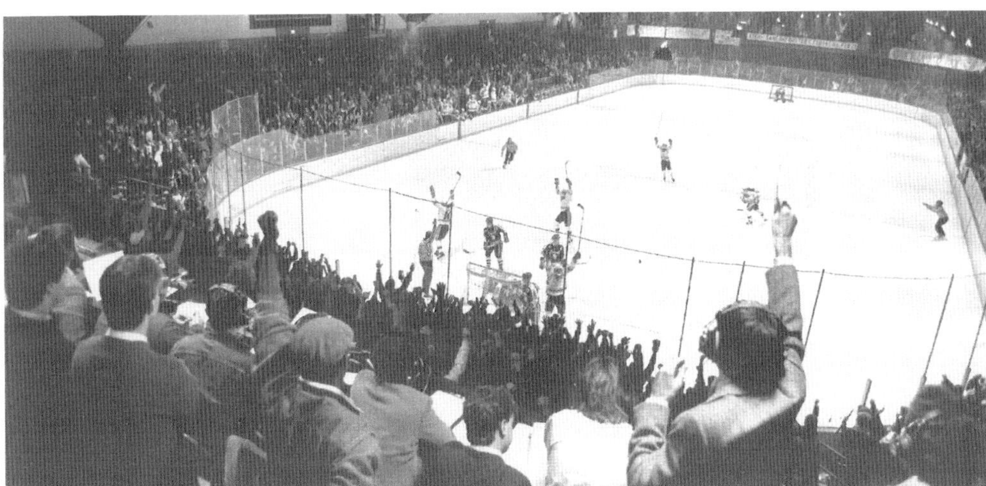

UNBIASED ANNOUNCER CHEERS MAINE SCORE. With the Black Bears' rise to national prominence, other media outlets began to broadcast and televise games. The Black Bear Radio Network was formed and includes stations WLOB in Portland, WDME in Dover-Foxcroft, and WEGP in Presque Isle. WABI TV began to broadcast Maine hockey as well as WPFO-TV 23, covering the Portland market. The New England Sports Network also began to broadcast games throughout New England.

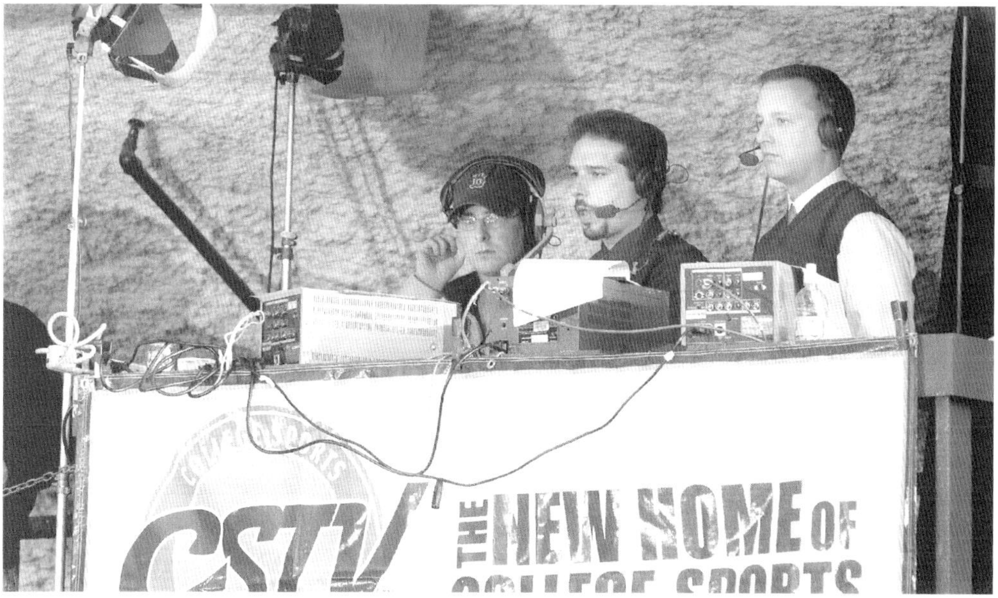

BEARS GOING PRIME TIME. Black Bear games are now being carried nationwide on the College Sports Television, a subsidiary of CBS. UMaine hockey was first seen on television in 1986, when Maine beat Providence at Alfond Arena. The game was seen on the New England Sports Network.

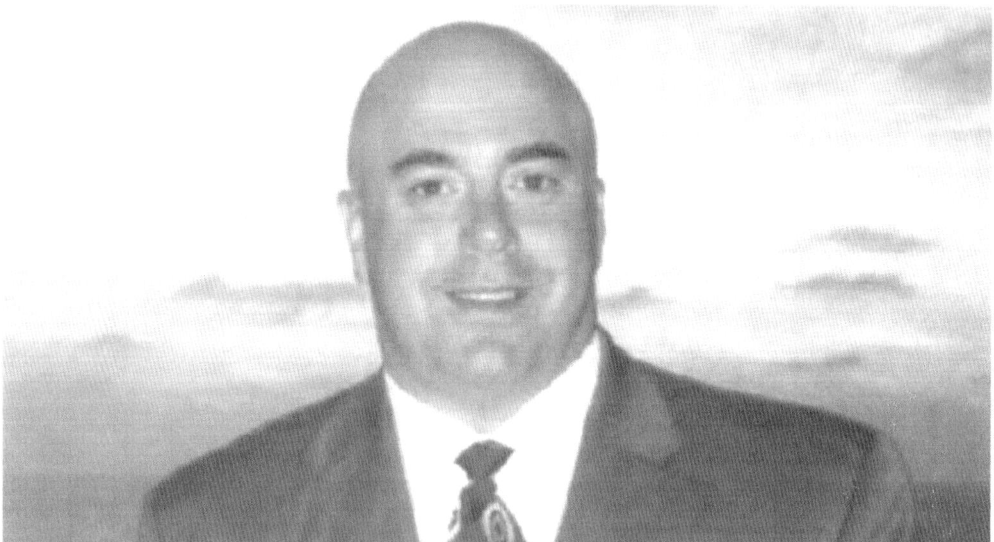

JOE KENNEDY, THE FACE BEHIND THE VOICE. The decade of the 1990s has been called the decade of Black Bear, and the voice of Black Bear hockey was Orono native Joe Kennedy. Kennedy, a lifelong fan, grew up on College Avenue just down the road from the Alfond Arena. As a college student, he ran the scoreboard for high school games and men's leagues before landing his dream job as the announcer at UMaine home games. Kennedy said that while players are the spotlight, the crowd controls the energy.

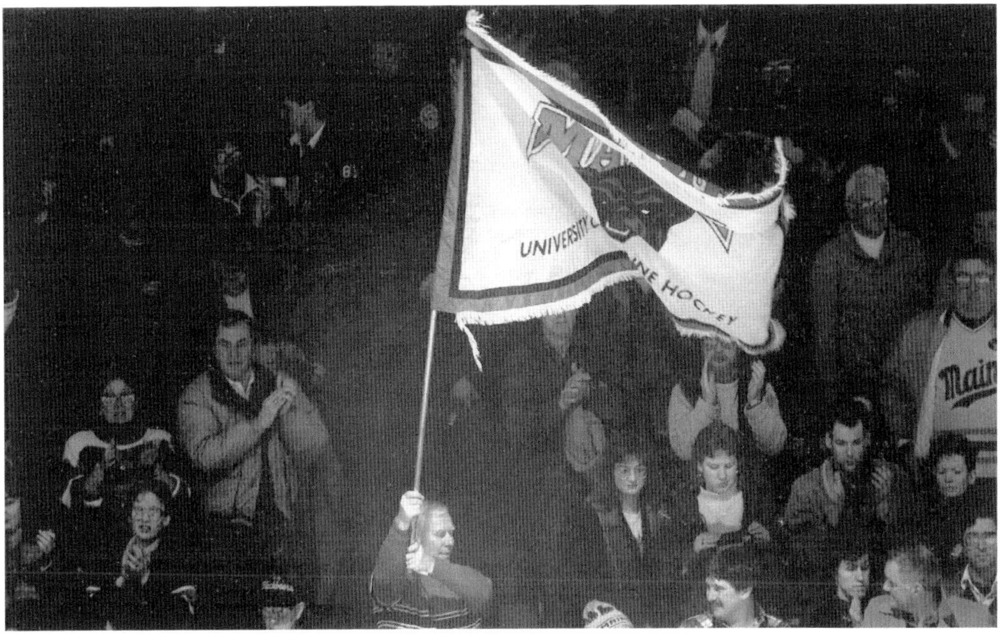

FANS WAVE MAINE BLACK BEAR BANNER AT ALFOND. Talent and preparation are not the only elements that make championship teams. Intangibles like loyal, enthusiastic fans can play a legitimate seventh man and give teams a true home ice advantage.

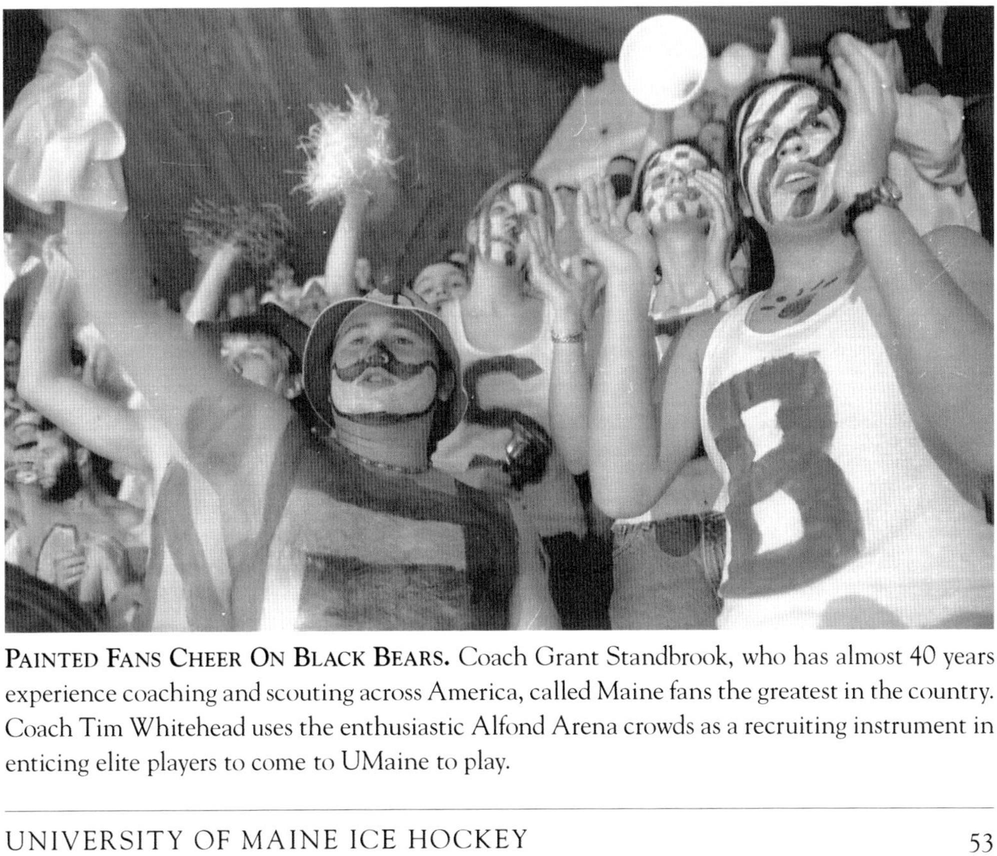

PAINTED FANS CHEER ON BLACK BEARS. Coach Grant Standbrook, who has almost 40 years experience coaching and scouting across America, called Maine fans the greatest in the country. Coach Tim Whitehead uses the enthusiastic Alfond Arena crowds as a recruiting instrument in enticing elite players to come to UMaine to play.

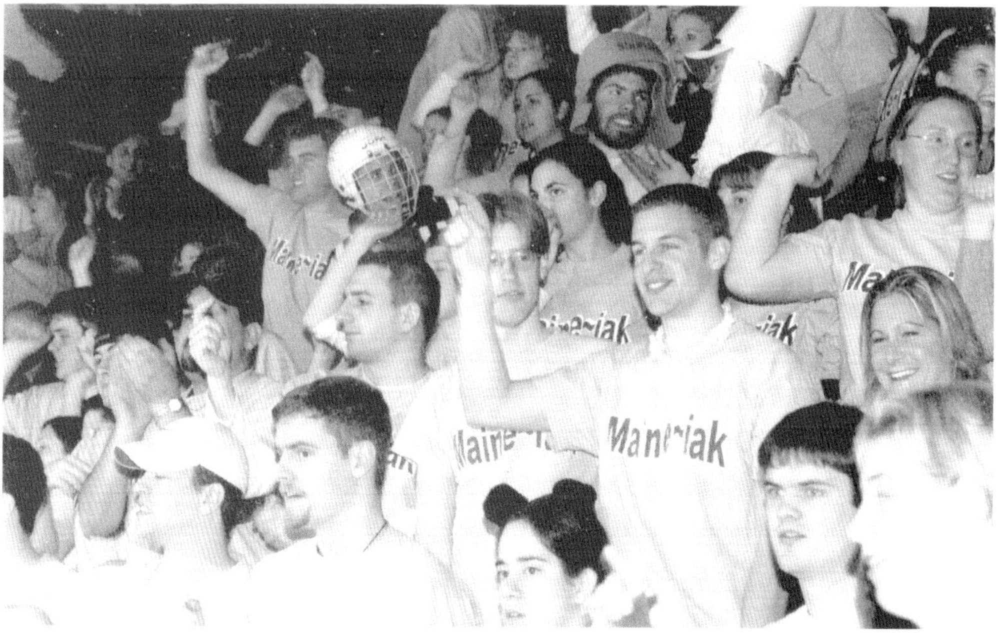

Go Maine! UMaine has its own version of the "Bleacher Bums" and the "Royal Rooters." The "Maine iaks" are an exclusive group of UMaine students who encourage Maine players, heckle the opposition, and question every call made against the Black Bears. Requirements are a $10 fee and plenty of energy to expend.

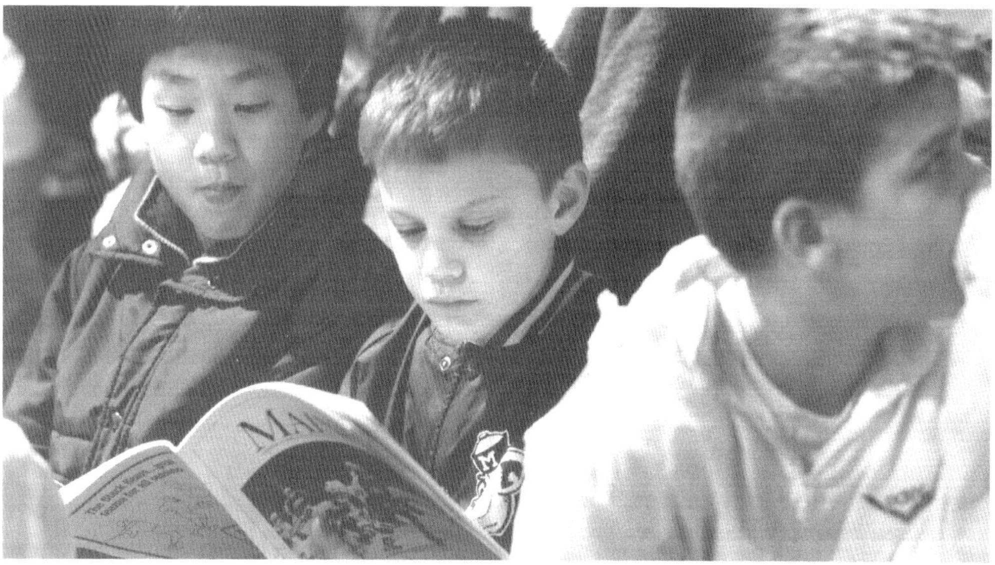

Students of the Game. Crowds at the Alfond Arena are an eclectic mix. Attendance has increased from 30,450 in the 1977–1978 season to 107,969 in 2005–2006. A significant addition of seats and skyboxes were added to accommodate the growing numbers. Seven times UMaine has led Hockey East in attendance, and it is the hottest ticket in New England. Fans often wait in lines for hours to get the limited tickets available.

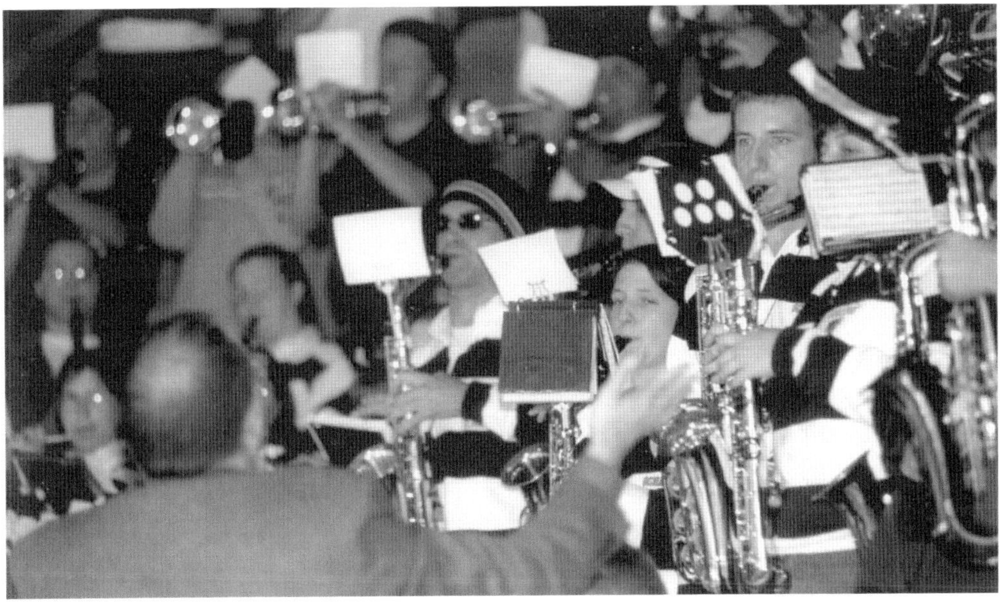

STRIKE UP THE BAND. Also contributing to the atmosphere at Alfond is the Screamin' Black Bears Pep Band, which breaks out into the "Stein Song" whenever Maine scores a goal. The band often follows the Black Bears to important away games and to the national playoffs. The pep band has become such an important part of Maine hockey that it received the Friends of Maine Hockey Madeline Bacon Spirit Award in 2006. It has been recognized nationally as one of the best pep bands in the country by CSTV.

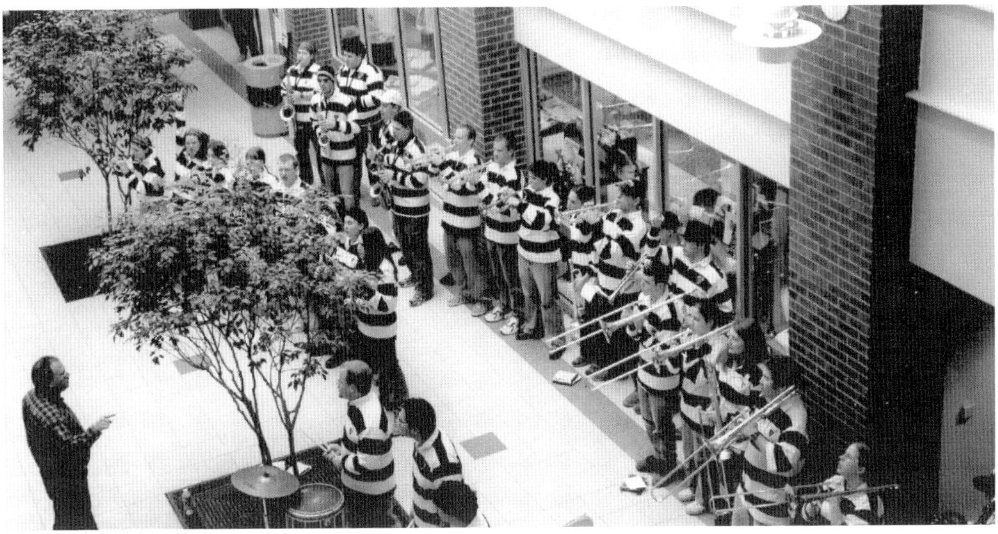

CHRIS WHITE DIRECTS THE UMAINE PEP BAND. The Screamin' Black Bears Pep Band and also the Pride of Maine Marching Black Bear Band are led by Chris White, UMaine director of sport bands. White has directed the bands for 15 years and calls it a part of the pageantry of college athletics. Coaches agree that a quality band and energy from fans can make a difference in the outcome of a close game.

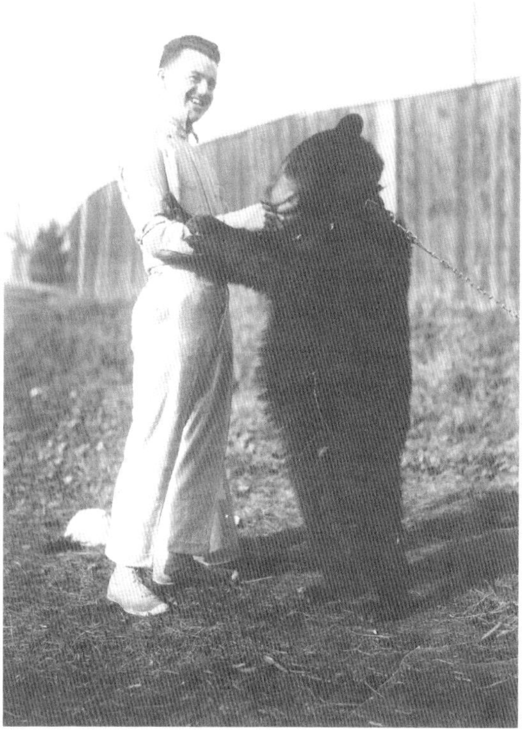

BANANAS UMAINE MASCOT. The original Bananas was a live black bear cub given to the university in 1914 by alumnus Lloyd Houghton, with the suggestion that the cub be called Bananas. A live Bananas prowled the sidelines for 15 generations, appearing primarily at football games until the death of Cindy Bananas in 1966. The service fraternity Alpha Phi Omega renewed the tradition in 1969 by supplying a human Bananas.

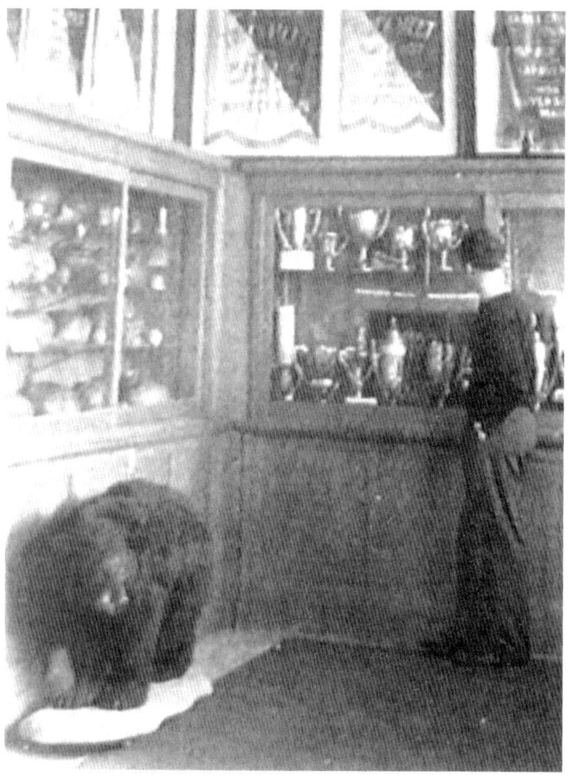

BANANAS IN TROPHY ROOM AT UMAINE IN THE 1940S. A stuffed Bananas resides in the Memorial Gymnasium after dying of ptomaine poisoning and being sent to a taxidermist for preservation. Although Bananas was the long-standing tradition, he may have not been UMaine's first mascot. Bolivar the elephant was captured from a downtown Bangor clothing exposition and forced to attend a football game in the early 1900s. History would have read differently had the school adopted the name the UMaine Elephants.

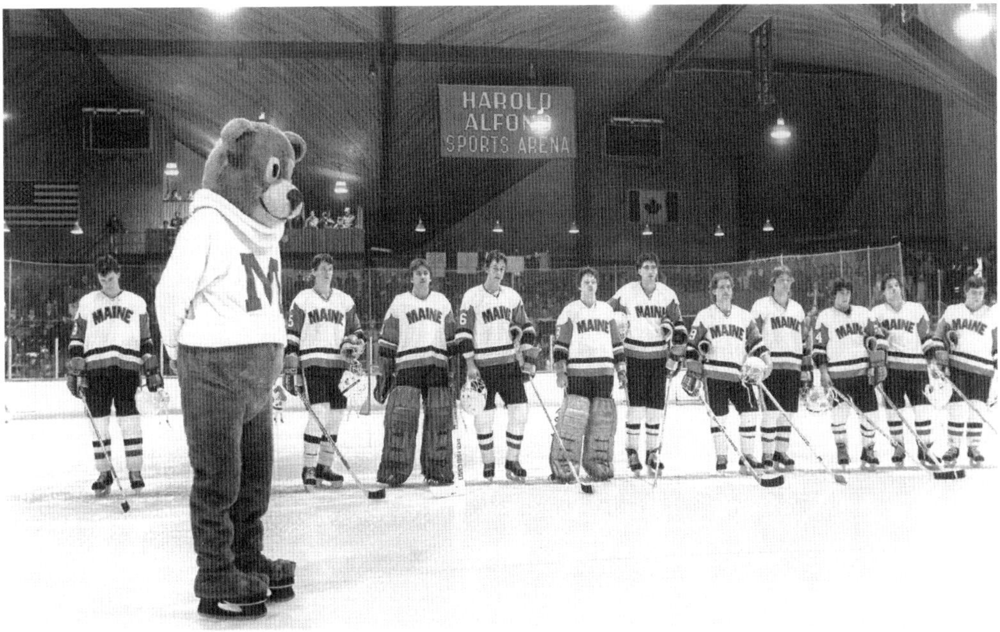

BANANAS T BEAR STIRS UP THE FANS AT ALFOND. A home game at Alfond would not be complete without an appearance by Bananas T Bear encouraging the crowd and cheering on the players.

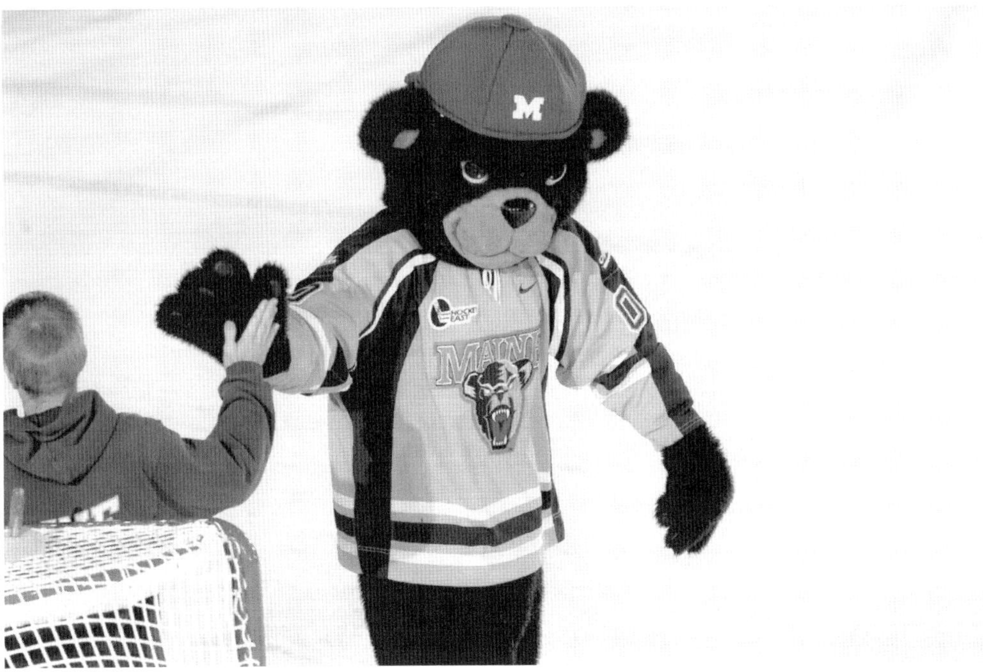

NEW AND IMPROVED BANANAS. In 2004, Bananas received a complete body and face lift. The university has also established the Bananas Cub Club for young UMaine fans. Membership entitles them to a free newsletter and a chance to meet their favorite players.

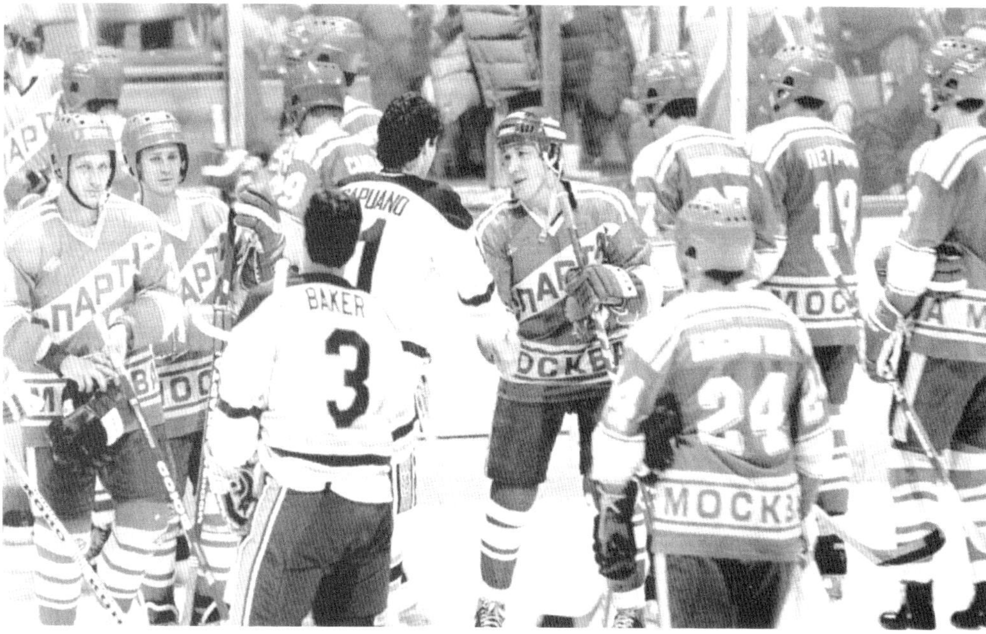

BLACK BEARS PLAY SOVIET TEAM, 1985. No cold war here, except on the ice. In 1985, UMaine played an exhibition game against the Soviet Union's Sokol-Kiev team, losing 11-1. It was the first time ever Maine played against an eastern European team. Coach Shawn Walsh believed the higher the caliber the opponent, the better his team could be. Walsh would often bring in all-star teams, Olympic teams, and semiprofessionals to play exhibition games at Alfond Arena against the Black Bears. Below, players stand at attention while both national anthems are played prior to the face-off.

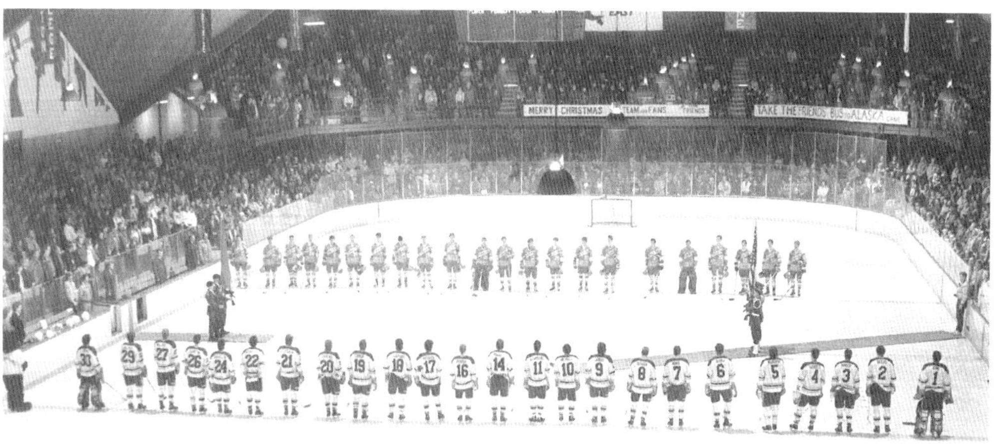

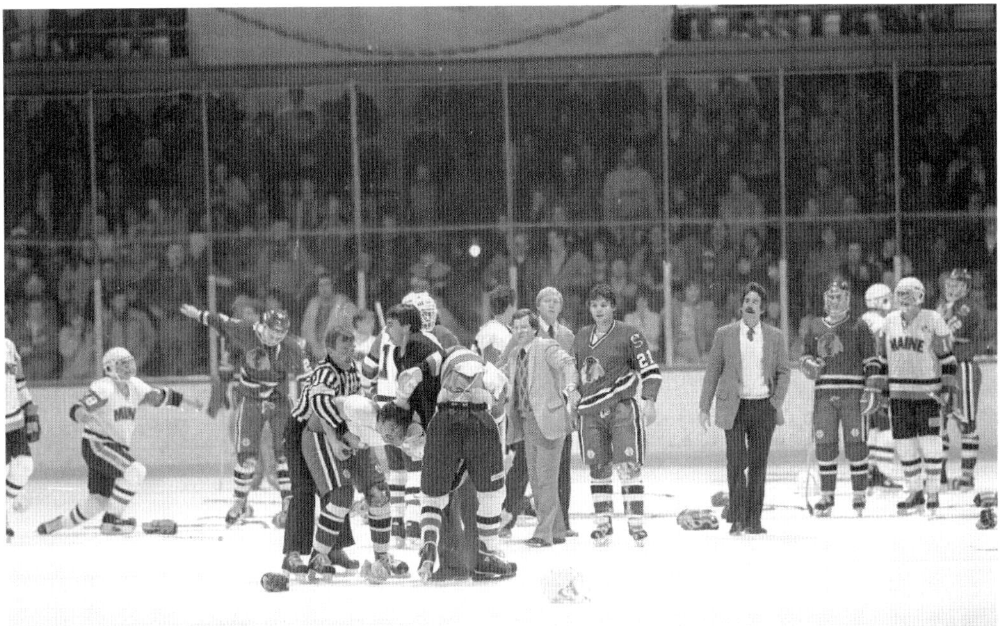

Coach Walsh Joins Altercation. Although gentlemen play it, no one has ever called hockey a gentlemen's game. Players are often exhorted to leave it all on the ice, and sometimes that includes helmets and gloves.

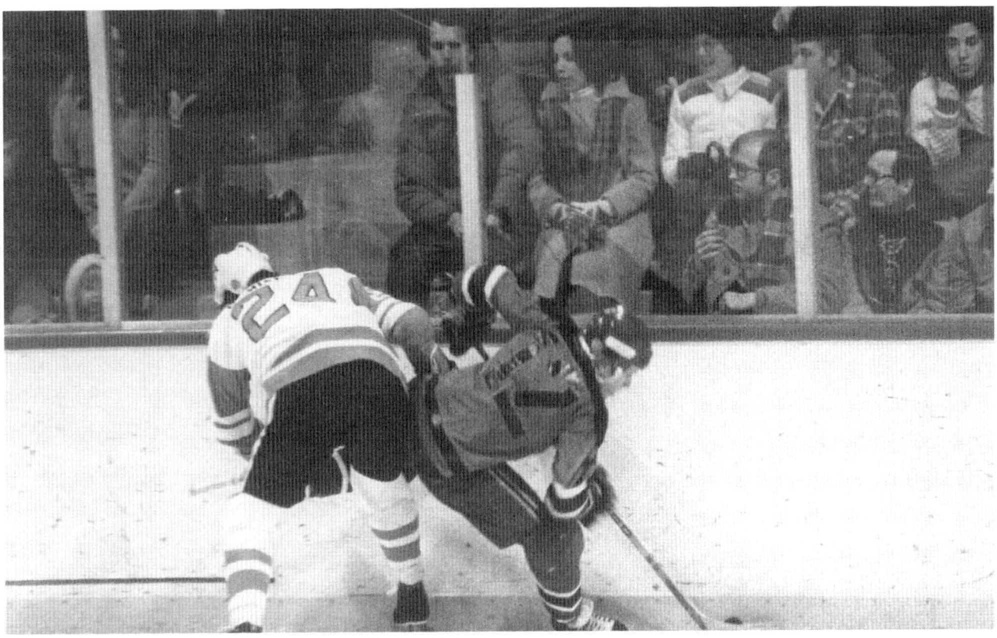

UMaine's Bill Demianiuk Delivers Check. The game of hockey is an aggressive contact sport, and inevitably tempers flare. Reforms concerning the violence of the sport, however, are being encouraged by the American College of Sports Medicine, which advocates a no-tolerance standard for violent acts and fighting.

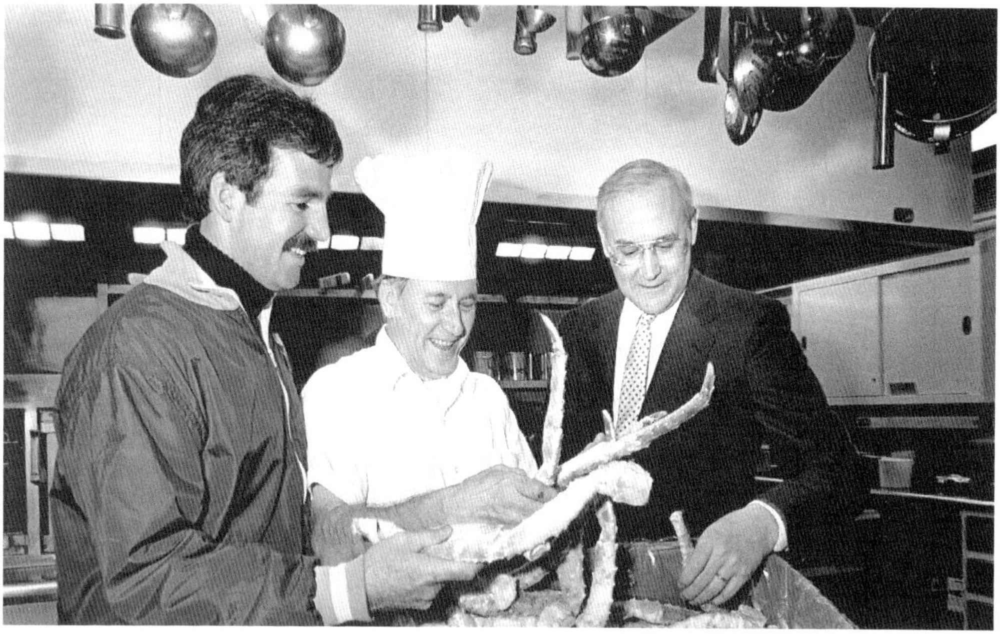

COACH WALSH AND UMAINE PRESIDENT DALE LICK WITH ALASKAN KING CRAB. To the winner go the spoils. Coach Shawn Walsh had a bet with the head coach of the University of Alaska Anchorage (UAA) team over the outcome of their game at Alfond on November 17, 1990. Prior to the contest Maine had had two losses and a tie against UAA. Maine won this time, 5-2.

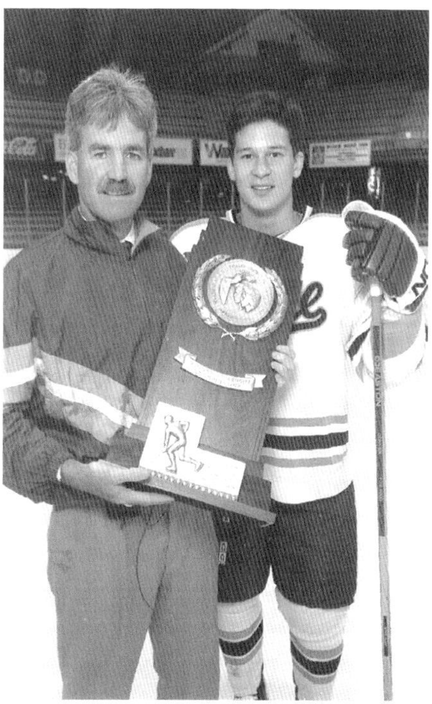

COACH WALSH CELEBRATES NATIONAL CHAMPIONSHIP. Walsh undoubtedly enjoyed this feast more.

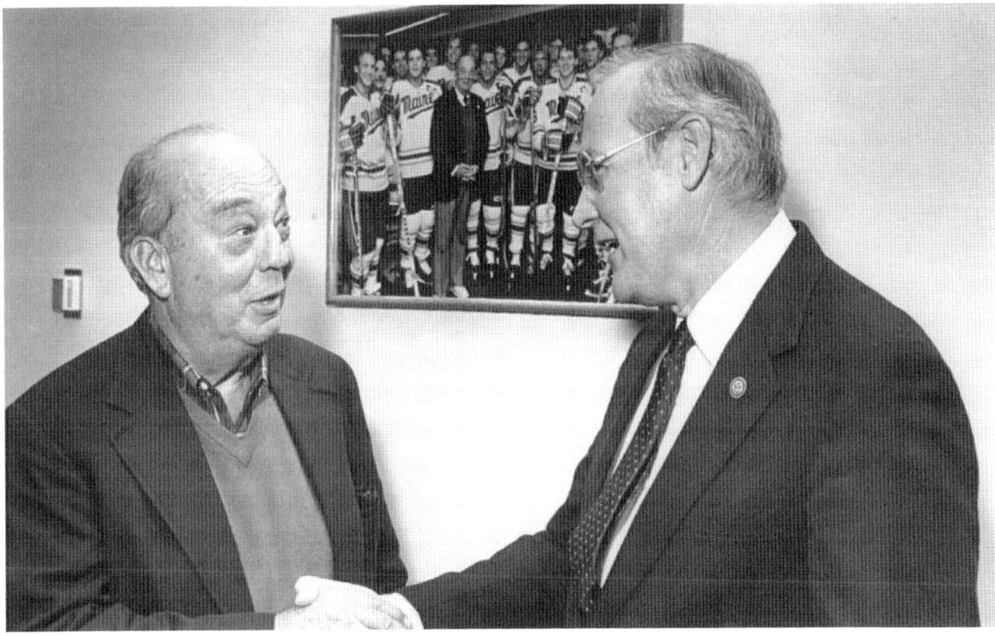

Harold Alfond with UMaine President Dale Lick. In the competitive arena that is Division I hockey, championship-caliber teams are not forged without money for scholarships, arenas, and talented coaching staffs. The generosity of faithful patrons like Harold Alfond has helped to defray the cost of the program and keep it moving forward. Although hockey generates more revenue than any other sport at UMaine, approximately $1.8 million in ticket sales alone, it only consumes 10 to 12 percent of the total athletic department budget.

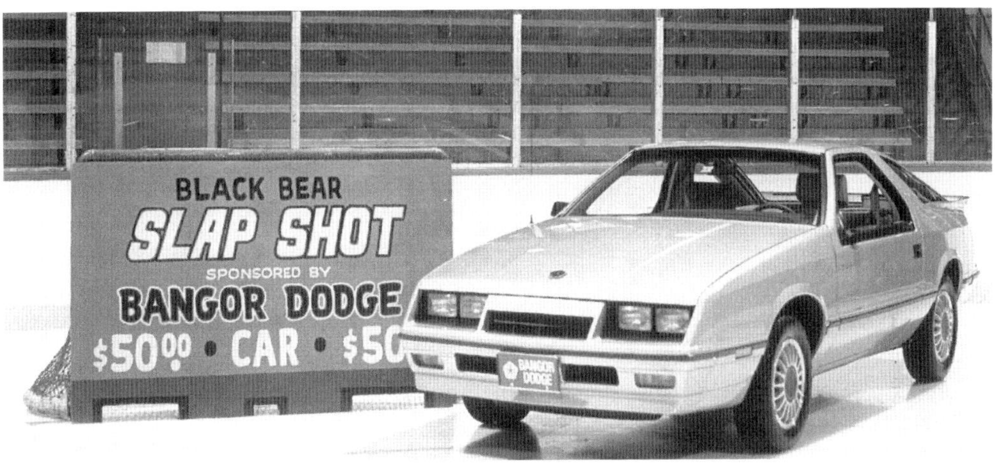

Car Offered in Slap Shot Contest, 1988. Externally generated income accounts for almost half of the resources needed to sustain the hockey program at UMaine. Groups such as the Black Bear Club and the Friends of UMaine Hockey have been major contributors to the cause. Local businesses have also helped by supplying promotional activities like this one sponsored by Bangor Dodge. In 1988, 13-year-old Jason Cyr beat the odds and won himself a Dodge Daytona.

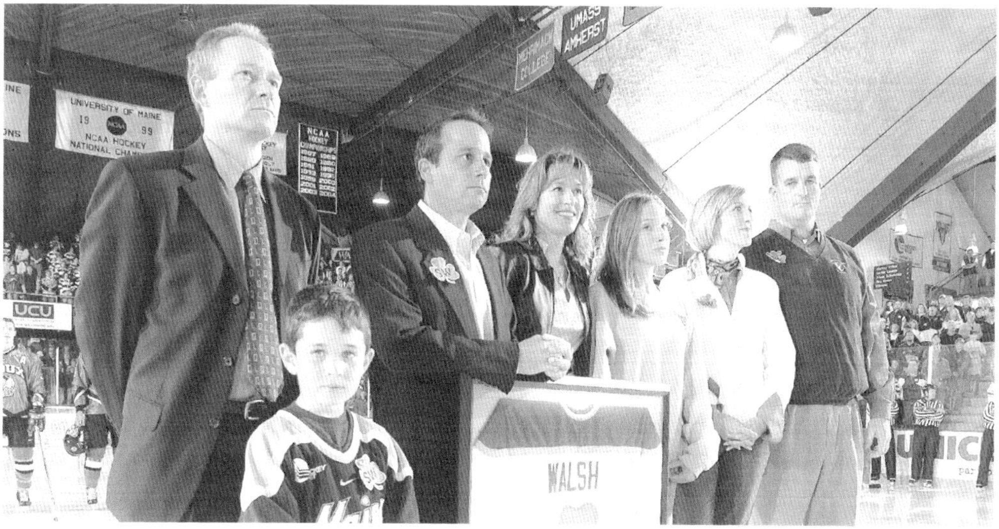

A CHAMPION IN LIFE AND DEATH. In 2000, the hockey world was shocked by the news that Shawn Walsh had been diagnosed with cancer, requiring the removal of a kidney and a lung. His courageous battle ended on September 24, 2001, as he was preparing for his 18th year as UMaine coach. For 16 months, Walsh fought the greatest opponent of his life. Whether he won or lost depends upon perspective. He certainly won the hearts of Mainers, former critics, and players with a courage that never waned. Days before his death, he was on the ice with a team that played its way to the Frozen Four in his honor.

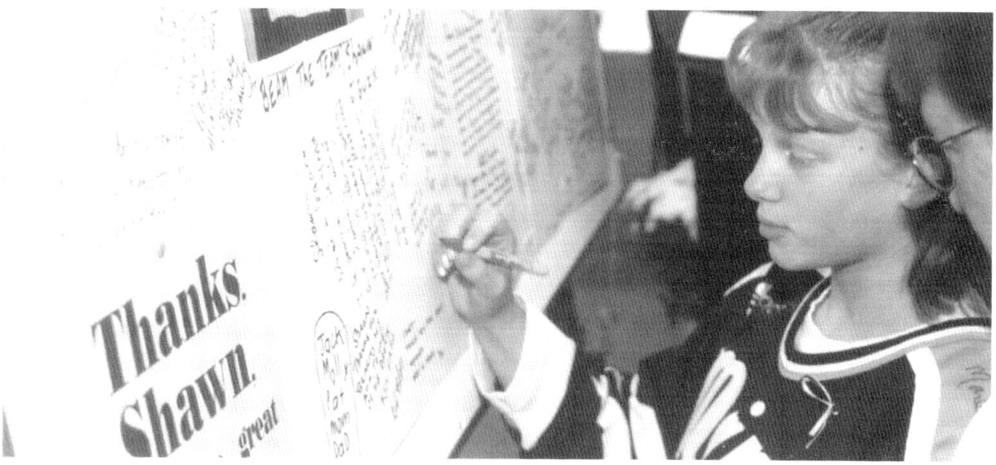

A LIVING LEGACY. Walsh's life and legacy are best summed up by those who played for him. "Coach liked the phrase: the definition of a man's character is the way he handles adversity," said Peter Metcalf, captain of the 2001–2002 team. "This is exactly what he was talking about," said Garth Snow, Walsh's goalie on the 1993 national championship squad, in an interview with the *Bangor Daily News*, "I owe everything I have ever accomplished in my field to him. One, he convinced me to come to Maine. Two, he helped me turn my hockey career and personal life around 180 degrees." Walsh is best remembered for his favorite axiom: "If you don't have the best of everything, make the best of everything you have."

4

GREAT TEAMS

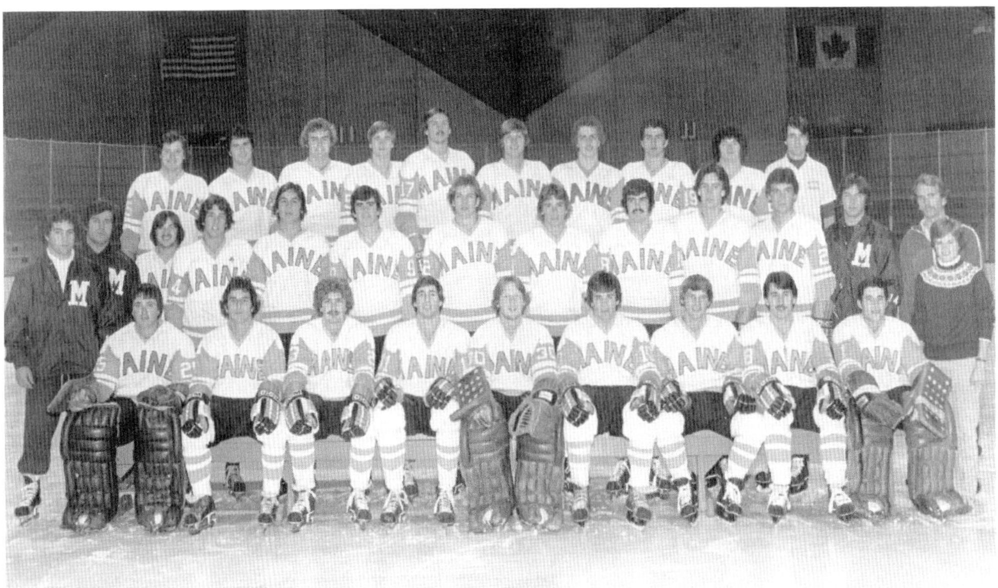

THE 1977–1978 UMAINE MEN'S BLACK BEAR ICE HOCKEY TEAM. Great teams are not always determined by won and lost records or tournament appearances. In the Black Bears' inaugural season of the modern era, coach Jack Semler did a remarkable job of transforming a hockey club into a varsity sport. Coach Semler had no blueprint to work from, no returning veterans, and few at the university with hockey expertise. He relied heavily on the efforts of athletic director Harold Westerman, who was determined to establish a quality program at Maine. Semler and lone assistant Ted Castle led the squad to a respectable 15-12-0 record, just missing the playoffs while playing in the East Coast Athletic Conference Division II East league.

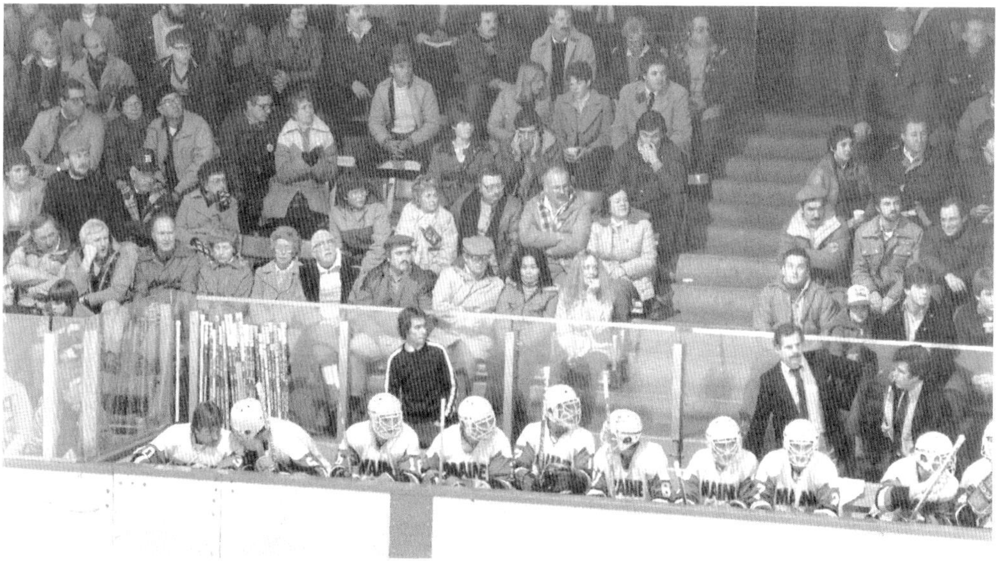

Coach Semler Giving Instruction in 1977 Game at Alfond. With a squad of 28 players, 27 of whom were freshman, Jack Semler had the youngest hockey team in the nation. The team moved forward quickly, and in 1978–1979, posted a 25-8-1 record with wins over Division I opponents Northeastern and the University of Vermont. The season earned the team an invitation to be granted Division I status by the NCAA the following season. Semler was awarded New England Coach of the Year honors.

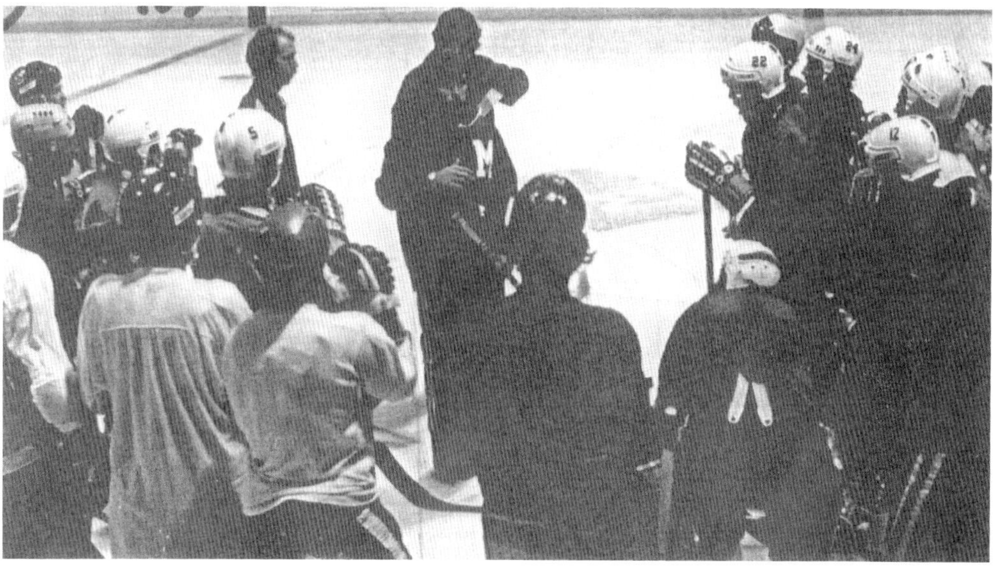

Coach Semler at Practice. Semler's philosophy as a coach was to have his players work hard on every shift and play clean, hard hockey. They were encouraged to know that win or lose the sun always comes up tomorrow. "We tried to have fun and be humble in victory, and not get down on ourselves in defeat," Semler said. "Everybody was expected to go hard all the time and talent didn't guarantee playing time."

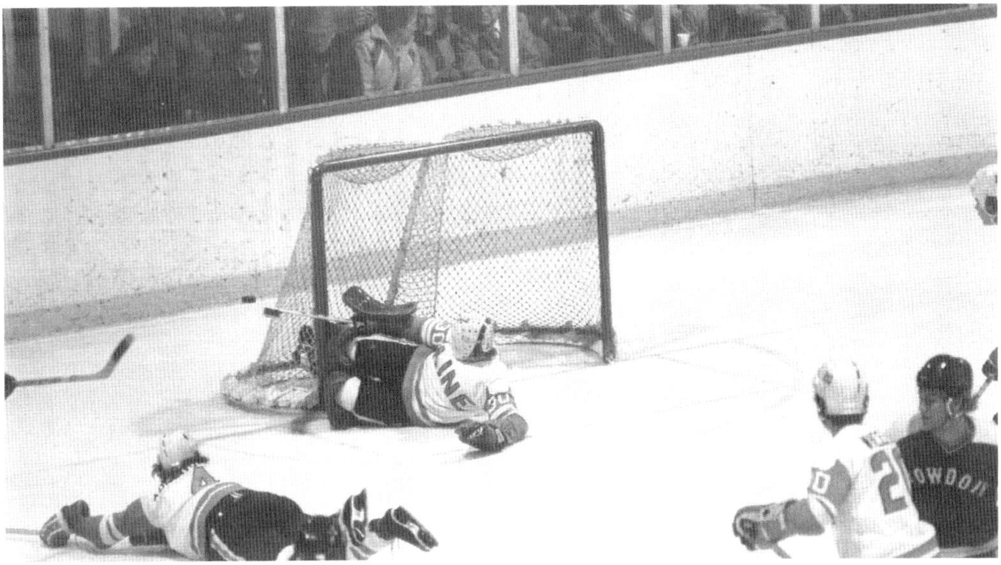

JEFF NORD STOPPING A SHOT DURING THE 1977–1978 SEASON. Tending goal the initial season were Jeff Nord (No. 30) and Jim Tortorella (No. 1). Nord would have a four-year career with the Black Bears, starting 62 games and winning 38. He had a .887 save percentage while recording 1,795 saves. He is helped out above by Dwight Montgomery (No. 4).

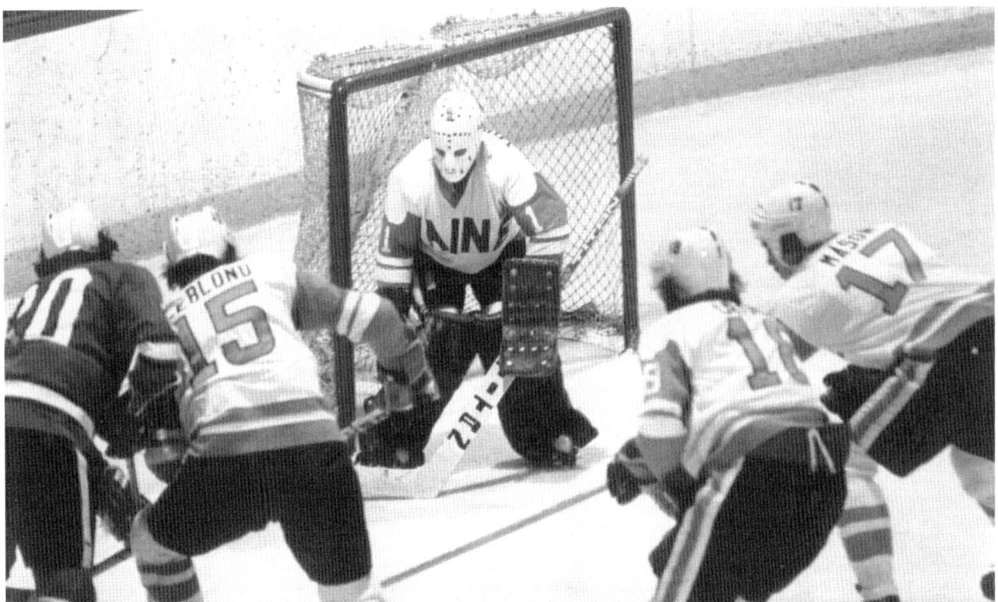

WITH A LITTLE HELP FROM HIS FRIENDS. Jim Tortorella also had a four-year career at Maine. He compiled an 8-5 record in 1977–1978. He went on to play in 68 games for the Black Bears, recording 1,941 saves and 38 career wins. Tortorella later went on to be a successful coach at Colby College, where he is the all-time coaching wins leader and the 2005–2006 NESCAC coach of the year.

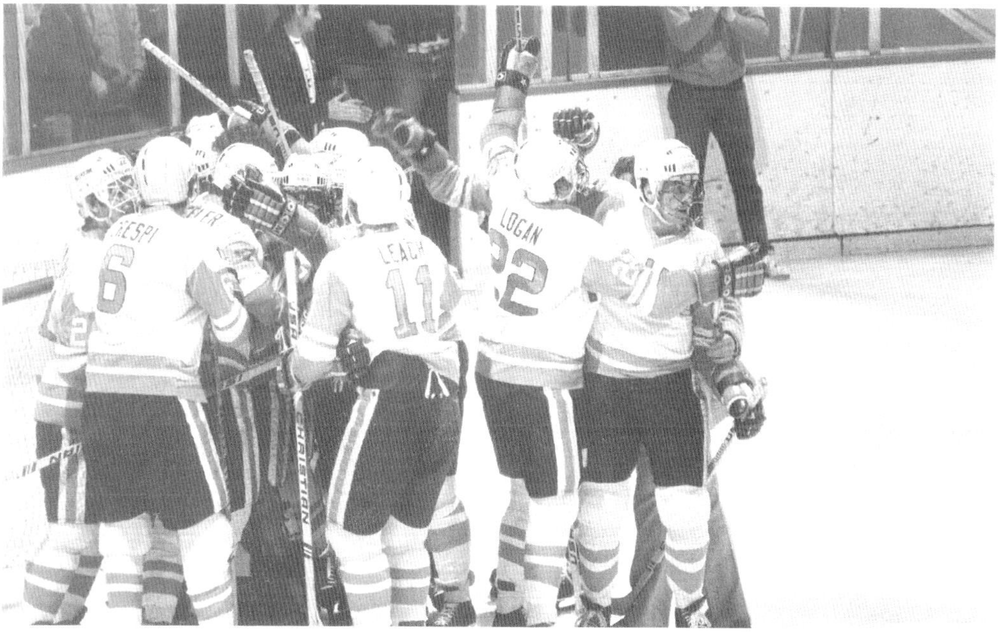

TIME TO CELEBRATE. Joe Crespi, Jon Leach, and Jamie Logan congratulate teammates after a regular-season win at Alfond Arena. Semler's teams would be characterized by hard, clean, selfless play. A fitting tribute came from an opposing player who told the *Bangor Daily News*, "They're all hustlers who give 100 percent. They have good coaching and discipline, play their positions and stay cool in their own end."

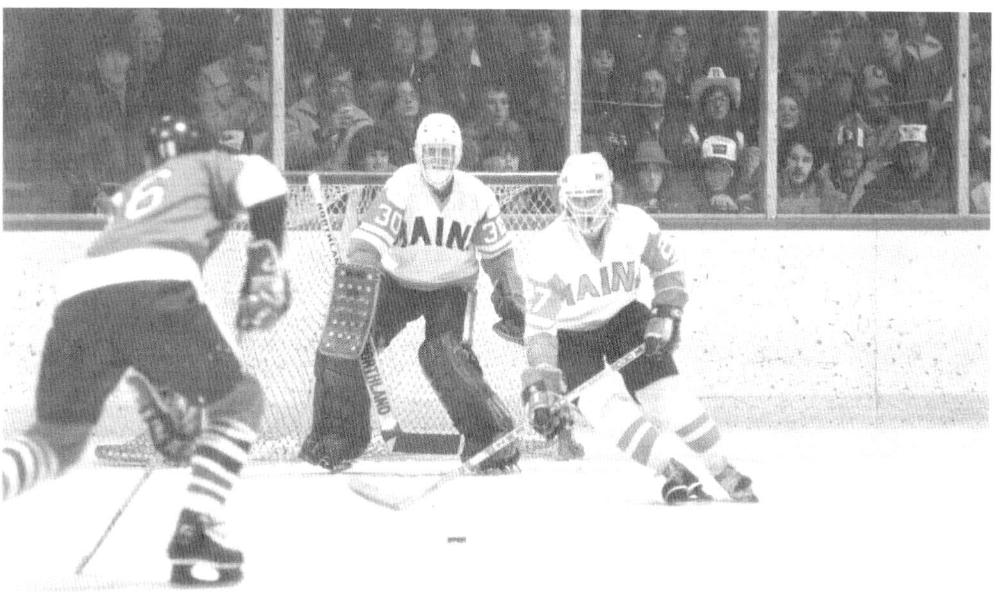

ANDRE AUBUT CHASING THE PUCK OUT OF THE MAINE ZONE. Defenseman Andre Aubut (No. 27) aids goalie Jeff Nord (No. 30). Gifted with the puck, Aubut was a great scorer and skillful defender. In 1980, Aubut would be the first Black Bear to be named to the All-American team.

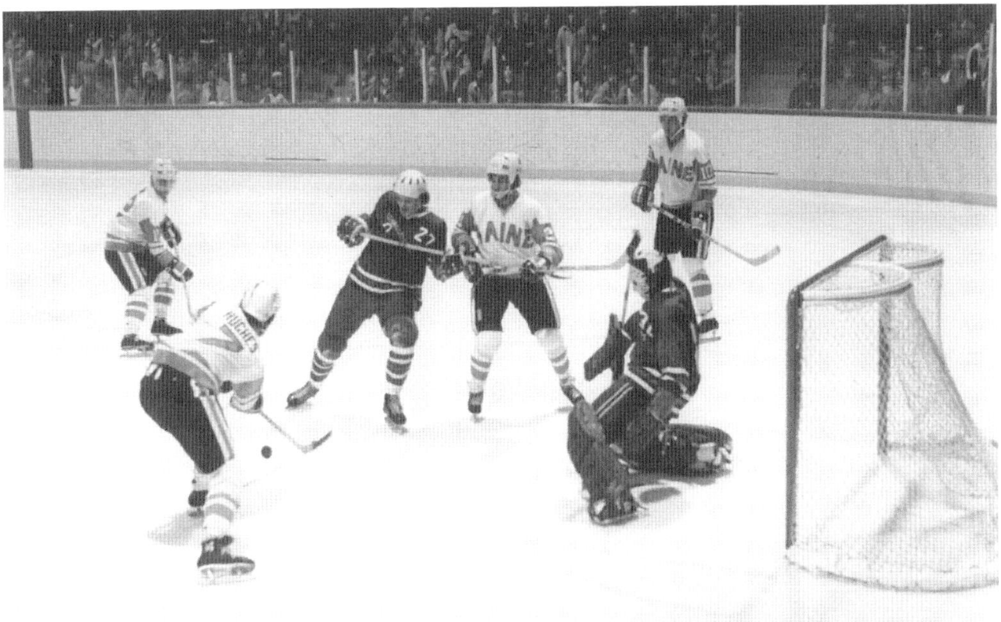

MAINE POWER PLAY IN ACTION. Brian Hughes (No. 7) looks to pass with Dave Walsh (No. 10) waiting for a rebound. Hughes was a steady player who finished second to Gary Conn in scoring with 14 goals and 28 assists in 1977–1978.

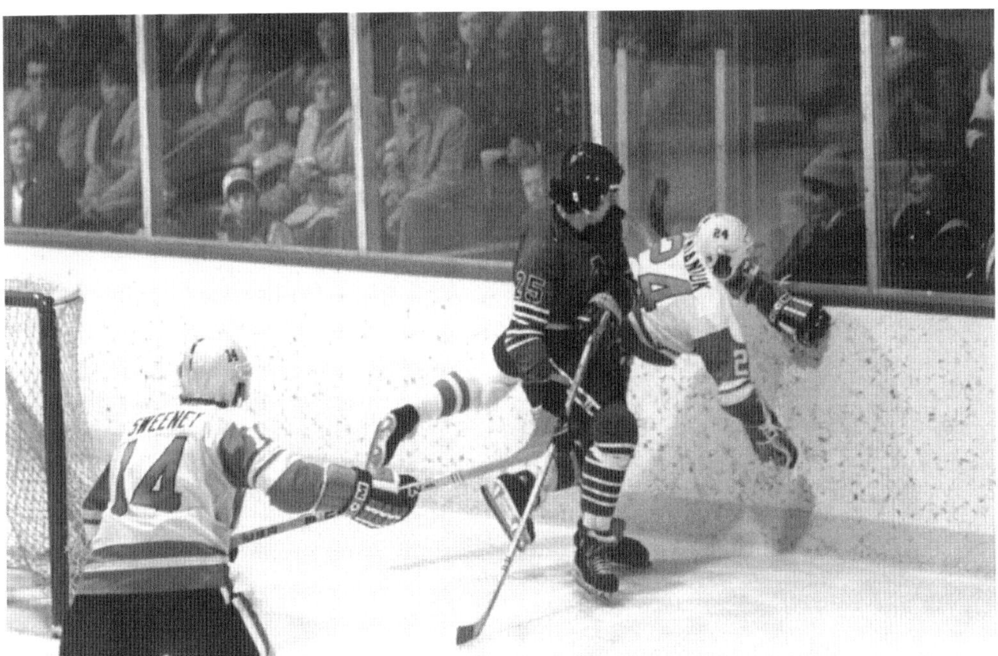

BILL DEMIANIUK CHECKED HARD INTO THE BOARDS AT ALFOND. The heart and soul of the team was Bill Demianiuk (No. 24), who would captain the team the next two seasons. Coming to his aid is Dan Sweeney (No. 14), who also played football and baseball at UMaine.

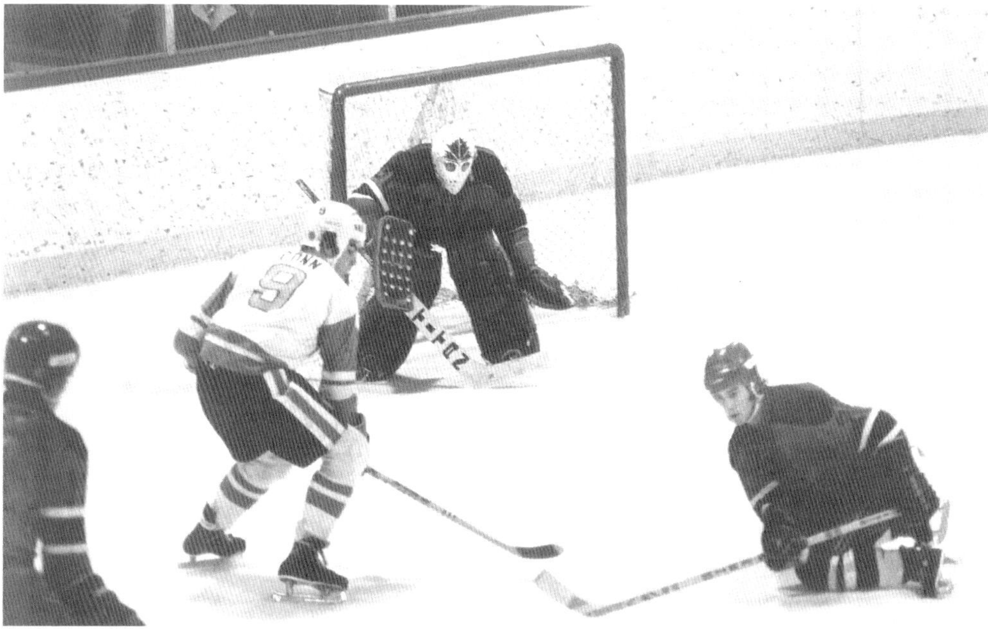

READY TO SCORE. One of Maine's first hockey superstars, Gary Conn (No. 9) led the inaugural campaign in scoring with a team-high 21 goals in a 27-game schedule. He would lead the team in scoring each of the Black Bears' first four years. Conn scored the first goal in the history of the modern era of Black Bear hockey.

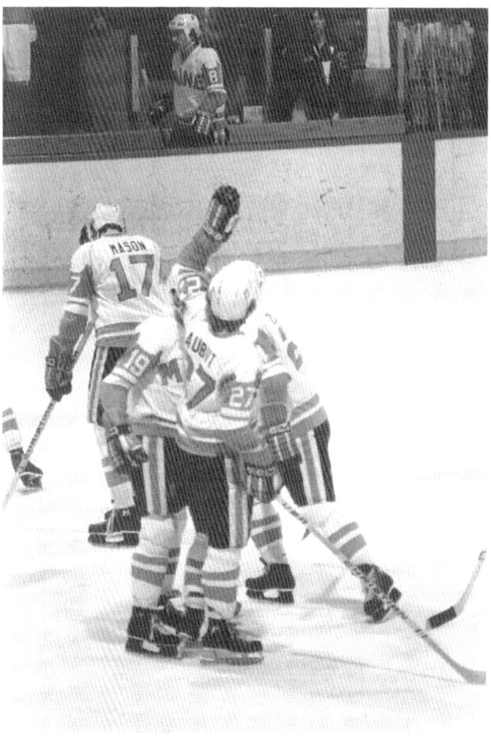

THINGS ARE LOOKING UP FOR UMAINE HOCKEY. While in Conn and Andre Aubut, Jack Semler had two future All-Americans, he had a core of workhorse players around them, including Robert Lafleur, David Ellis, Donald Mason, and Art Demoulas.

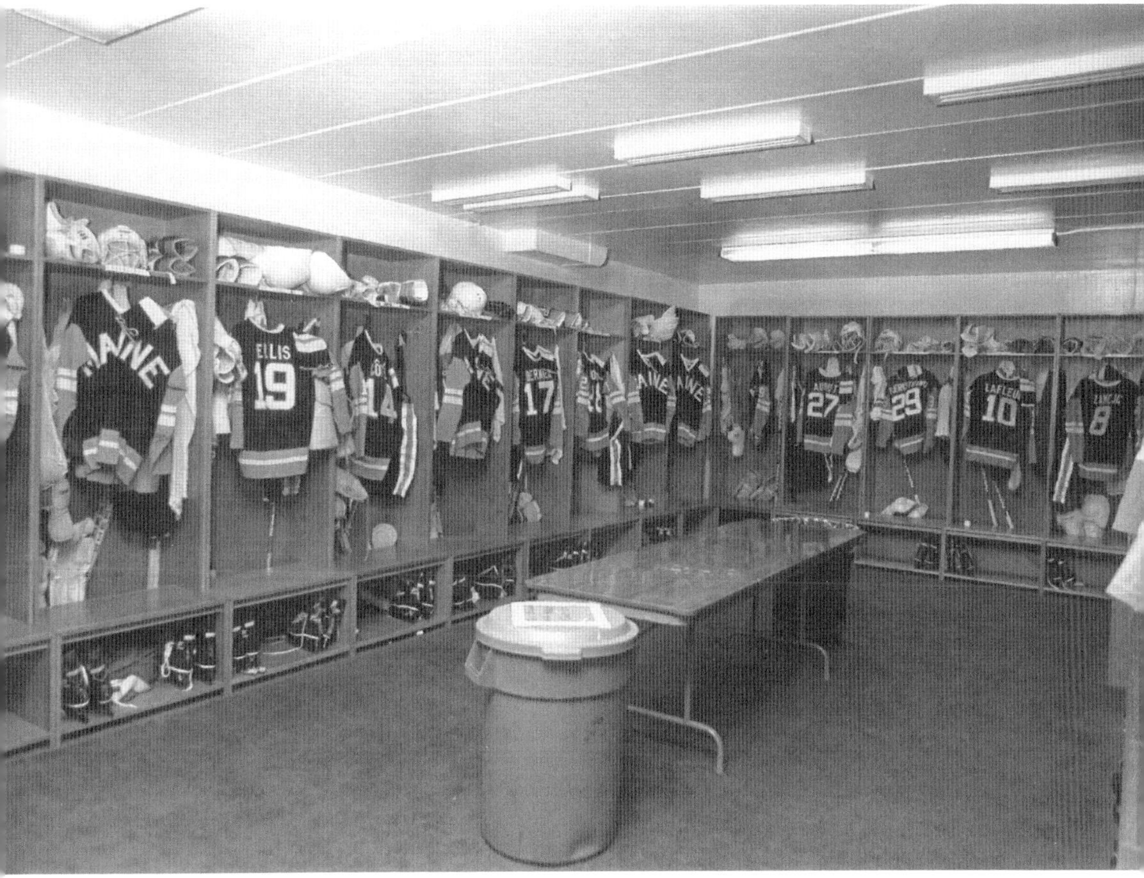

The 1980–1981 UMaine Men's Ice Hockey Team. Semler's team entered the 1980–1981 season with high expectations. Players who were freshmen on the first team were now seniors, and newcomers Rob Zamejc and John Tortorella added more firepower to the squad. The team did not disappoint. It compiled an overall 23-11 record before losing to Cornell 7-4 in the postseason tournament. In their first four seasons, the Black Bears compiled an impressive 78-47-2 record. But most important, they proved themselves a legitimate Division I program and one on its way to becoming a hockey power.

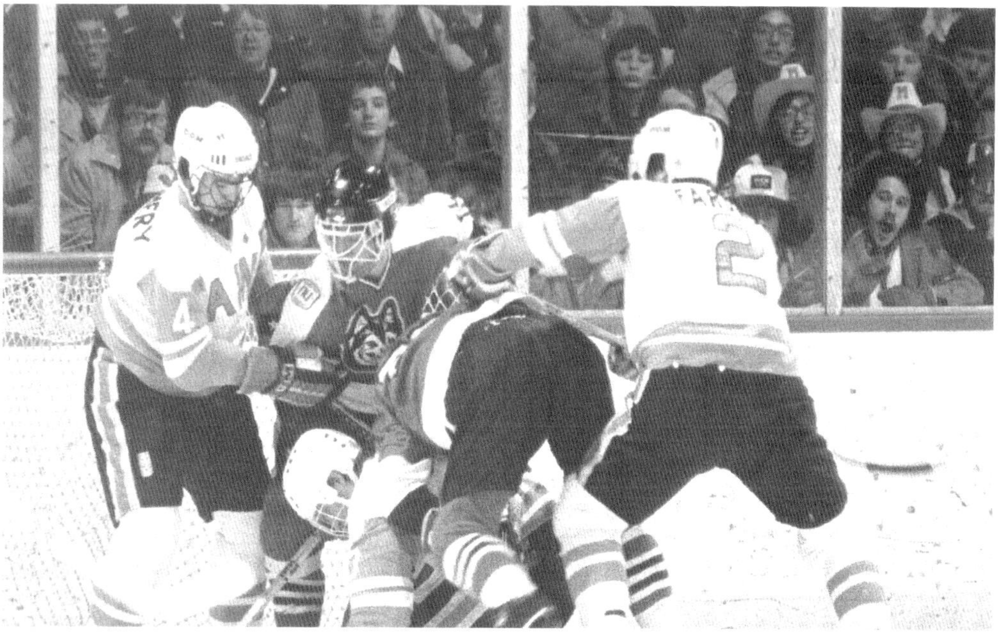

Jam in Front of the Northeastern Goal. Dwight Montgomery (No. 4) and Ken Fargnoli (No. 2) scramble for a loose puck. The scrappy veteran team seemed to play best at Alfond Arena where it compiled a 12-3 record.

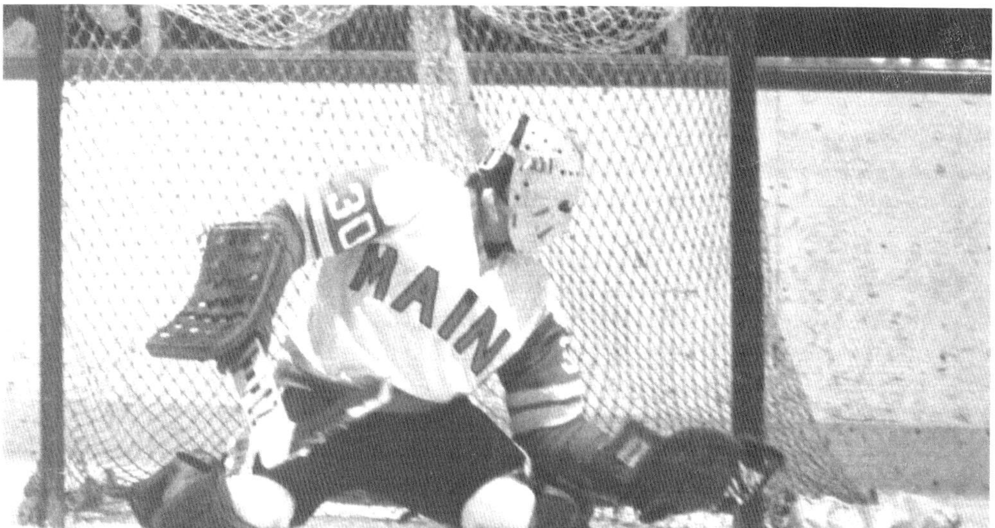

Glove Save by Goalie Jeff Nord (No. 30). Jack Semler called goalies Jeff Nord and Jim Tortorella the best in the east. They were backed by the solid play of defensemen Andre Aubut, Dwight Montgomery, and David Ellis. Midway through the season, Tortorella became the first Eastern College Athletic Conference (ECAC) goalie to score a goal. His clearing pass bounced off the side board, over the opposing goalie's stick, and into the net. Both Tortorella's stick and the puck are on display at the United States Hockey Hall of Fame.

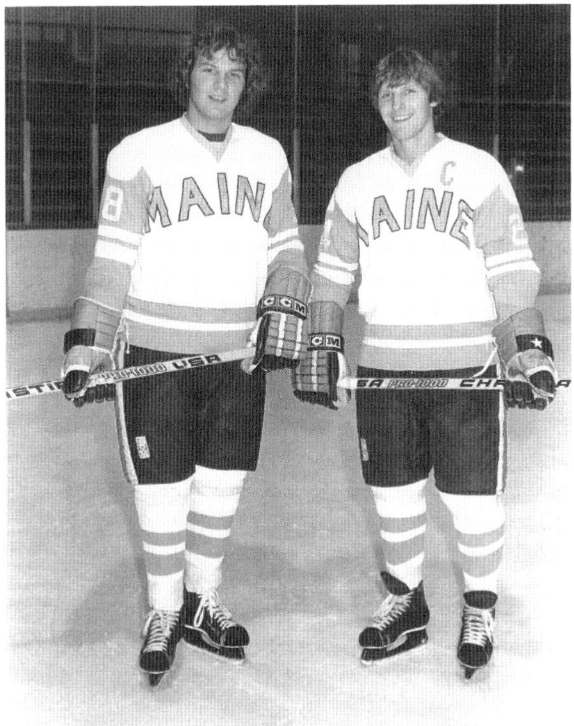

Gary Conn and Team Captain Bill Demianiuk. Leading the team was captain Bill Demianiuk and leading scorer Gary Conn. Conn led the team in scoring for the fourth consecutive year with a team-high 30 goals and 33 assists while compiling 63 points.

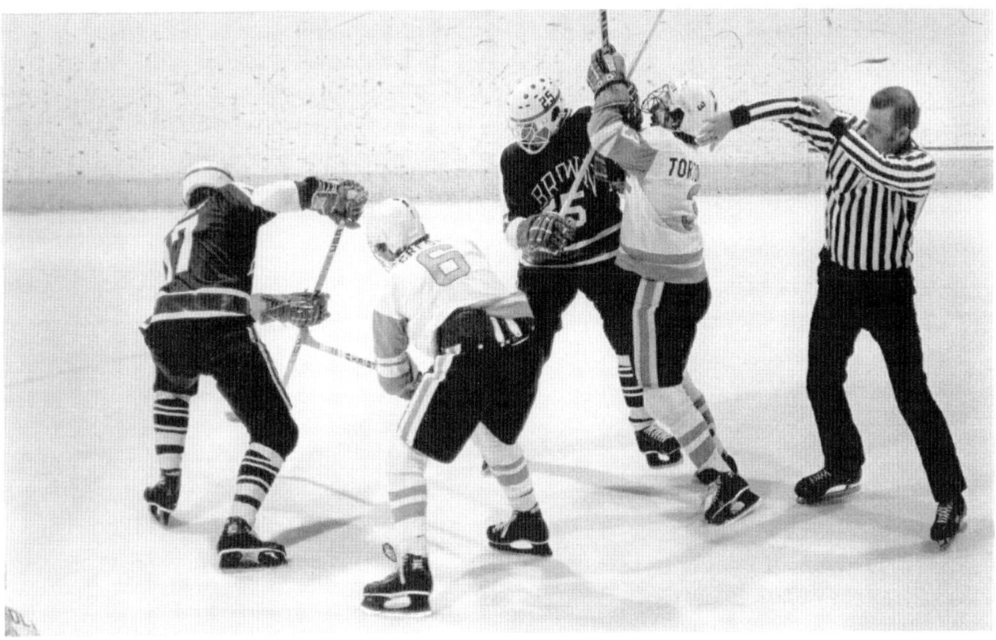

Joe Crespi Digging Puck from Brown Player. Another solid performer for the 1980–1981 squad was Joe Crespi (No. 6), seen here battling for the puck with teammate John Tortorella in a game against Brown. Crespi had a distinguished four-year career with the Black Bears, finishing 7th on the all-time goals scored with 78 and 10th in total points with 168.

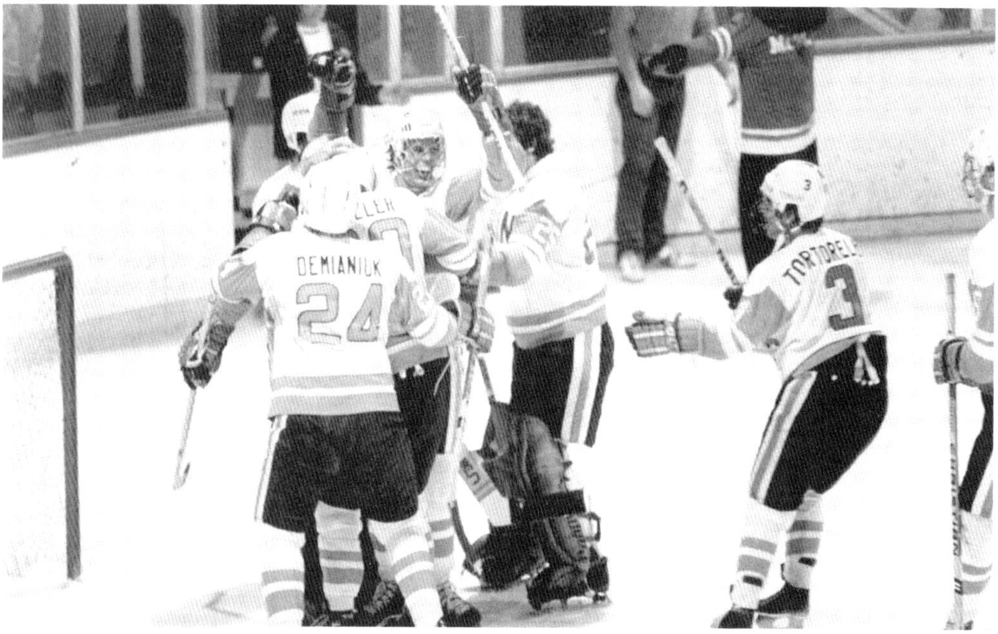

UMAINE CELEBRATION OF WIN AT ALFOND. Celebrating a UMaine win are John Tortorella (No. 3), David Hunt (No. 25), Paul Wheeler (No. 20), and Bill Demianiuk (No. 24). The team compiled a 12-3 record playing at Alfond Arena.

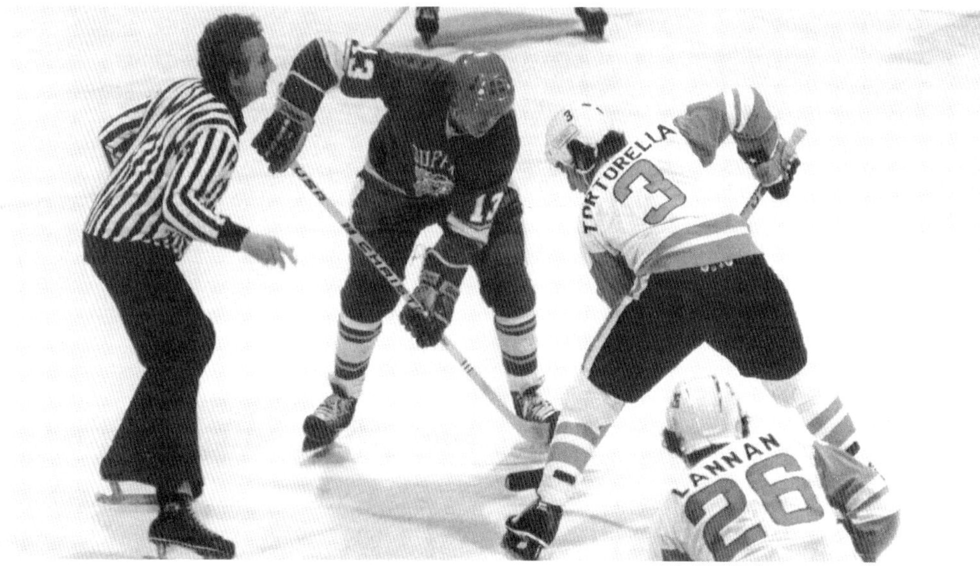

JOHN TORTORELLA WINS FACE-OFF. John Tortorella played three seasons at UMaine before signing with the Hampton-Roads Gulls in the Atlantic Coast Hockey League (ACHL). After retiring as an active player in 1986, Tortorella went on to become the head coach of the Virginia Lancers before serving as an assistant coach in the NHL for the Buffalo Sabers, Phoenix Coyotes, and New York Rangers. In 2001, he was named head coach of the Tampa Bay Lightning, where his 2003–2004 team won the Stanley Cup Championship.

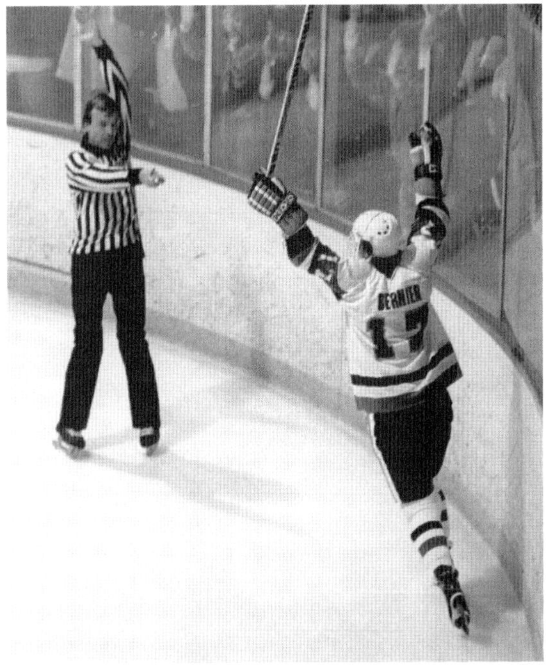

GAETAN BERNIER (NO. 17) SCORES FOR THE BLACK BEARS. A successful season was dampened by a 7-4 loss to Cornell in the postseason playoffs. Graduation would take its toll on a senior-laden team, but new recruits were on the horizon. Pete Smith, who played at Maine the following season, was the first Black Bear selected by an NHL team, drafted in the 12th round by the St. Louis Blues in 1981. Jay Mazur, seen below, was the second, taken in the 12th round by the Vancouver Canucks in 1983. UMaine has become one of the leading contributors to professional hockey with over 50 former Black Bears seeing action in the NHL.

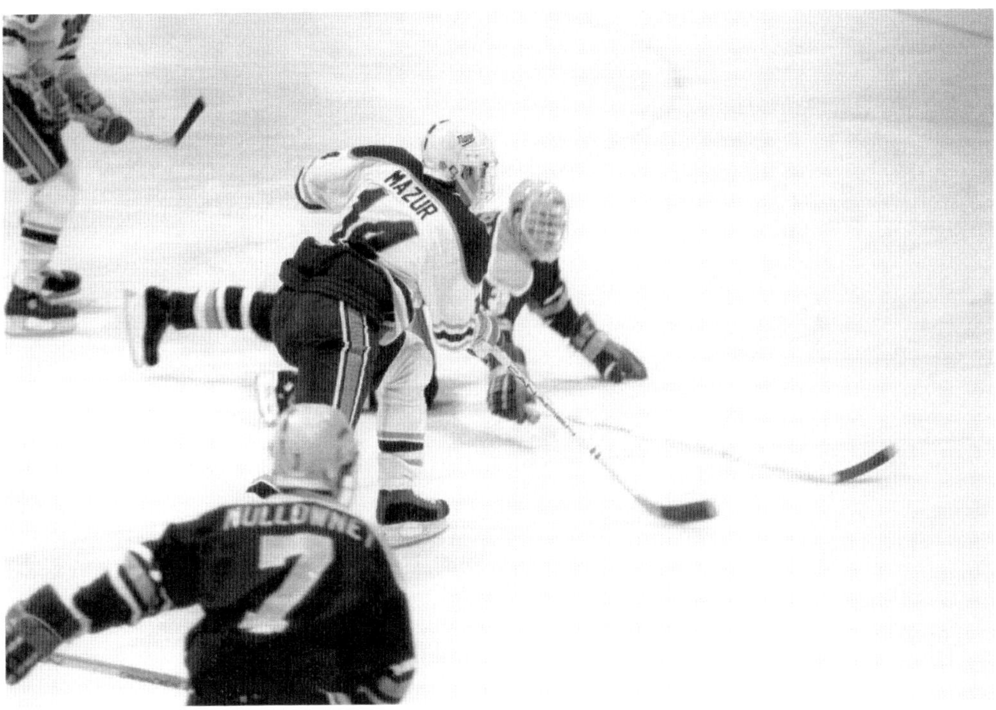

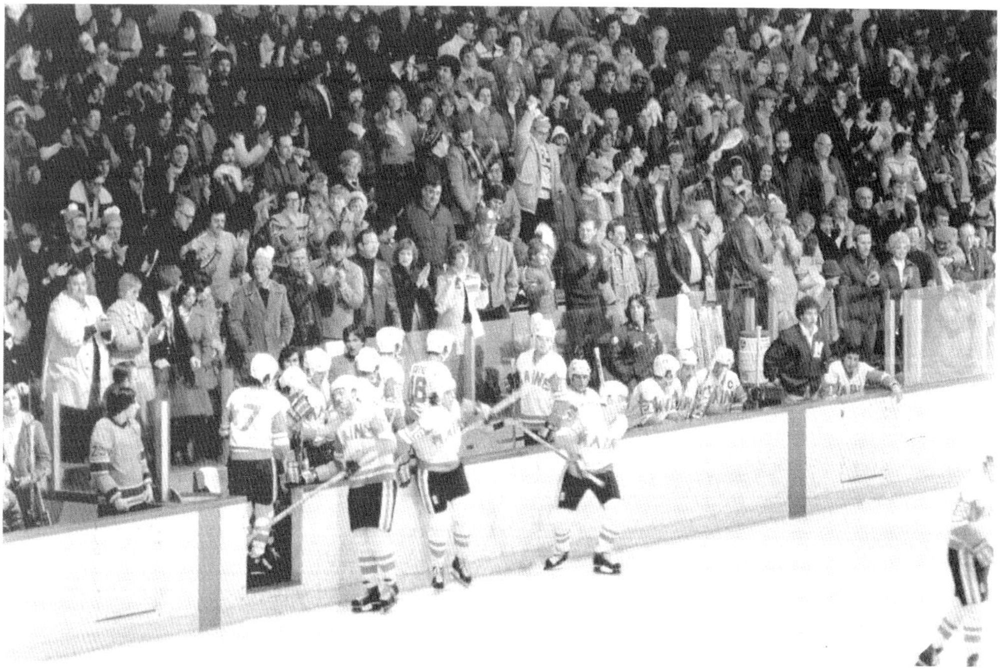

CHANGE OF THE GUARD. The Jack Semler era came to an end on February 27, 1984, in a home game against his alma mater, the University of Vermont. Below, Semler is seen walking off the ice with his old coach Jim Cross, who was also coaching his last game. Vermont won the game 6-5 in overtime. Semler left the coaching ranks to work in the human services field in Vermont and start his own stoneware business. In 2006, he returned to the college coaching ranks as an assistant at Skidmore College.

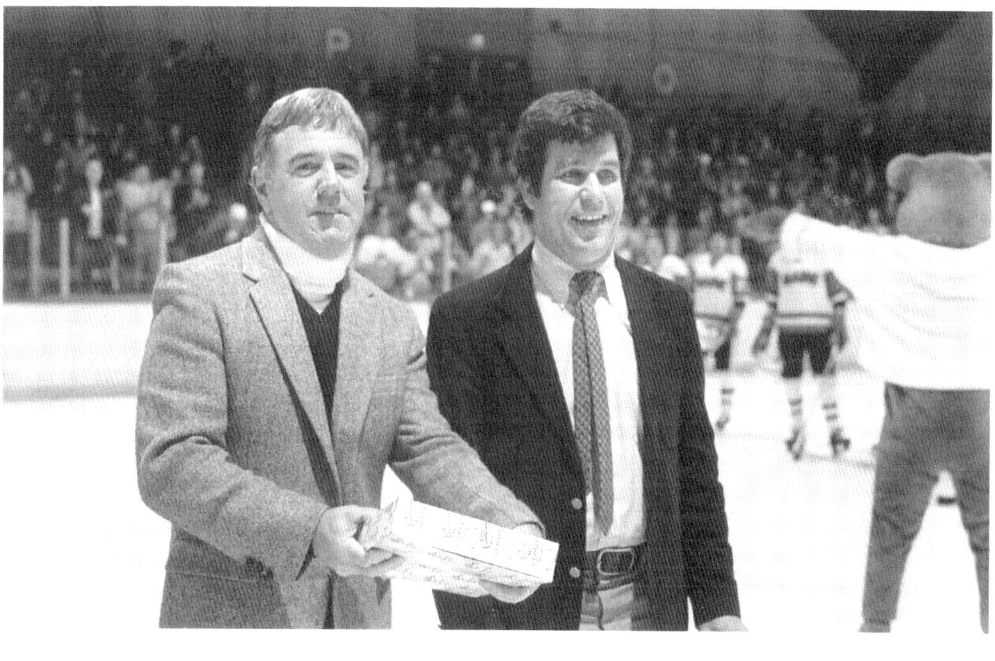

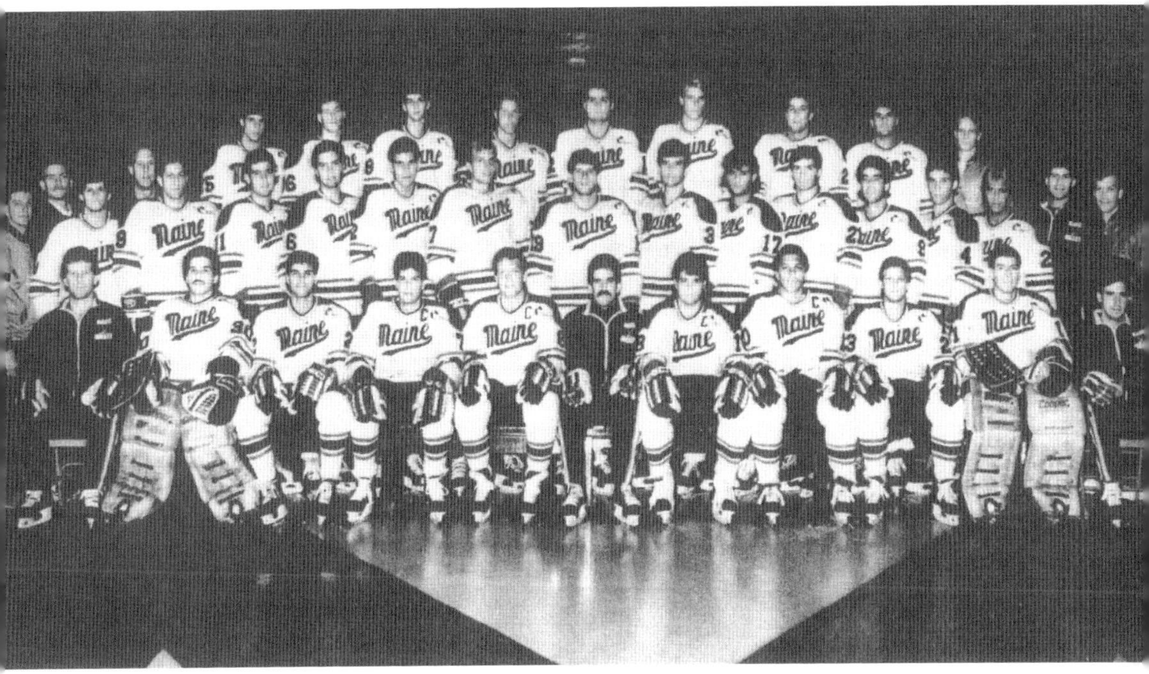

THE 1987–1988 MAINE BLACK BEAR MEN'S ICE HOCKEY TEAM. On April 19, 1984, a little-known college assistant coach and former backup goalie at Bowling Green was hired to replace Semler. At 28 years of age, Shawn Walsh was the youngest Division I coach in the nation. He struggled through his first two years, compiling a record of 23-57-2 before turning things around in 1986–1987 when the team went 24-16-2. In coach Walsh's fourth year at the helm, the Black Bears would have their greatest season to date. Despite losing All-American defenseman Eric Weinrich most of the year to the U.S. Olympic Team, and facing one of the toughest schedules in the country, the Black Bears posted an impressive 34-8-2 mark. They finished the regular season with the best winning percentage in NCAA Division I and became the top seeded team in Hockey East. The Black Bears would go deep into the postseason tournament before finishing third in the nation.

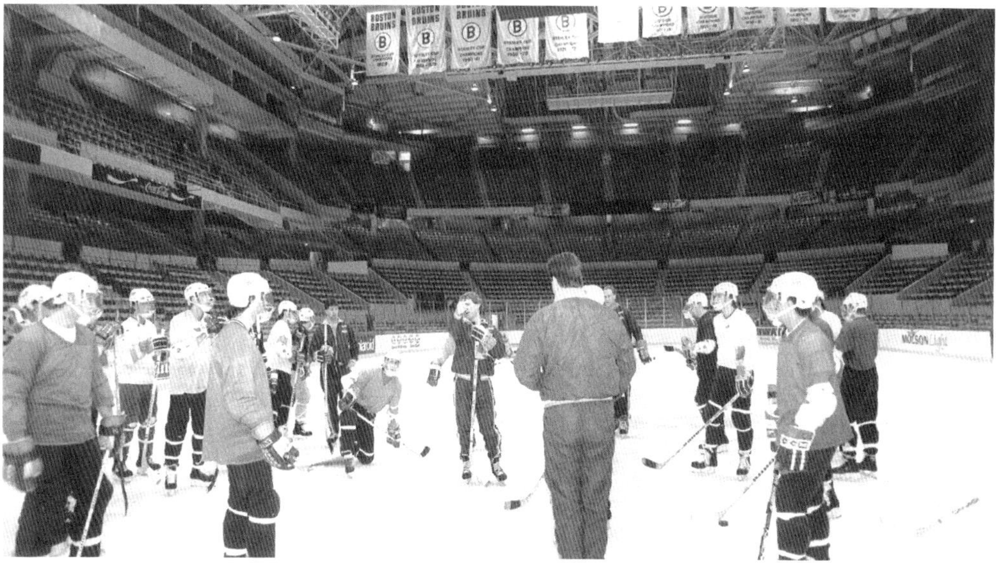

MAINE PREPARES FOR PLAYOFFS. Practicing in front of the championship banners at Boston Garden in 1988, Shawn Walsh hoped one day to be hanging some of his own. The 1986–1987 season ended on a high note with the Black Bears being competitive in the postseason and finishing fifth in the nation. The season was highlighted by a 5-2 victory over Providence at Alfond Arena, the team's first ever Division I playoff win.

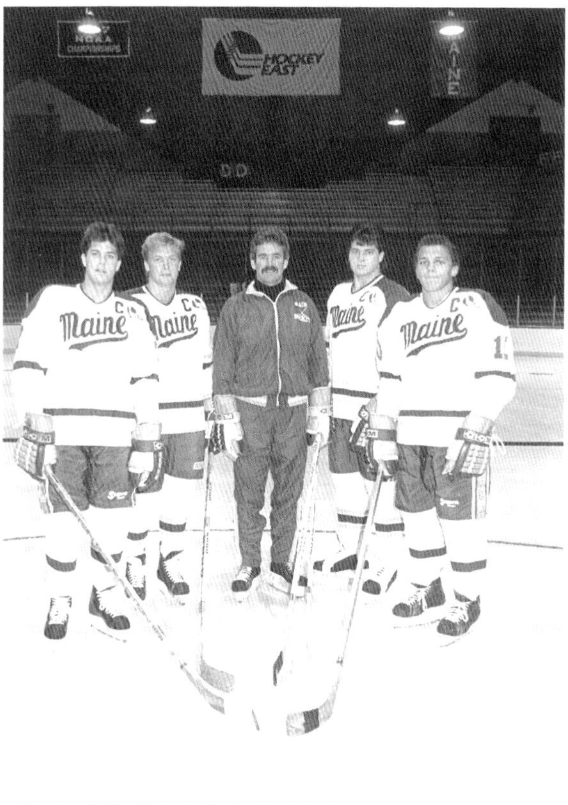

MAINE CAPTAINS. Joining coach Walsh are Mike Golden, Dave Nonis, Jack Capuano, and Mike McHugh. A big step in Maine's progress up the hockey ladder came in 1985 when the Black Bears became a part of Hockey East. One of the strongest conferences in the country, Hockey East consists of 10 Division I programs. In the past 14 seasons it has produced 22 of the 56 berths in the NCAA Frozen Four championship tournament, producing four winners. Hockey East has also been a seed bed for players moving up to play at the professional level, with 54 players from Hockey East schools playing in the NHL in 2005–2006.

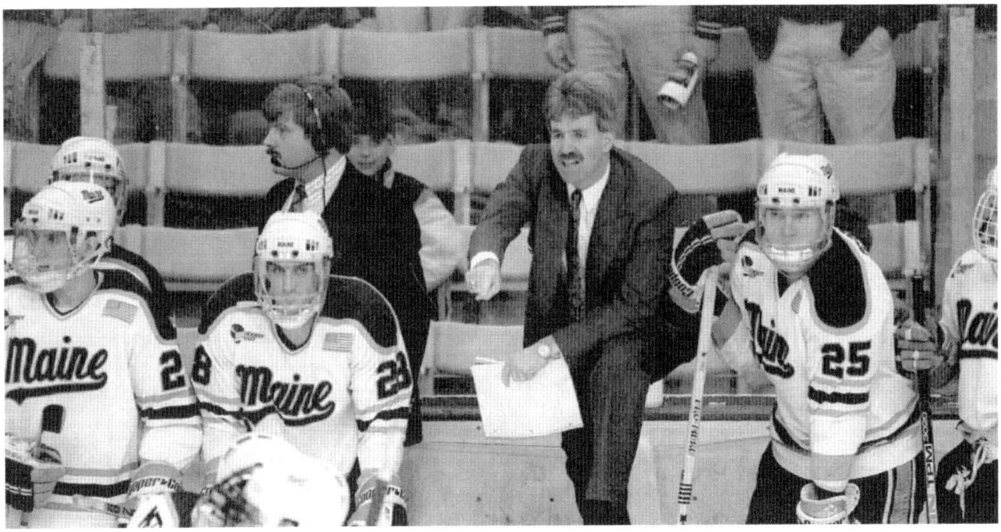

Coach Walsh Instructing Players. Coach Walsh was quickly earning a reputation around Hockey East as a great recruiter and bench tactician, and having a knack for getting the best out of his players. He began to snatch players once thought to be the exclusive property of the elite colleges. Hockey East commissioner Joe Bertagna would later say of Walsh that his preparedness and recruiting raised the bar for the whole of Hockey East. *Portland Press Herald* writer Steve Solloway wrote, "On the ice, Walsh couldn't skate a lick. Off the ice he was a master tactician. He knew how and when to squeeze the best performance out of his players." On the bench with coach Walsh, below, seen to the right, is assistant Joe Clark, who served two terms under Walsh, 1996–1998 and again 1991–1992. Clark went on to coach professional teams in Denmark, Norway, and Texas. He is presently coaching an affiliate of the New York Islanders, where he joins former UMaine stars Garth Snow and Jack Capuano.

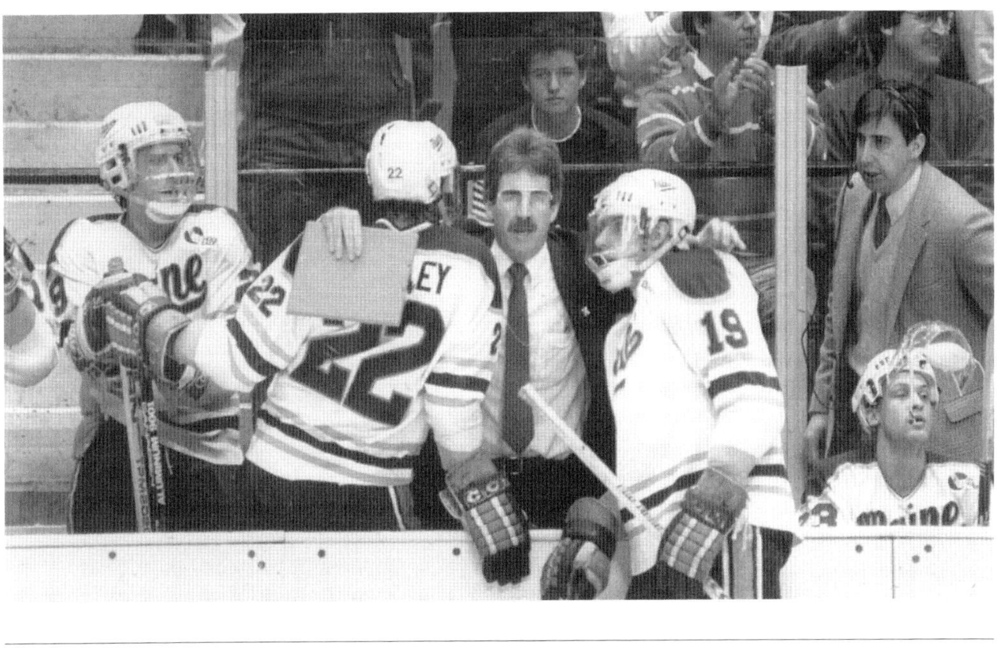

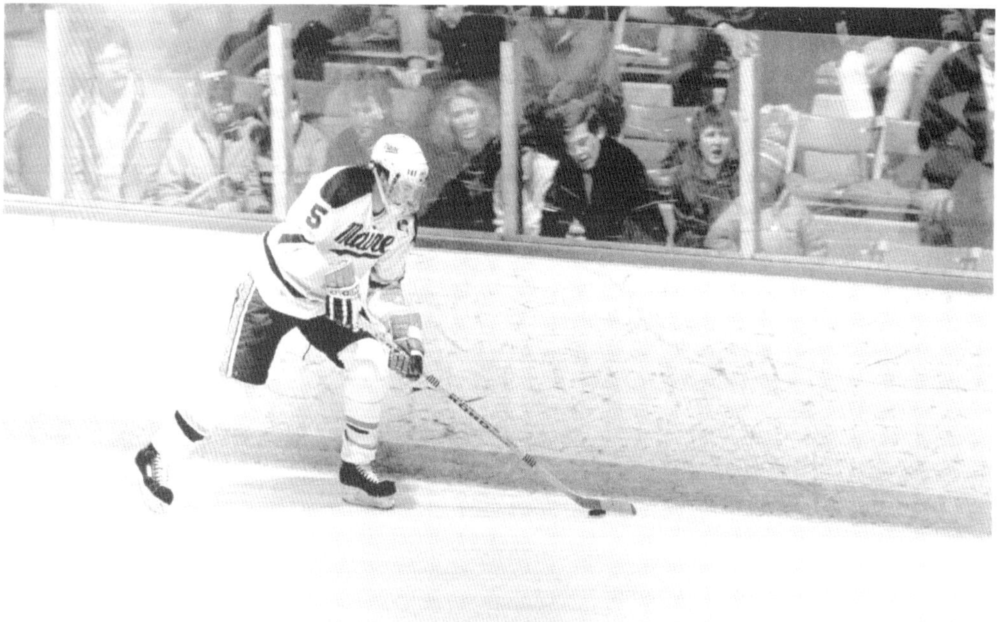

MISSING IN ACTION. The 1988 Olympic team robbed the squad of one of its most outstanding players, defenseman Eric Weinrich. Weinrich, who had been selected to the All-America team in 1987, would rejoin the team for the last regular season game and the postseason playoffs.

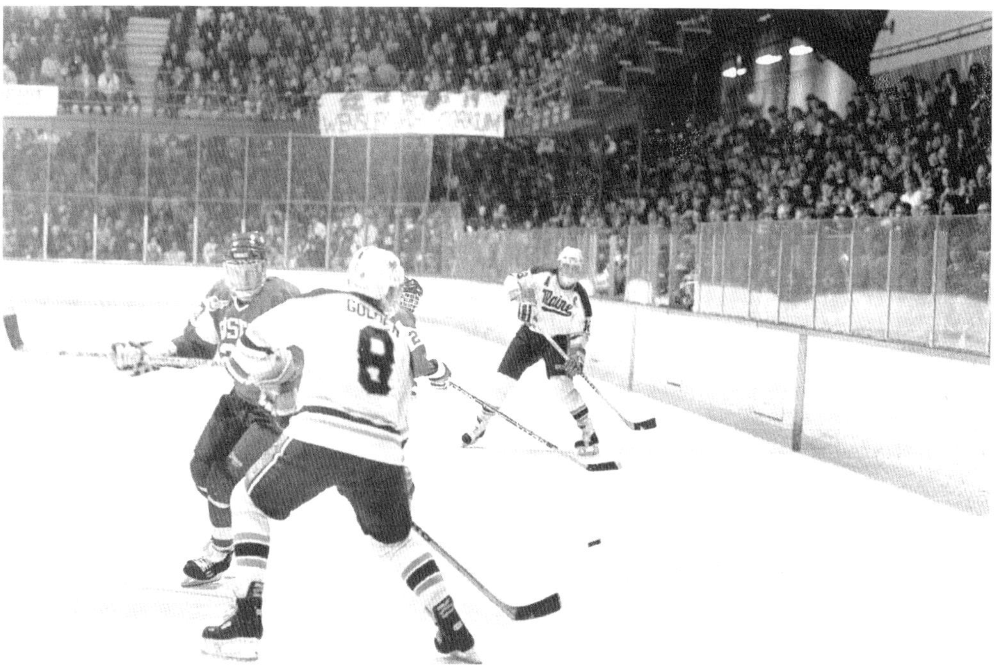

GOLDEN LOOKS TO SCORE. Mike Golden waits to receive a pass from Jack Capuano (No. 18). Capuano was on his way to an All-America team selection, and led the team in goals scored, assists, and points scored. The two would represent UMaine on the All-America team.

MAINE CAPTAIN MIKE MCHUGH. Team captain Mike McHugh helped pick up the slack for Weinrich's absence by scoring 29 goals and providing veteran leadership. He was a second-team All-America selection at the end of the season.

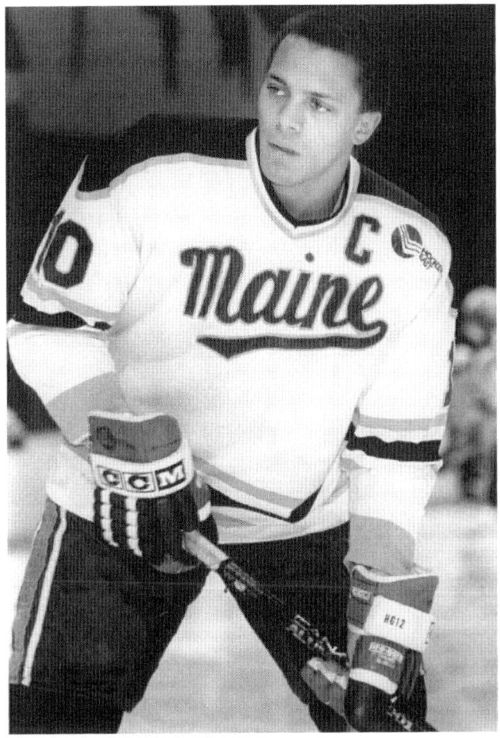

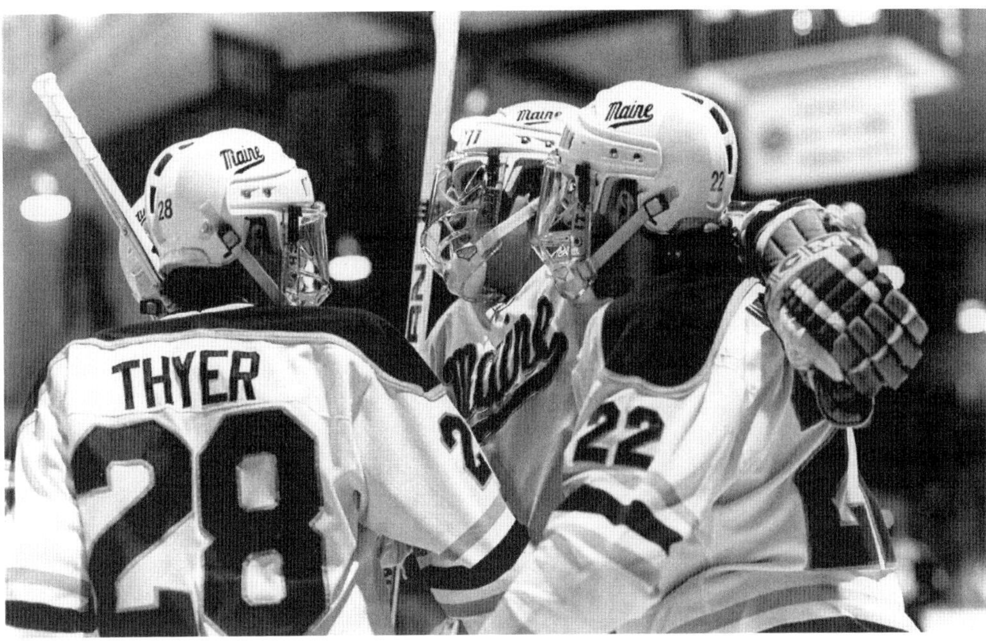

FRESHMAN PHENOM MARIO THYER. Mario Thyer (No. 28) is greeted by David Wensley (No. 22). Thyer had a huge freshman year, earning the 1988 Hockey East Rookie of the Year Award and All-Tournament Team selection. Thyer would only play two seasons with the Black Bears before signing with the Minnesota North Stars.

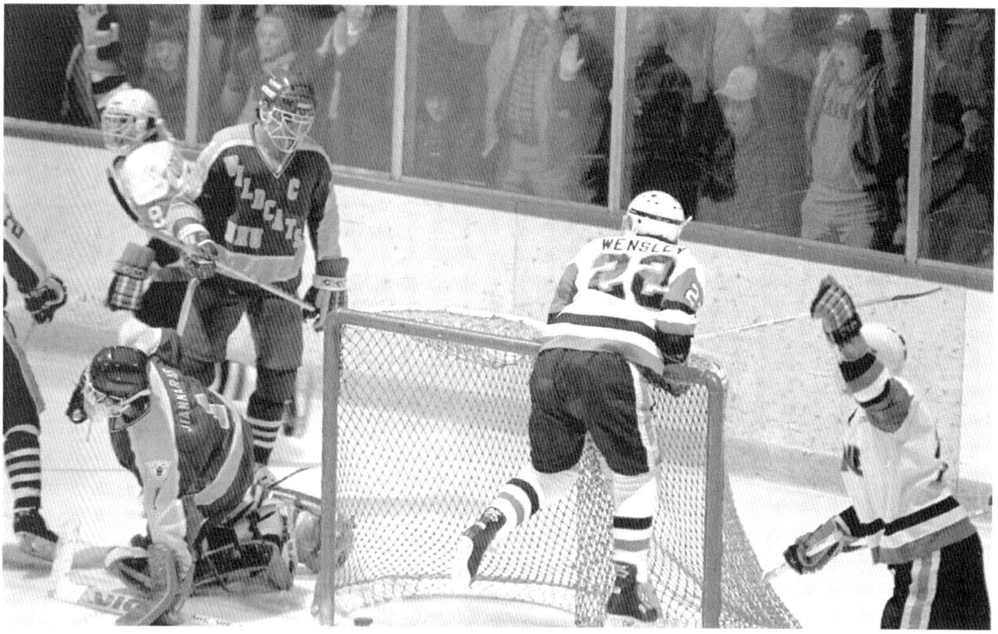

David Wensley Scores Against Wildcats. This team also enjoyed the friendly confines of Alfond Arena, posting a 19-4-1 record, with one of those losses coming to the U.S. Olympic team in an exhibition game. UMaine also lead Hockey East in attendance, drawing 107,309 spectators.

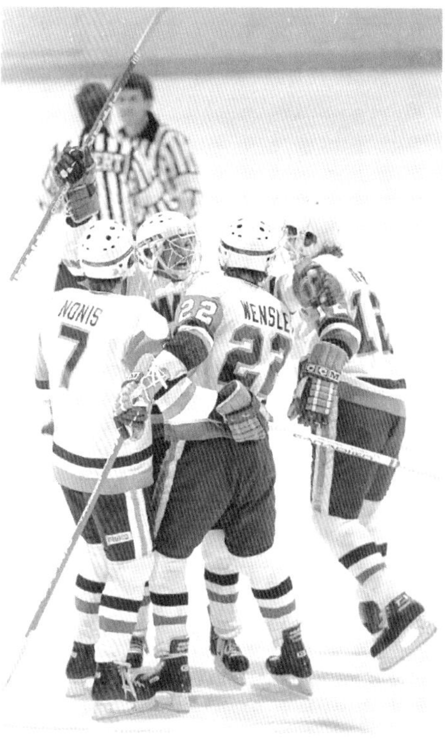

David Wensley and Captain Mike Nonis. Mike Nonis (No. 7) and David Wensley (No. 22) confer on the ice as referees sort out the situation.

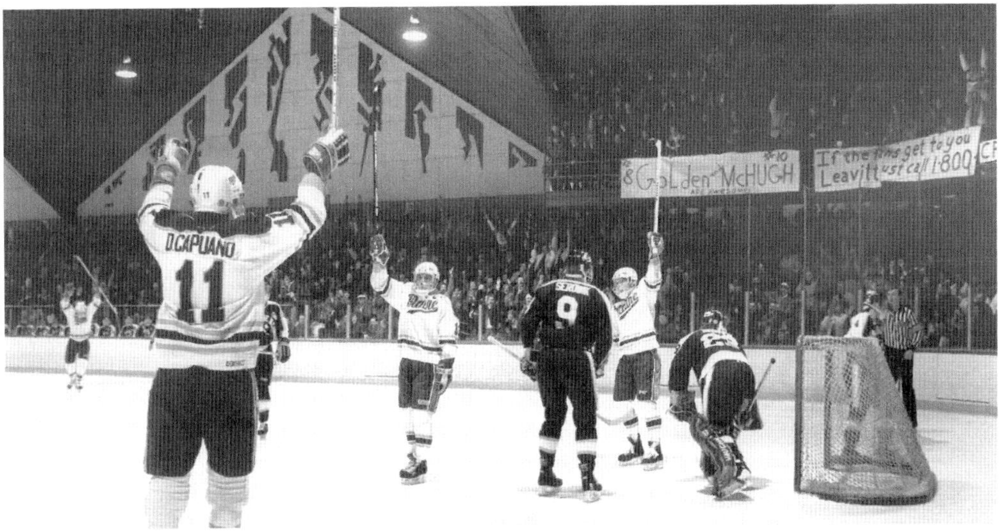

Fan Support. Team achievement led to individual honors. The 1987–1988 season was a season of accolades for several UMaine players. Fan favorites Mike Golden (No. 8) and Mike McHugh (No. 10) were voted second-team All-Americans. David Capuano and Jack Capuano became the first brother combo to be named first-team All-Americans in the same season. Mario Thyer was the nation's leading freshman scorer and Hockey East Rookie of the Year. Mike Golden and David Capuano were Hobey Baker Memorial Award finalists for the best college player in the nation.

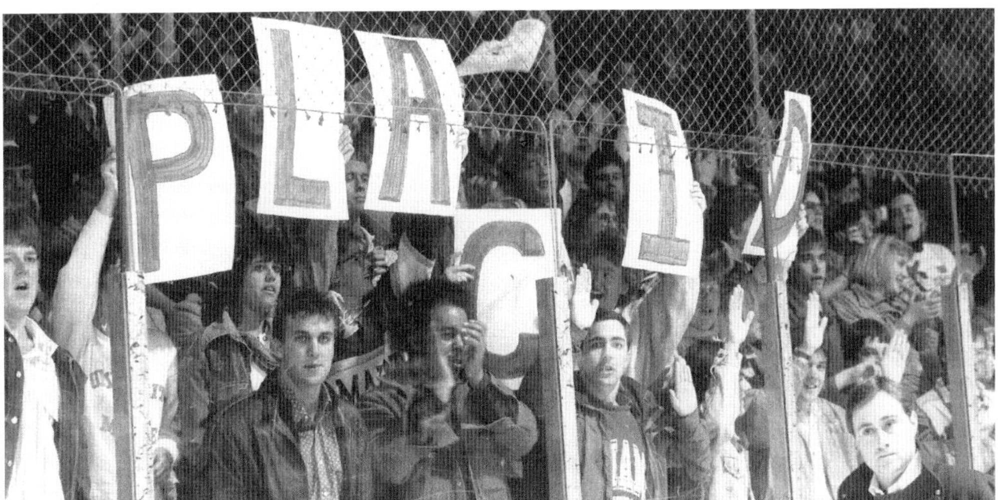

On to Lake Placid. After receiving a first-round bye, the Black Bears entertained Bowling Green State University at Alfond Arena, where they swept a two-game series and moved on to the NCAA tournament at Lake Placid, New York. After taking an early first-period lead on goals by David Capuano, Lake Superior State (LSSU) rallied to a 6-3 win. LSSU went on to win the national championship while UMaine finished third in the nation, beating Minnesota in the consolation game 5-2.

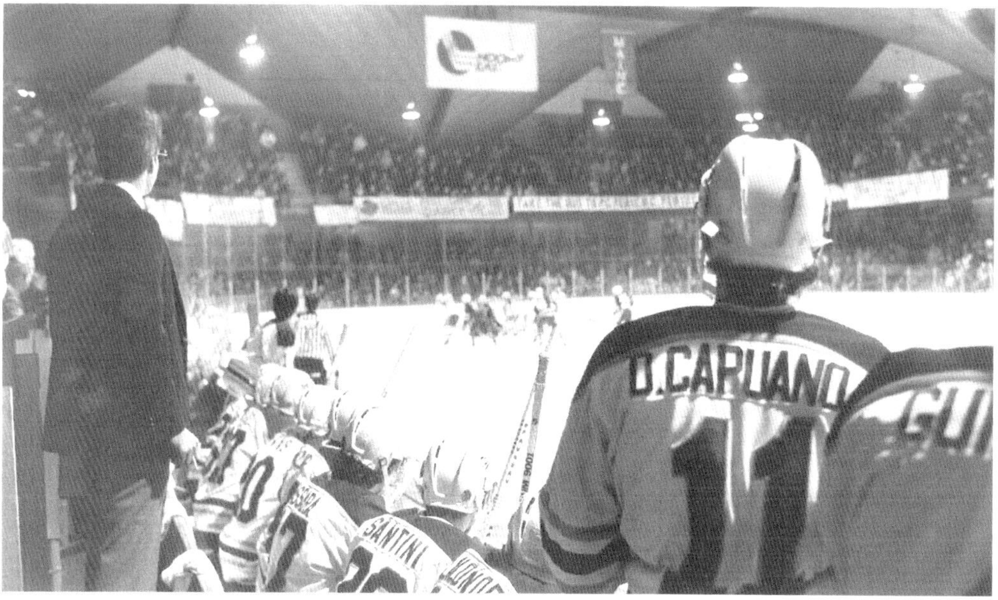

Players View Action from the Maine Bench. The 1980s were a transitional time for hockey at UMaine. The Black Bears had established themselves as a legitimate Division I contender. They began play in Hockey East, one of the strongest conferences in the nation, and quickly rose to the top. The media and the fans could not get enough of the team, and Black Bear Hockey fever was spreading across the state. In coach Shawn Walsh, the program had one of the brightest, most energetic coaches in the country. Walsh would go on to be named Hockey East Coach of the Year four times and National Coach of the Year in 1995. With up-and-coming talent like Mario Thyer and Martin Robitaille, and a newcomer named Jim Montgomery, the light was sure to come on often for UMaine in the 1990s.

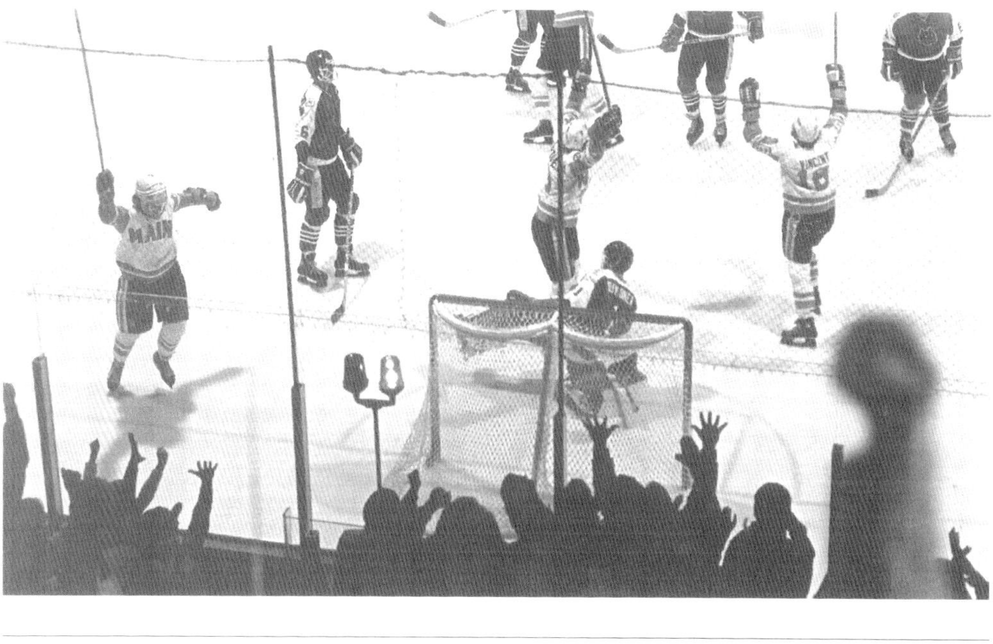

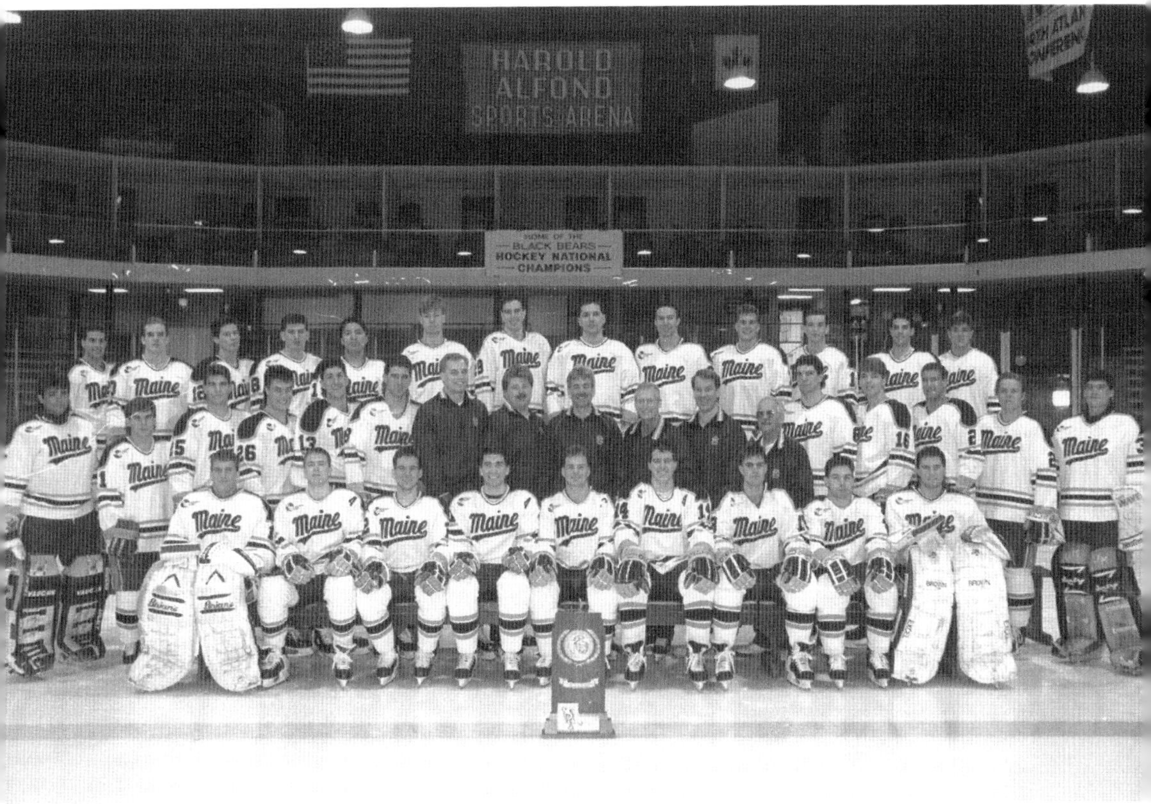

UMAINE BLACK BEARS MEN'S ICE HOCKEY TEAM, 1992–1993. The 1990s became known in college hockey as the decade of the Black Bear. The team compiled an on-ice record of 285-86-31. The Black Bears won three Hockey East championships, had six trips to the NCAA tournament, and won two national championships. The Black Bears also gained notoriety through a scandal that made them ineligible for the postseason and nearly stripped them of their 1993 national title. In all, the NCAA accused the hockey program of 27 violations involving eligibility, recruiting, and favoritism issues. The school suspended coach Shawn Walsh for one year without pay when the allegations broke.

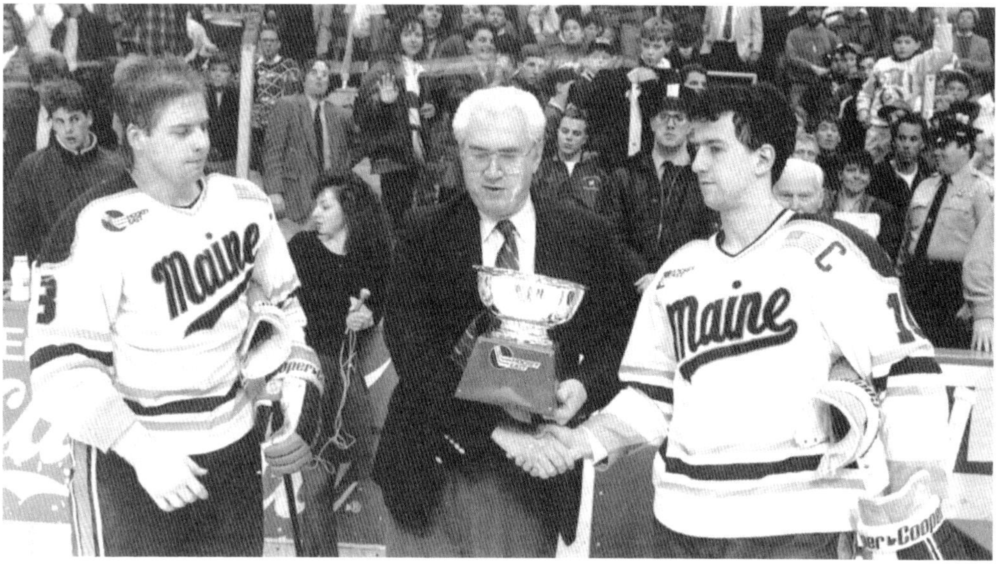

Maine Captains Receiving Hockey East Award. Team captains Scott Pellerin and Martin Robitaille receive a trophy for winning the Hockey East title in 1992. The Black Bears entered the 1992–1993 campaign with many question marks. The 1991–1992 team had won 32 games and made it to the final four in the NCAA tournament, but graduation had significantly depleted the team. Not returning would be Scott Pellerin (No. 8), who had been voted the top college hockey player in the nation in 1992.

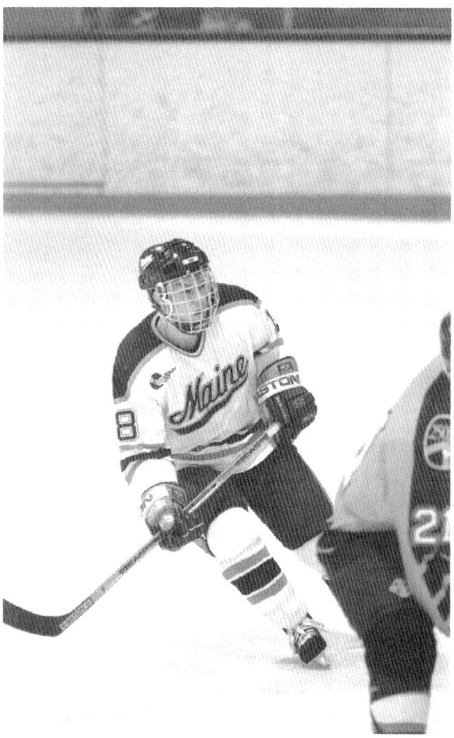

Scott Pellerin Looks to Receive Pass. It would be hard to replace a Hobey Baker Award winner, but another was waiting in the wings.

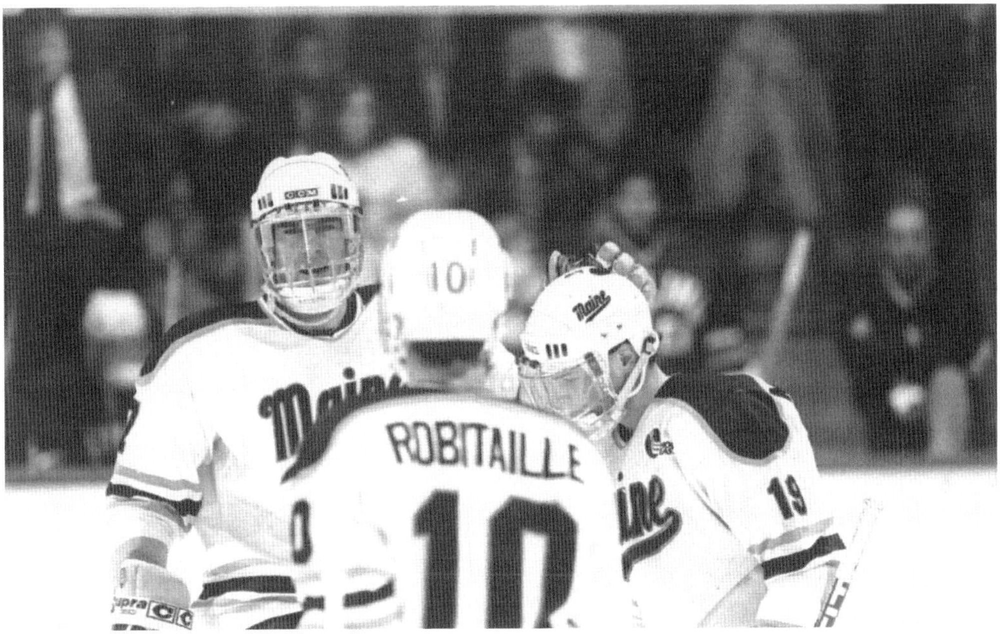

TWO-TIME TEAM CAPTAIN MARTIN ROBITAILLE. It is said that the most difficult accomplishment in all of sports is continued excellence. It is especially true at the collegiate level where every four years the roster is guaranteed to turn over. Graduation meant the loss of veteran leadership in two-time team captain Martin Robitaille (No. 10), seen above. And three-time All-American and UMaine's all-time leading goal scorer Jean-Yves Roy, seen below, would turn professional and also not be returning.

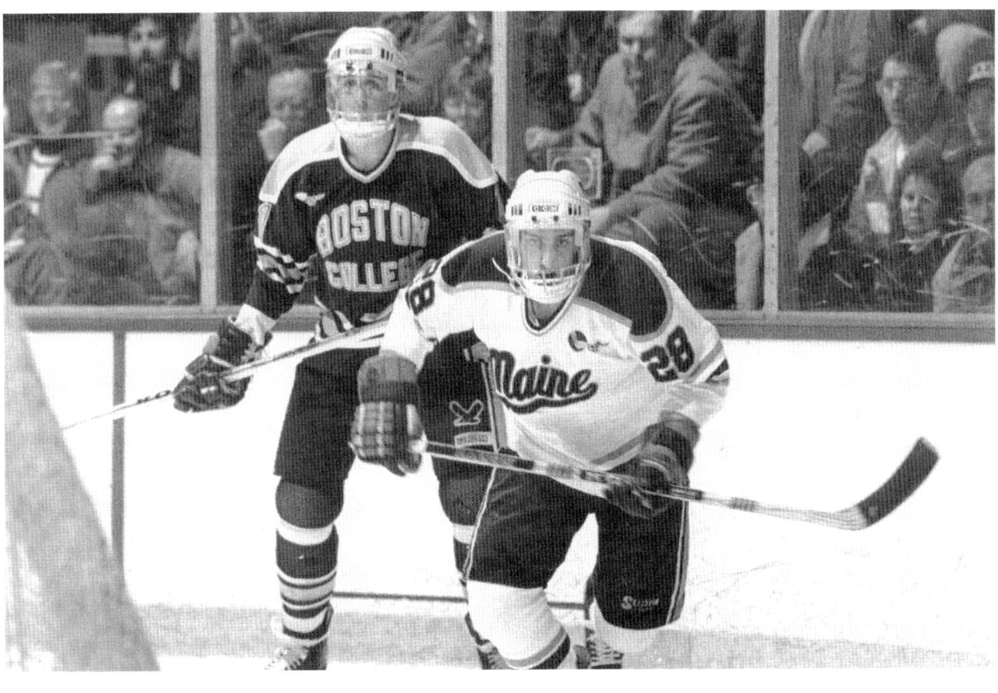

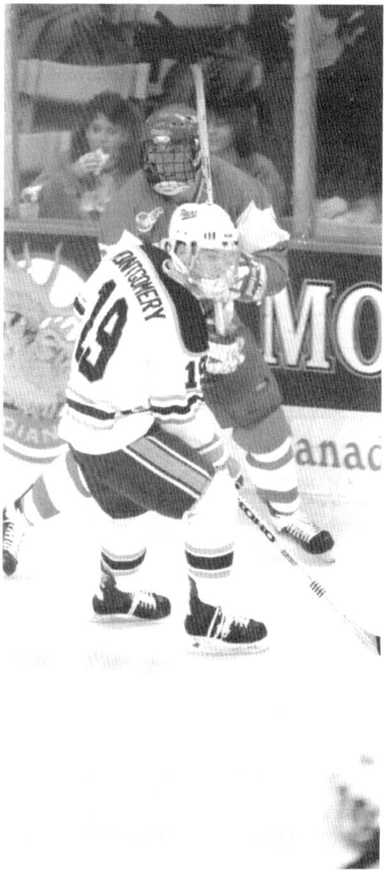

Jim Montgomery in Action. Shawn Walsh had to look to new faces to get the job done in the 1992–1993 season. The team was led by senior captain Jim Montgomery, who would be named to the All-America team for the second time in three years. Montgomery and line mates Paul Kariya and Cal Ingraham became college hockey's most prolific scoring line, totaling 280 points in 1992–1993. Kariya had a remarkable freshman season, scoring 25 goals with 75 assists to score 100 points. He was awarded the 1993 Hobey Baker Award, the first freshman to win the honor. He would lead the team to the most wins, an undefeated record on the road, and the best win-loss percentage in the nation. The only blemishes on a near-perfect season were a 7-6 loss in overtime to Boston University, a 3-3 tie against Providence College, and a 4-4 tie against Clarkson. Montgomery would save his best for last. Trailing Lake Superior State 4-2 entering the final period, Montgomery scored three goals to give the Black Bears a national title in a 5-4 come-from-behind victory. Montgomery was named the tournament's most outstanding player.

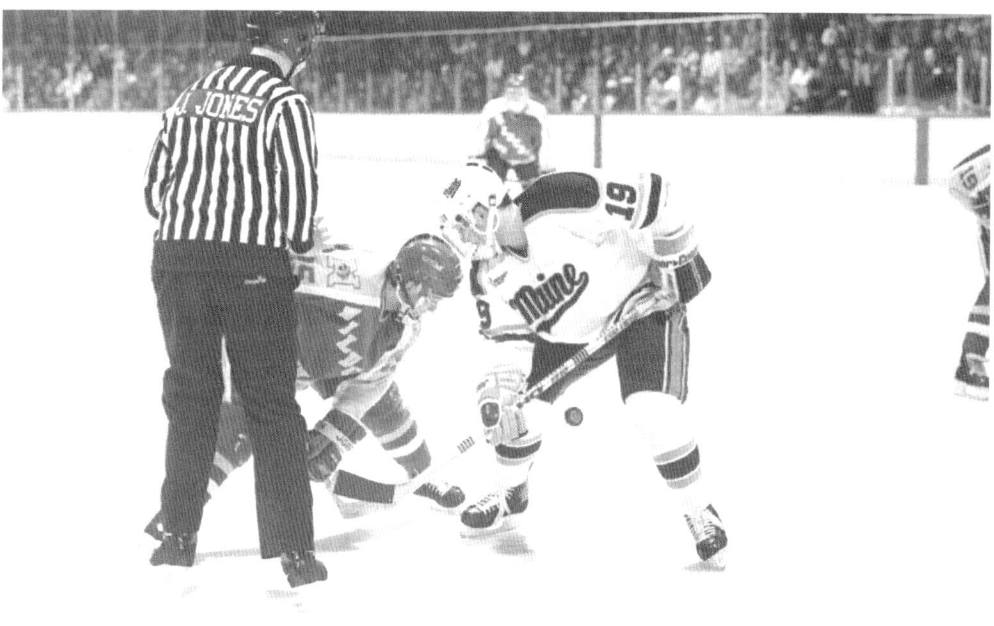

UMaine Goalie No. 1 Mike Dunham. The high-powered offense was backed by a stingy defense led by senior Mike Dunham, who was named to the All-America team. His .893 save percentage was among the best in the nation. He compiled a 21-1-1 record for the season and was named a first-team All-American. Dunham and teammate Garth Snow were considered one of the top goaltending duos in the nation, and both would become standout goaltenders in the NHL.

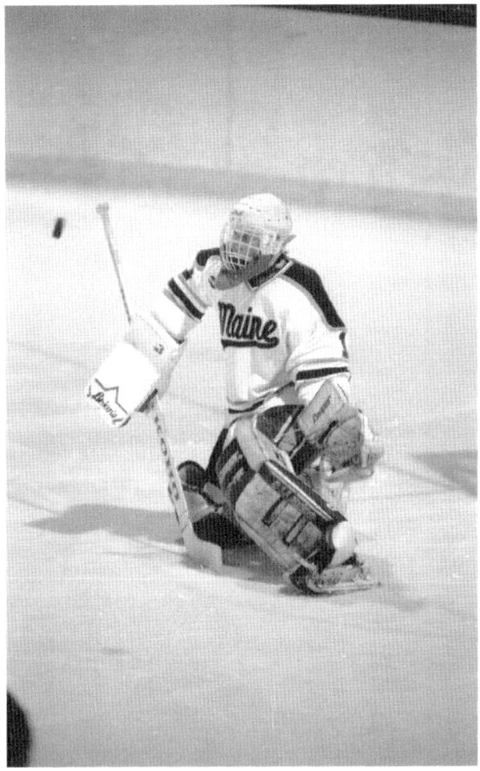

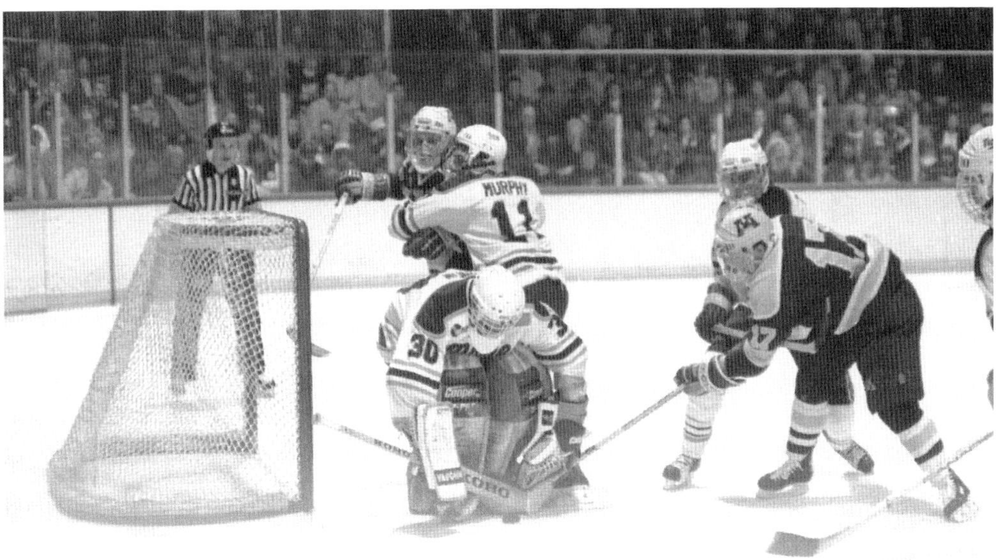

Garth Snow No. 30. Garth Snow provided veteran leadership and sported a 21-0-1 record in the net. Both goaltenders were used in the 1993 championship game. The teammates' association in hockey would continue after their college days. Snow would later become the general manager of the New York Islanders, and in 2007, Dunham started 17 games in goal for the Islanders.

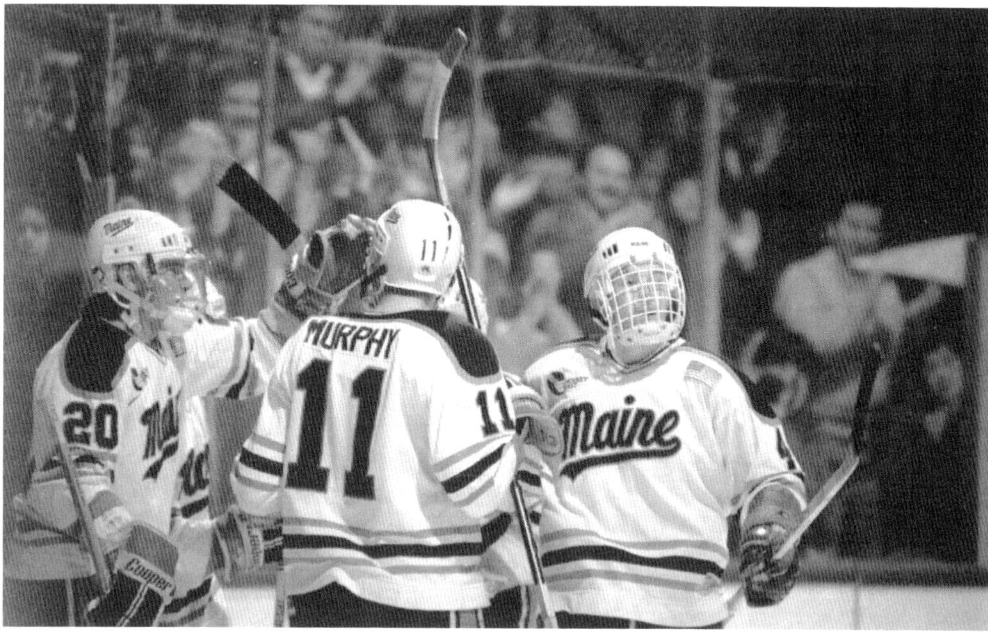

DAN MURPHY. On a squad that had five All-Americans and the Hobey Baker Award winner, there was a need for role players to pave the way. Senior Matt Martin was a solid performer along with Dan Murphy (No. 11).

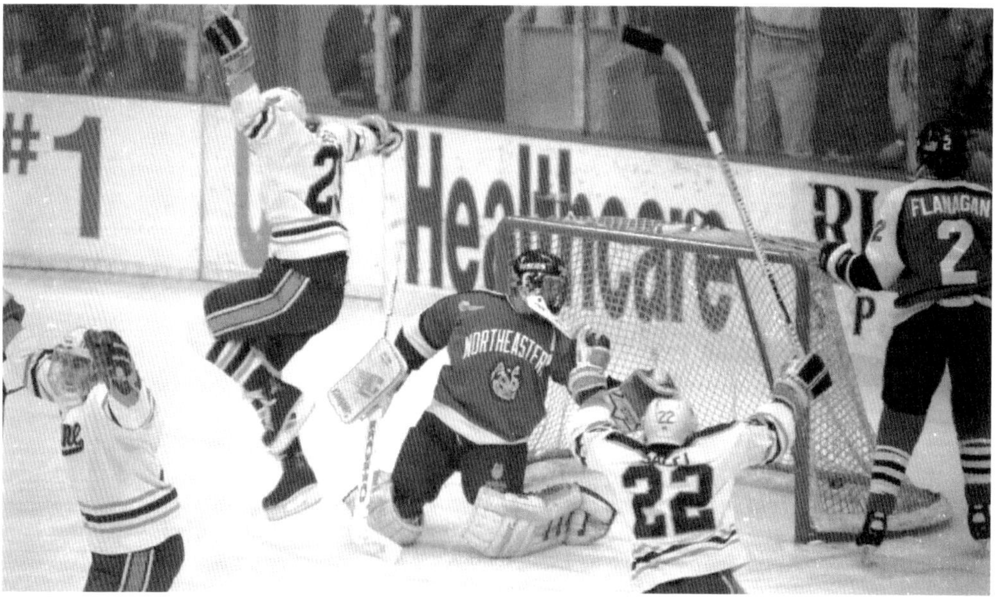

KENT SALFI CELEBRATES A 5-4 PLAYOFF VICTORY AT ALFOND. Longtime Alfond Arena announcer Joe Kennedy said one of the challenging things for him during the 1993 season was announcing Paul Kariya's goals. "On more than one occasion the stats people were still gathering assist information, and before I would have a chance to announce Paul's first goal, he had already scored another one."

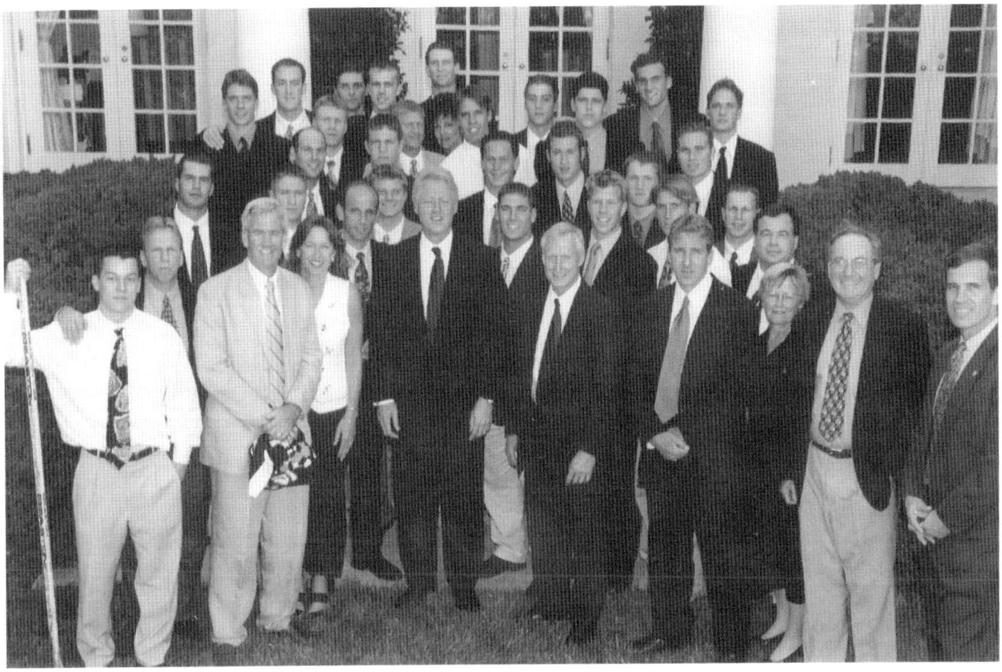

National Championship Team with the President. The year culminated with a trip to the White House to receive congratulations from Pres. Bill Clinton. Clinton chided, "In my state football is a slightly more popular sport than hockey. We don't have a lot of ice. But after spending three months getting banged around in this town, I can understand a little more about hockey than I did before I came here." The glitter of the 1993 championship was tarnished by the recruiting controversy that hovered over the program. Nobody felt worse than Shawn Walsh, whose place was taken by assistant Greg Cronin midway through the 1995–1996 season. Walsh handled his exile with grace, humility, and a passion to return his team to the top. In 1999, the Black Bears would be national champions again, no questions asked.

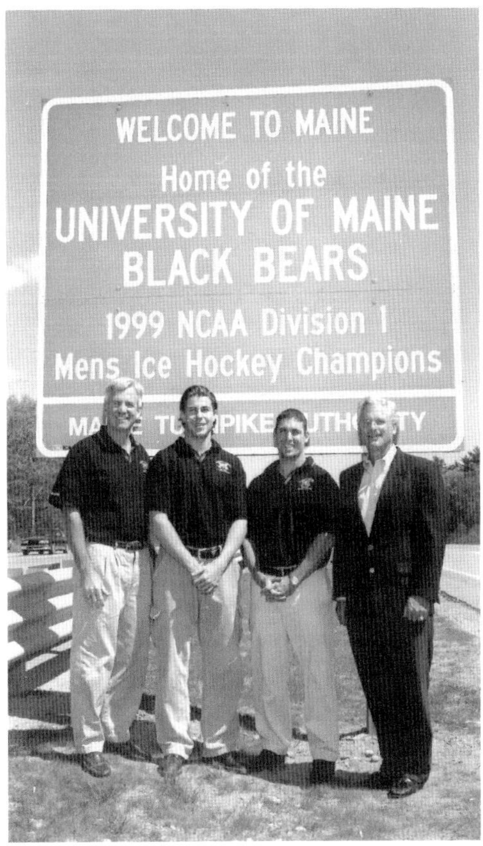

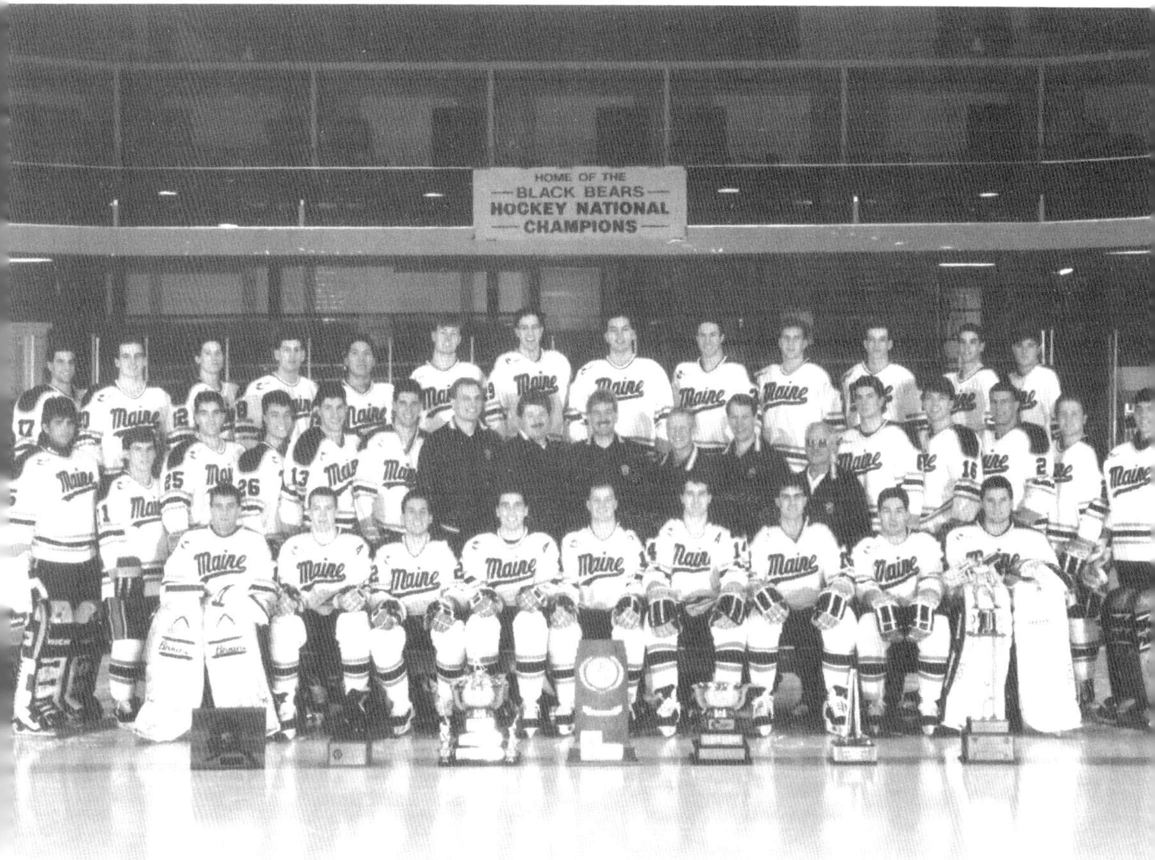

THE 1998–1999 UMAINE MEN'S ICE HOCKEY TEAM. By some accounts the 1998–1999 championship season was coach Shawn Walsh's greatest achievement as Black Bears coach. Unlike the 1993 champions that were laden with talent, there were no superstars, although Steve Kariya and David Cullen were named All-Americans. The previous year the team had floundered with a 17-15-4 record, dismal by UMaine standards. Although Walsh would lead the 1998–1999 team to a 31-6-4 record, it was not good enough to win Hockey East. The team would have to scratch and claw its way to another Frozen Four appearance, beginning with two big victories against UMass Amherst at Alfond Arena. The team would exact revenge over Hockey East champion New Hampshire in a thriller for the national championship.

COACH WALSH WELCOMED BACK BY MAINE FANS, 1997. In 1997–1998, Walsh's first full year back, the team struggled, going 10-11-3 in Hockey East, the division it once owned. During his suspension Walsh was capably replaced by assistant Greg Cronin. Cronin is now the head coach at Northeastern.

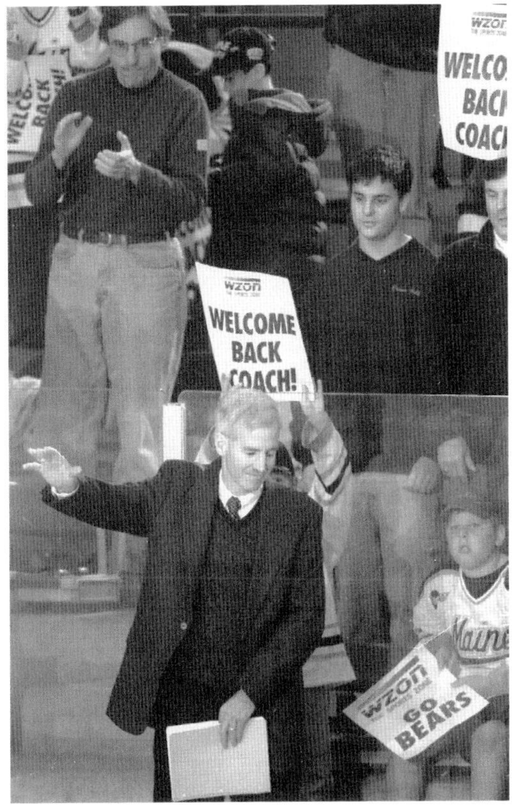

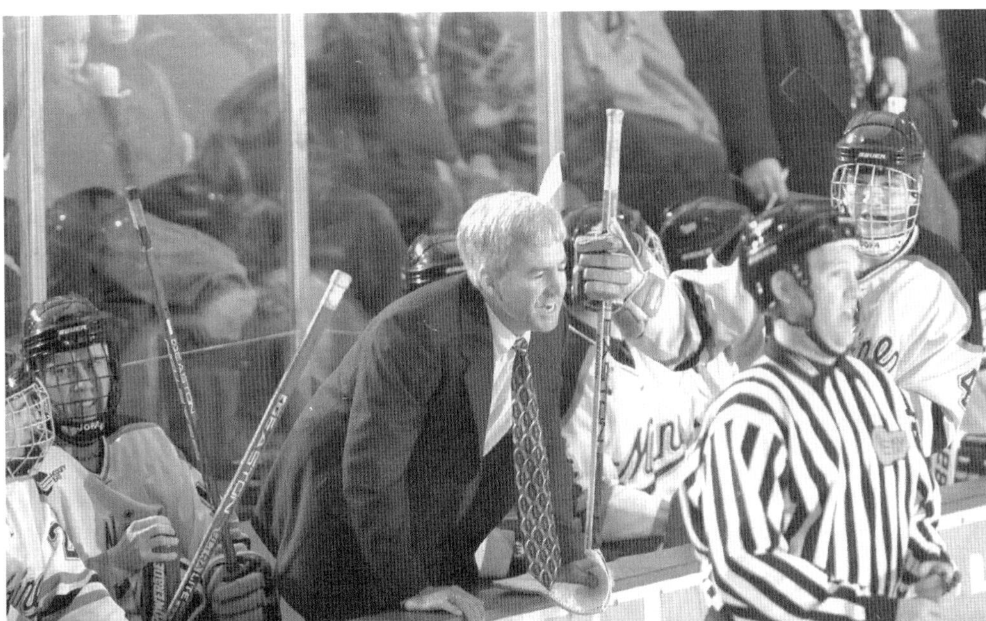

COACH WALSH ARGUES CALL. Perhaps not everyone was thrilled to see coach Walsh back in the game.

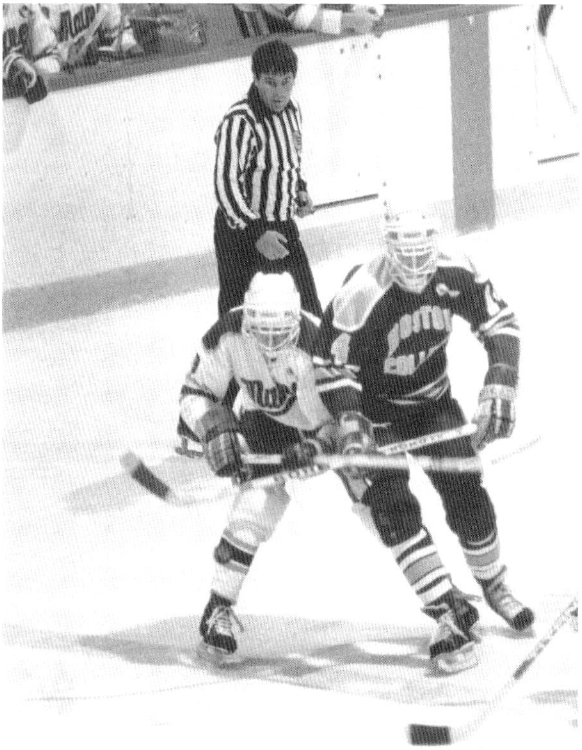

STANDOUT WINGER STEVE KARIYA. One of the few similarities between the 1993 and 1999 championship teams was a player with *Kariya* on the back of his jersey. This time it was Steve Kariya (No. 18), who would lead the team in scoring with 27 goals and 38 assists while serving as team captain. He was a finalist for the Hobey Baker Award and was named a first-team All-American. He capped a stellar season by making the academic honor roll and being named a College Sports Information Directors of America (CoSIDA) Academic All-American. A four-year letterman at Maine, Kariya went on to join brother Paul in the NHL.

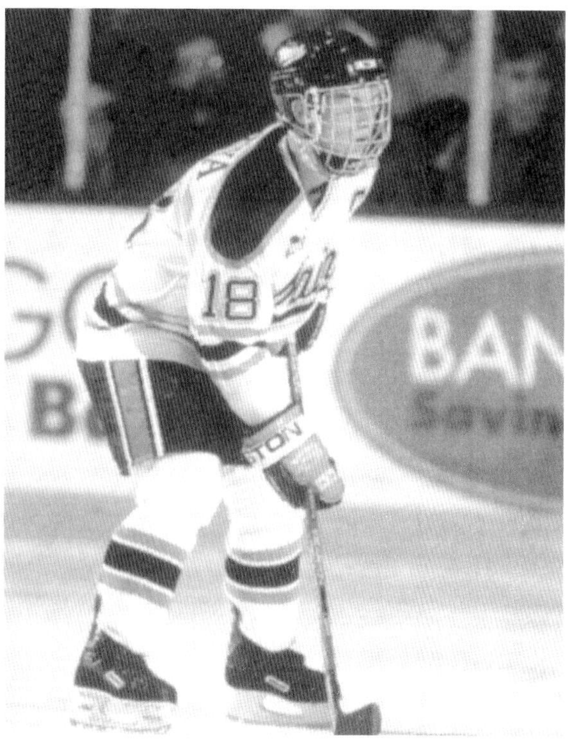

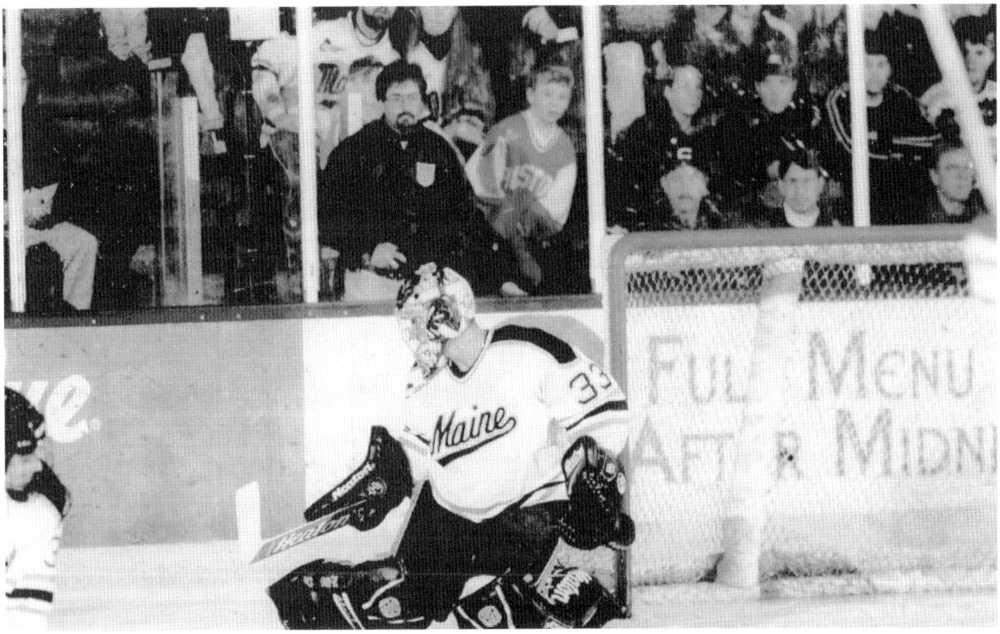

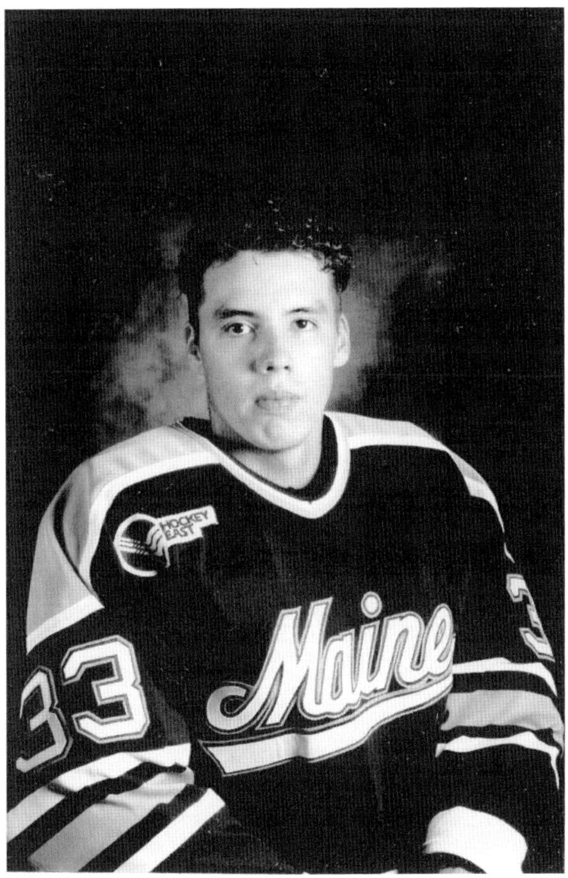

Goalie Alfie Michaud. Alfie Michaud (No. 33) led a tenacious UMaine defense. For three years Michaud led UMaine goalkeepers in goals against, saves, and save percentage. He was the MVP of the NCAA 1999 tournament and was named the Harold Alfond MVP. Michaud allowed an average of 2.32 goals a game in 1998–1999 and had a save percentage of .910. Michaud would save his best for last. Against rival New Hampshire in the national championship game, Michaud turned back 46 shots in preserving a 3-2 overtime victory.

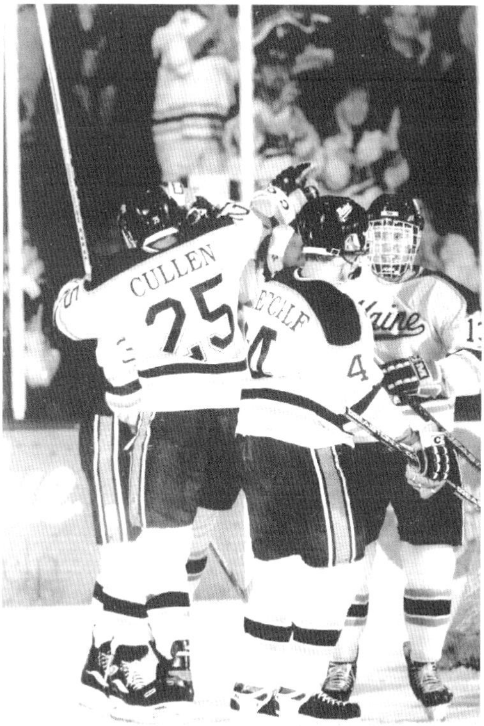

DAVID CULLEN (NO. 25) CELEBRATING WITH PETER METCALF (NO. 4). After a great season, David Cullen would be named a first-team All-American. Cullen had a spectacular postseason and was named to the NCAA All-Tournament Team.

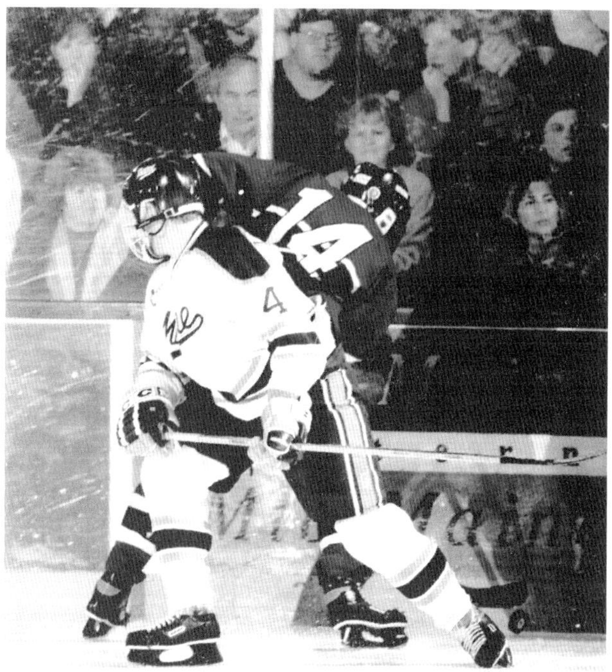

METCALF SKATES AROUND DEFENDER. Freshman sensation Peter Metcalf played an important role in the championship season. He made the All-Rookie Team and academic honor roll. In 2002, Metcalf would be named a second-team All-American.

1993 NCAA Championship Game

					April 6, 1993
Lake Superior State	1	3	0	- 4	**Bradley Center**
University of Maine	2	0	3	- 5	**Milwaukee, Wis.**

Goals:	Period 1	Maine - Tardif (Latendresse), 0:28
		Maine - C. Ferraro (Imes, P. Ferraro), 7:10
		LSSU - Bachusz (Angelelli, Ness), 17:02
	Period 2	LSSU - Beddoes (unassisted), 7:01
		LSSU - Hendry (Beddoes), 15:46
		LSSU - Strachan (Hulett), 18:42
	Period 3	Maine - Montgomery (Kariya), 4:19
		Maine - Montgomery (Kariya, Imes), 7:40
		Maine - Montgomery (Kariya), 8:54
Goalies:		Maine - Mike Dunham (12 shots, 8 saves), Garth Snow (8 shots, 8 saves)
		LSSU - Blaine Lacher (24 shots, 19 saves)

CHAMPIONSHIP BOX SCORE. The Back Bears breezed through the first two games of the Frozen Four, defeating Ohio State 4-2 and Clarkson University 7-2. Hockey East nemesis Boston College was up next, and Maine eked out a 2-1 overtime win. The Black Bears would face another Hockey East rival, New Hampshire, in the championship game. Thanks to Alfie Michaud's 46 saves, the Black Bears held close and won on a goal by Marcus Gustafson in overtime.

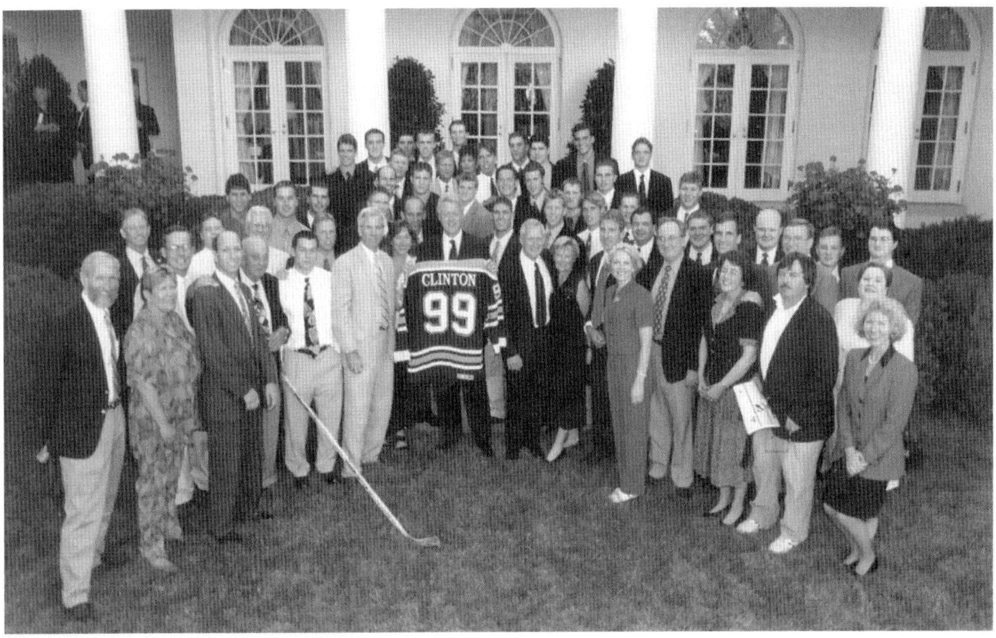

ANOTHER TRIP TO THE ROSE GARDEN. The Black Bears celebrate their second national championship in six years with a trip to the rose garden. The Black Bears presented Pres. Bill Clinton with a Black Bears jersey. A hockey stick may have been more appropriate, as Clinton was facing a scandal of his own.

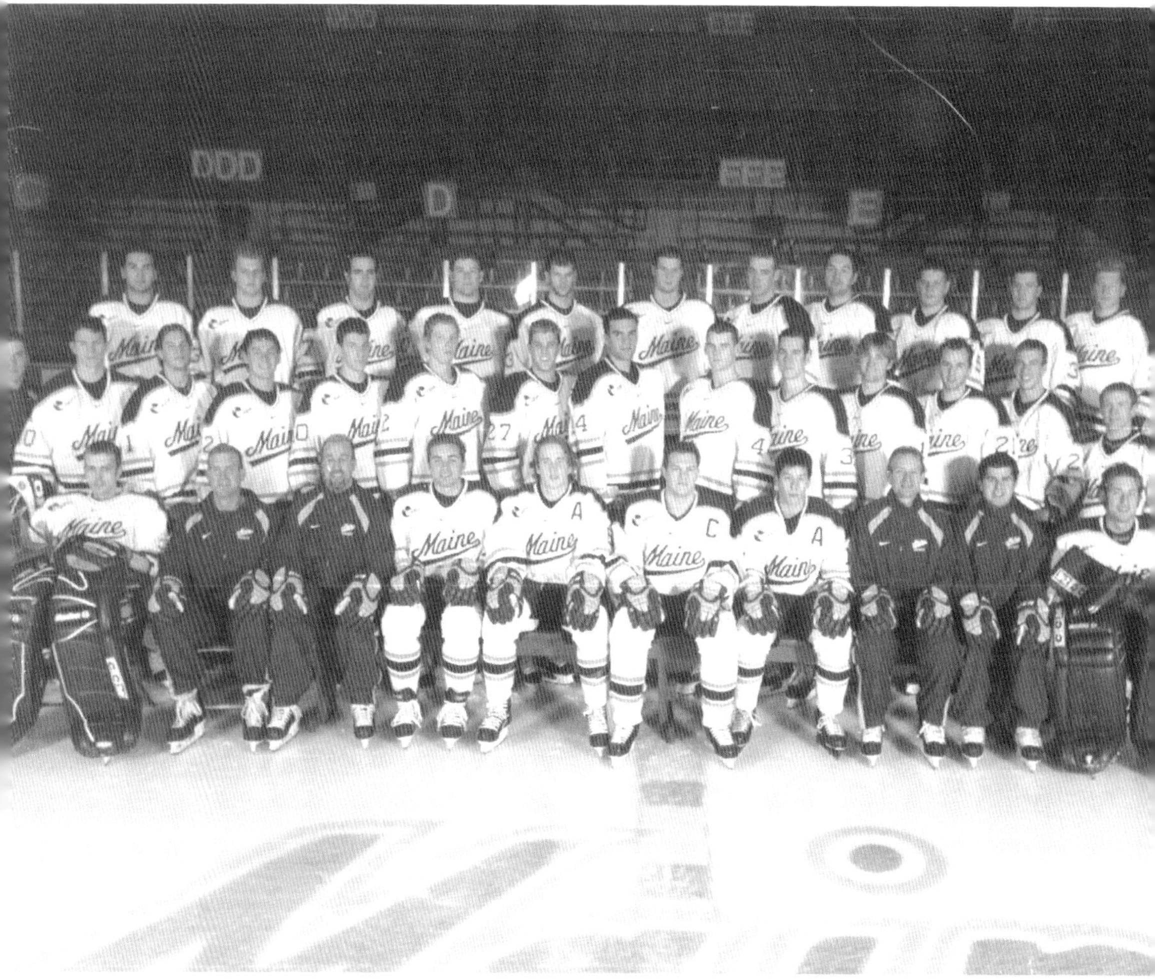

The 2001–2002 UMaine Men's Ice Hockey Team. On September 24, at 46, an age where most coaches are just hitting their prime, coach Shawn Walsh passed away, a scant two weeks before the team's season opener against Bowling Green. In a tribute written by members of the team, the following sentiments were shared: "Coach Walsh is so much more than a coach to us, he is a father figure to 33 guys on this team. . . . His passion for the game and for life will burn inside of us everyday . . . He taught us much more than hockey. As much as he works with you to make you a better player, he worked even harder to make you a better person . . . no one who has ever met him will ever forget what he brought into their lives."

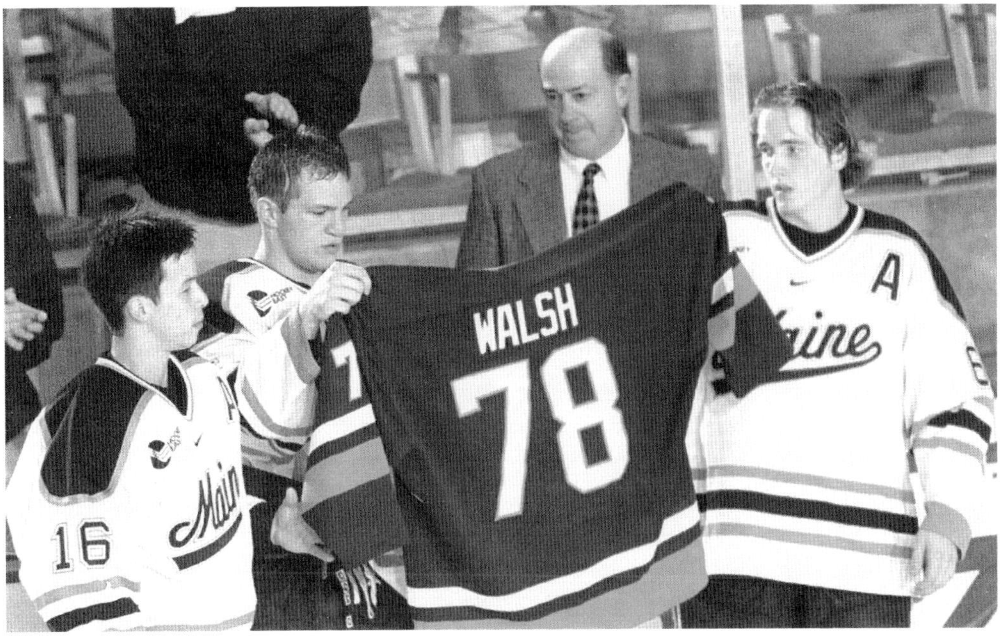

UMAINE CAPTAINS RECEIVING WALSH JERSEY. Ironically, UMaine's season opener was against Walsh's alma mater, Bowling Green University. Team captains Martin Kariya, Peter Metcalf, and Chris Heisten accept an honorary jersey before the face-off. An emotional 9-1 victory set the tone for the rest of the season.

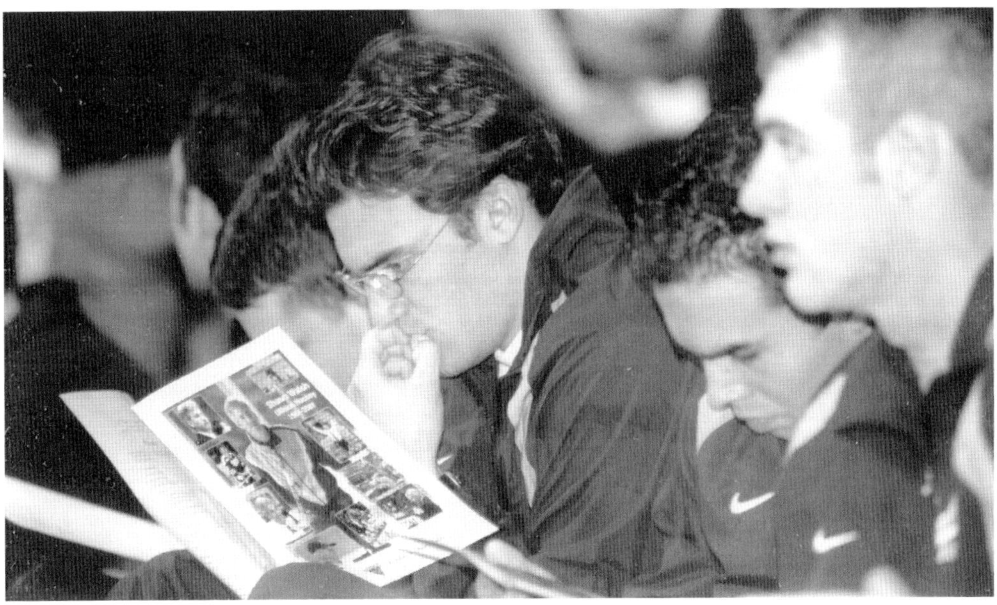

PLAYERS CELEBRATE WALSH'S LIFE AT MEMORIAL SERVICE. Players, fans, faculty, and students gathered at Memorial Union to pay tribute to coach Shawn Walsh. A funeral mass was held at St. John's Catholic Church in Bangor and was attended by several Hockey East coaches, former UMaine players, U.S. senators Olympia Snowe and Susan Collins, and Rep. John Baldacci.

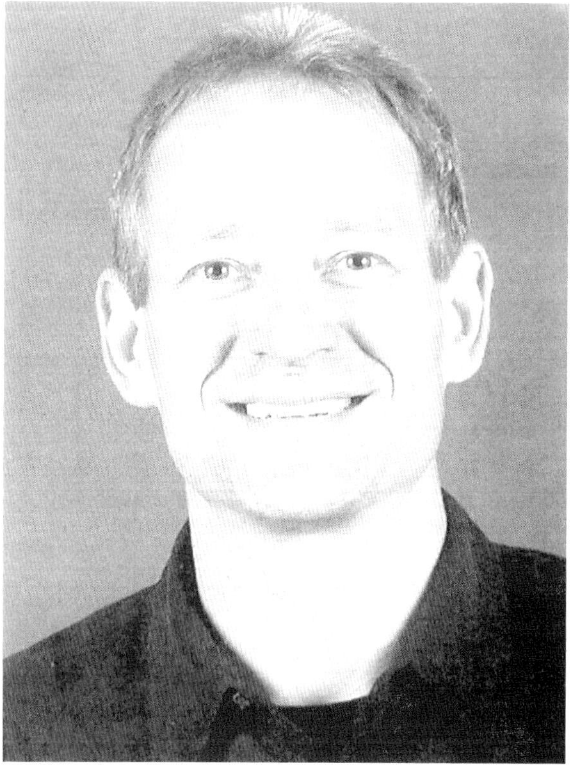

Head Coach Whitehead. Without much time or hesitation, the university named Tim Whitehead interim head coach. "I had to be true to myself and not try to be a Shawn Walsh," Whitehead said in comparing himself to Walsh. "We had different styles but had more in common than we did in difference."

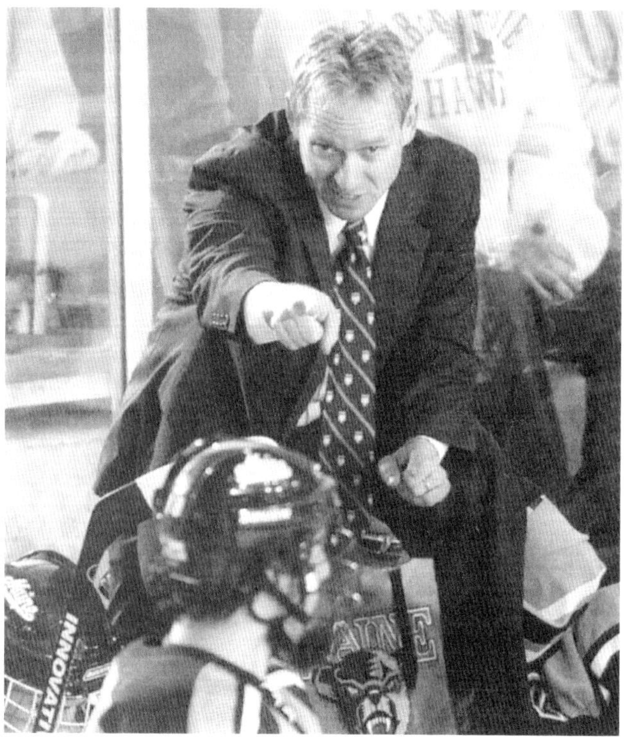

Coach and Team Focus on Game. The tale of the 2001–2002 season was something out of a Hollywood script. The death of a legend, the commitment to win a championship in his honor, the turnaround of a struggling team, and a postseason surge that came within one goal of winning another national championship.

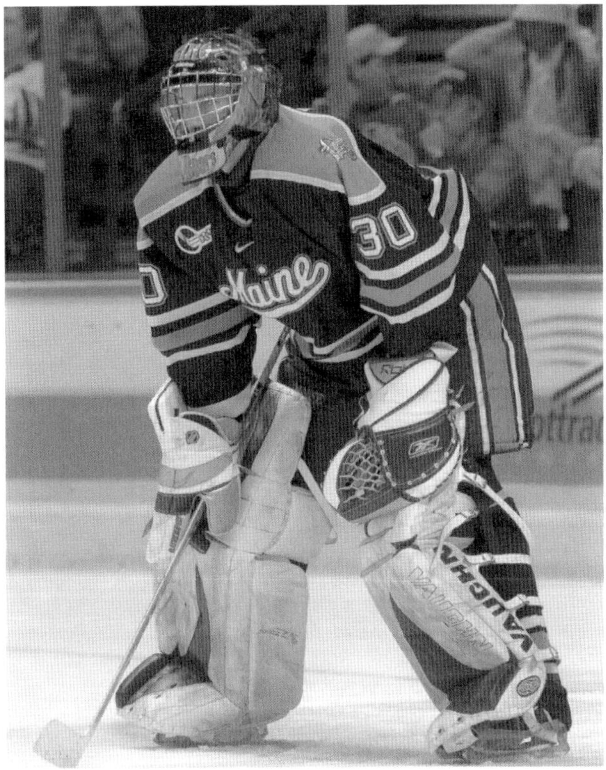

GOALIE MIKE MORRISON (NO. 30). Standouts on the 2002 team included goalie Mike Morrison, whose save percentage of .921 was one of the highest in team history. Morrison was named to the All-Hockey East team and All-New England team. Whitehead's team struggled through the first part of the year, barely winning half their games. After making some roster moves and challenging players to be true to their preseason pledges, the team caught fire, going 17-4-3 down the stretch.

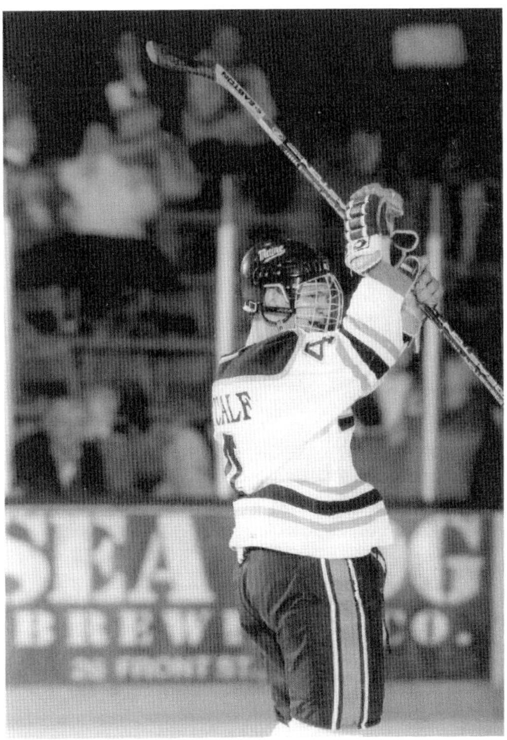

TEAM MVP PETER METCALF. Peter Metcalf was named a second-team All-American and All-Hockey East first-team member for his accomplishment in the 2001–2002 season. He shined in the postseason and was named to the Hockey East All-Tournament Team and NCAA All-Tournament Team. Maine began its tournament run by defeating Boston College twice at Alfond Arena. Maine swept trough the Frozen Four with victories over Harvard, Boston University, and New Hampshire before losing to Minnesota in a 4-3 overtime thriller.

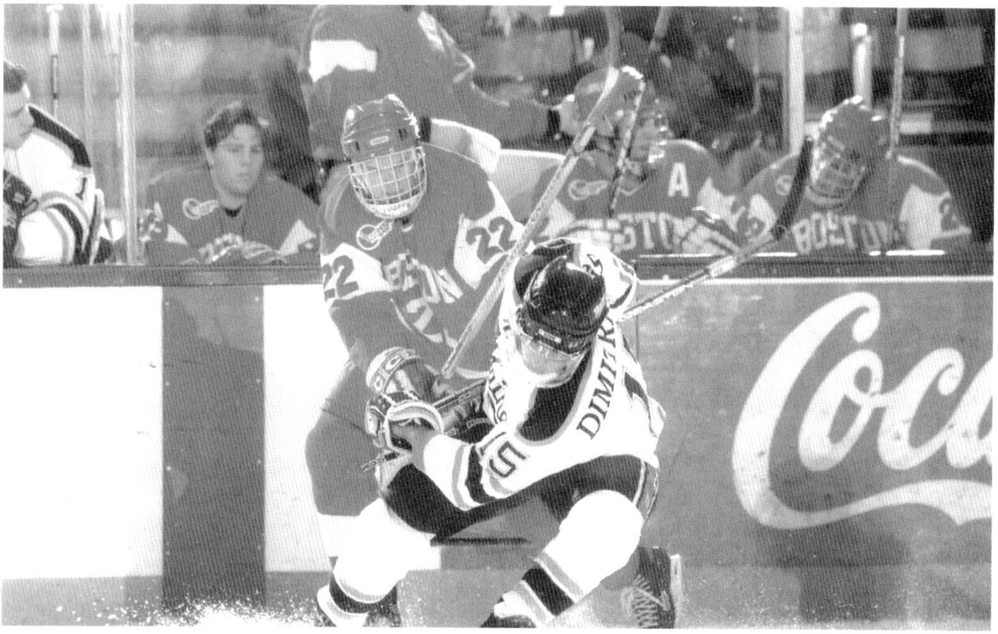

NIKO DIMITRAKOS (NO. 15) STRUGGLING FOR THE PUCK. Also having a banner season for UMaine was Niko Dimitrakos, who led the team in scoring with 20 goals and 31 assists. Dimitrakos would join Peter Metcalf as a second-team All-American.

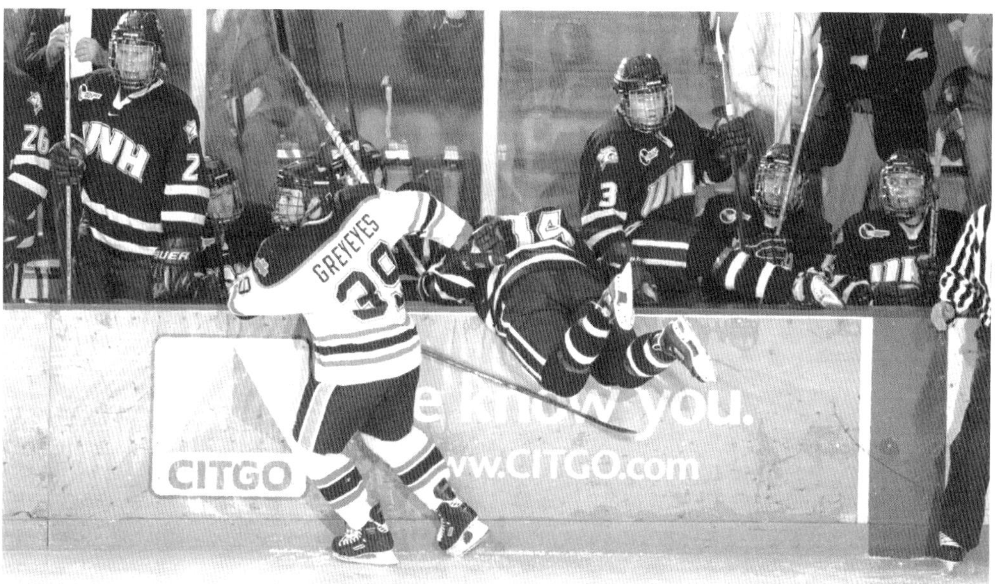

CHECKMATE. Matt Greyeyes (No. 39) avoids a check by a University of New Hampshire player. Postseason accolades were numerous for the 2001–2002 squad. The team had two All-Americans in Peter Metcalf and Niko Dimitrakos. Coach Tim Whitehead was awarded the Spencer Penrose Award as the national coach of the year. Whitehead would shortly lose his interim status and be signed by the university as head coach of men's ice hockey.

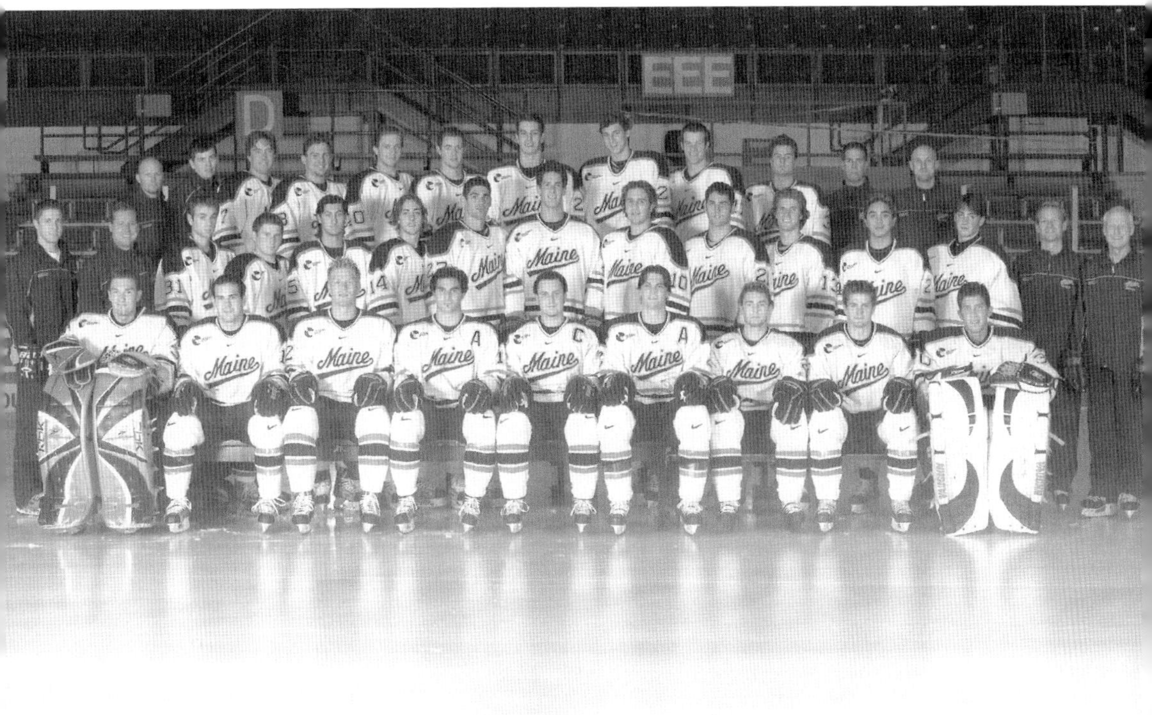

THE 2006–2007 UMAINE MEN'S ICE HOCKEY TEAM. In the first decade of the 21st century, the UMaine Black Bears have enjoyed the success that has made them one of the top college hockey programs in the nation. Since the 2000–2001 season, the Black Bears have a combined record of 154-69-26. They have advanced to the NCAA tournament all six seasons and played in four NCAA Frozen Four tournaments. Since 1998, UMaine has a winning percentage of .696, the best in the nation.

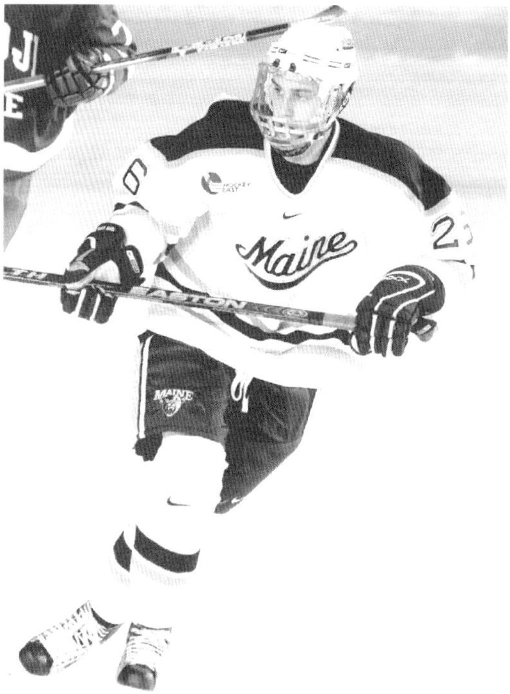

REBUILDING? In a program that seems to reload instead of rebuild, it appeared that coaches Tim Whitehead, Guy Perron, Dan Kerluke, and Grant Standbrook had their work cut out for them heading into the 2006–2007 campaign. The 2005–2006 season marked another banner year, with the team finishing with a 28-12-2 record and going deep into the playoffs, eventually losing to Wisconsin in the semifinal round. The team would look to newcomer Teddy Purcell (No. 26, left) for some offense. Purcell received the Hockey East Rookie of the Year Award in 2006–2007.

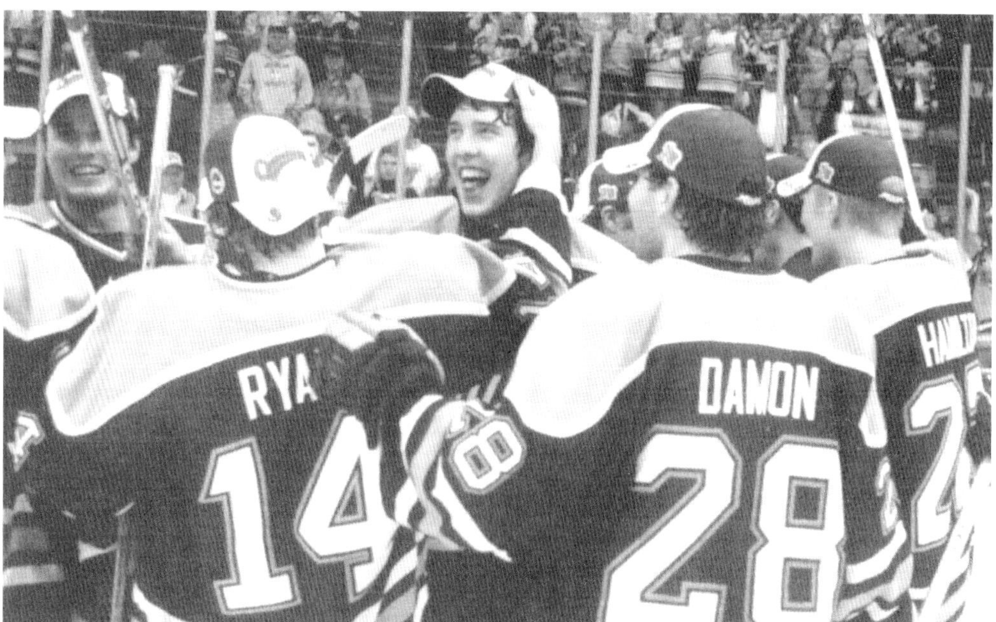

MISSING LEADERSHIP. Not returning was leading scorer Derek Damon (No. 28), who would graduate and turn professional. Damon is now skating for the Florida Everblades of the East Coast Hockey League (ECHL). Billy Ryan (No. 14) would be a solid contributor for the 2006–2007 squad, scoring 33 points with 13 goals and 20 assists.

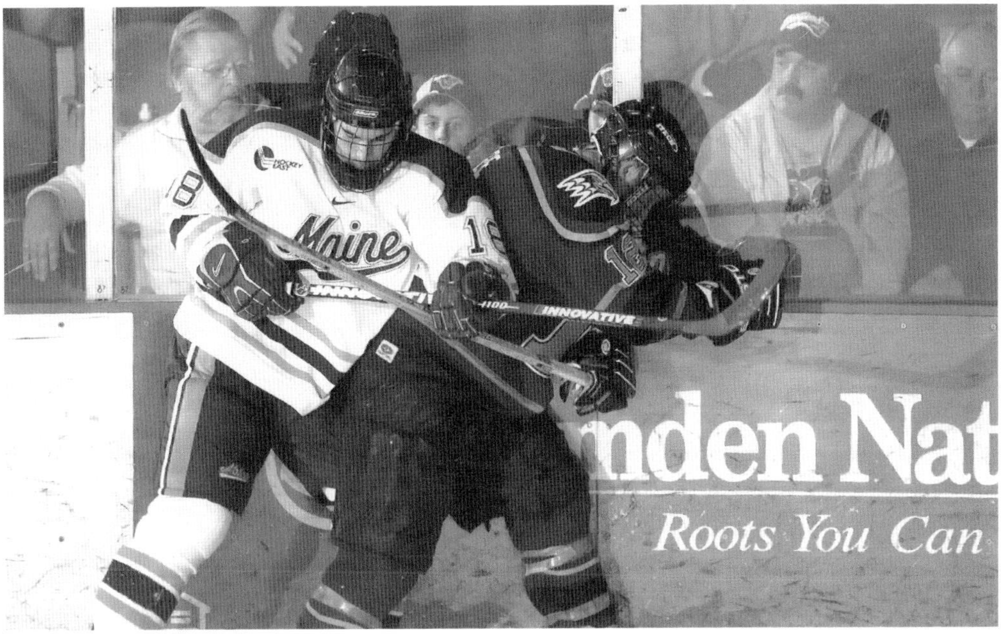

TOP GUN. Josh Soares (No. 18) had a big year for the Black Bears, leading the team in scoring along with Michel Leveille (No. 11). Coach Tim Whitehead called Soares "as good a player as there is in college hockey." Soares had back-to-back 40-point seasons. His efforts earned him Hockey East second-team selection and All-New England honors.

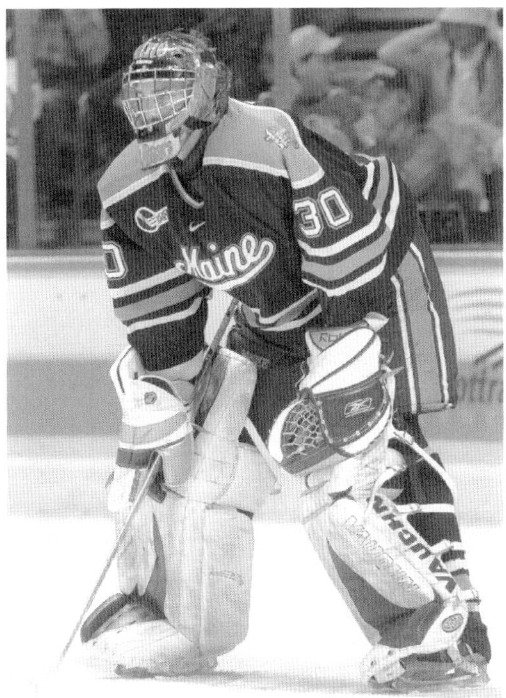

GOT YOU COVERED. At six feet seven inches and a matching wing span, good luck trying to get the puck by goalie Ben Bishop (No. 30). In 2006–2007, Bishop recorded 819 saves and had a stingy goals allowed average of 2.14 per game. Bishop recorded 35 saves in the NCAA regional, a 3-1 victory against Massachusetts.

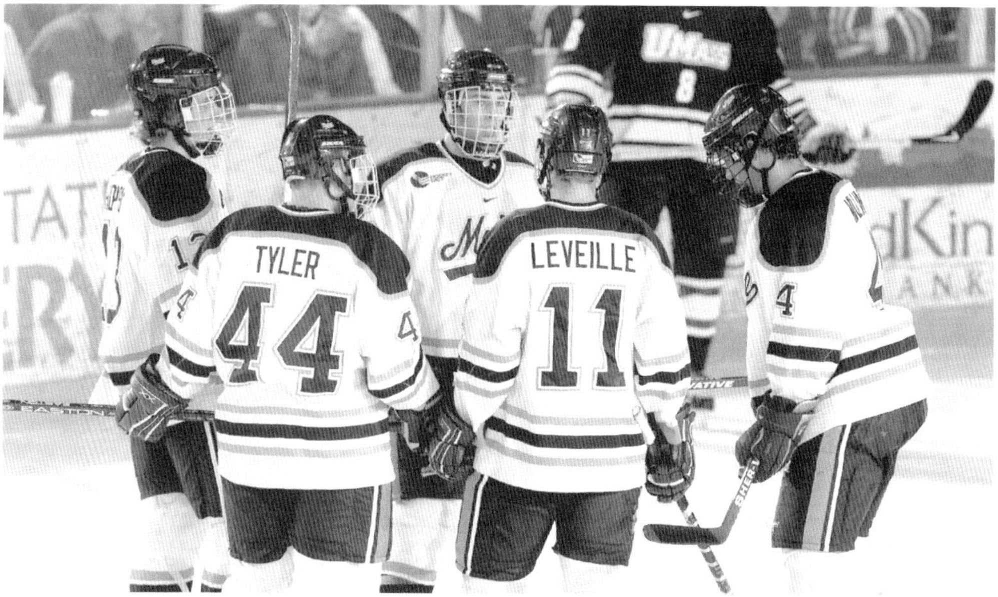

RISING STAR. Michel Leveille (No. 11) played in all 40 games for the 2006–2007 team, scoring 19 goals and adding 26 assists for 45 points. He leaves the Black Bears as a two-time All-American and one of Maine's all-time leading scorers. In his four years at UMaine, the team won 106 games and played in three Frozen Four tournaments.

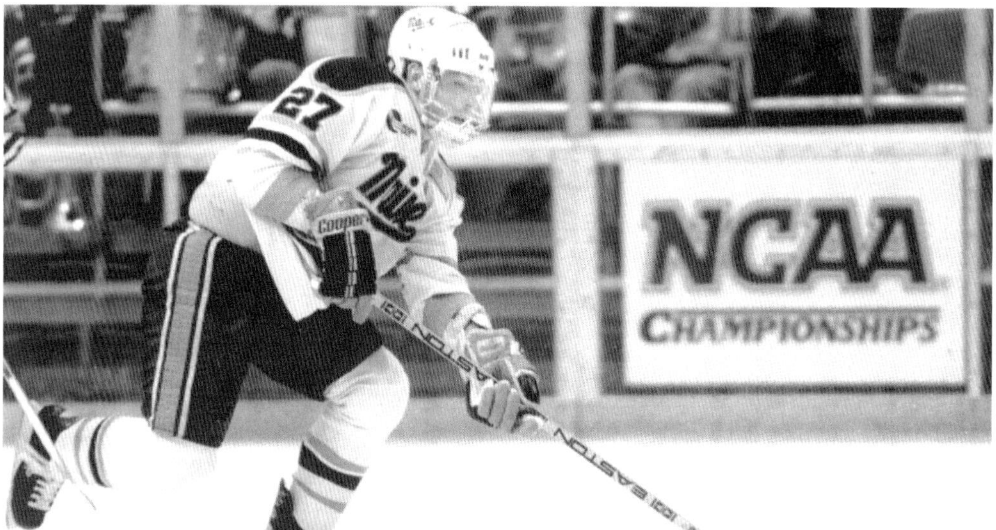

SKATING TO ANOTHER FROZEN FOUR. No. 27 heads up the ice in the NCAA playoffs. While the team struggled at times in compiling a 23-15-2 record, including four straight losses to Hockey East rival UMass, they were tough down the stretch, sneaking into the postseason and making it all the way to St. Louis to play in another Frozen Four.

5

Great Players

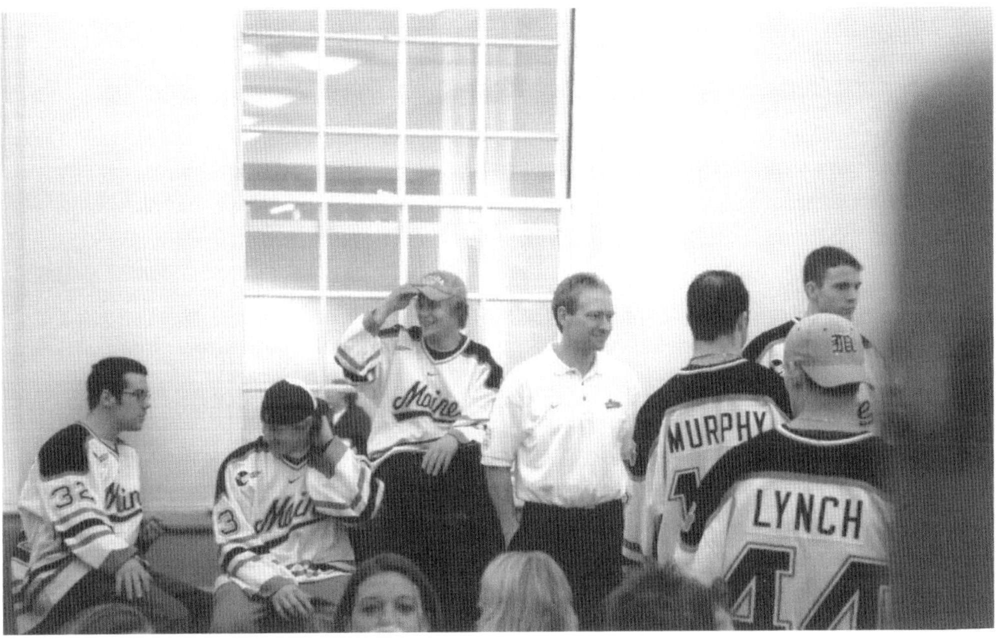

UMaine Hockey Alumni Reunion. It is a daunting task to sift through the playing resumes of the almost 300 young men who have worn the black and blue jersey of UMaine men's ice hockey. While each has made his own contribution, there stands out an elite group of players who have been thus recognized by their peers. That group includes 33 All-Americans, 11 Olympians, 9 Hobey Baker finalists, and 2 Hobey Baker Award winners. Over 50 UMaine alumni have reached the ultimate destination of playing in the NHL, while others have played for professional teams in Canada and Europe. Others have hung up their skates and had successful careers as coaches and administrators. This list of UMaine greats is broken down into the most influential players of their period.

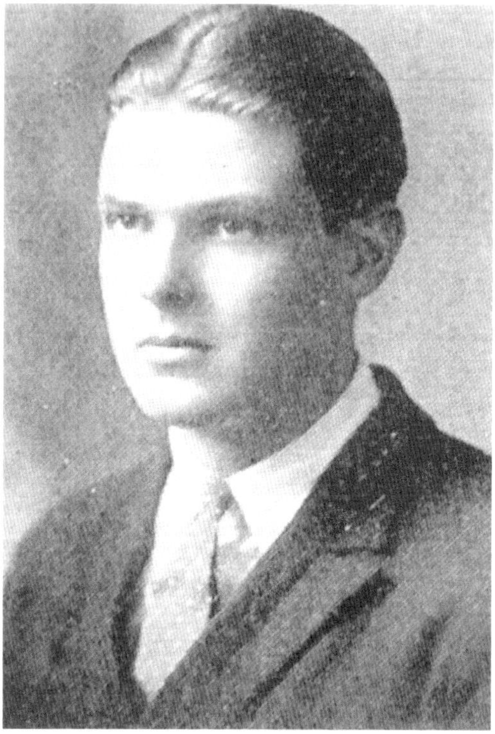

THE PIONEER. Although it was hoped that by the 1920s hockey at UMaine would be firmly established as a varsity sport, a hockey program at Maine continued to fall through the ice. One player who fought courageously that the program be continued was Charles Baxter (left, in his graduation photograph). A star player of the 1923–1924 squad, Baxter was elected captain for 1925–1926 only to have the season, and the program, cancelled. Baxter labored in vain to get the program reinstated, circulating petitions and meeting with administration. He did come away with a promise that if an indoor facility could be constructed, the hockey program would be reestablished as a varsity sport.

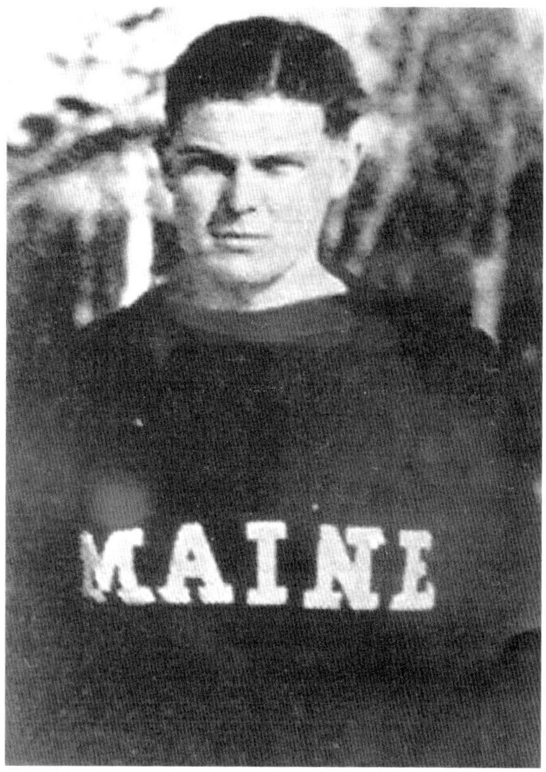

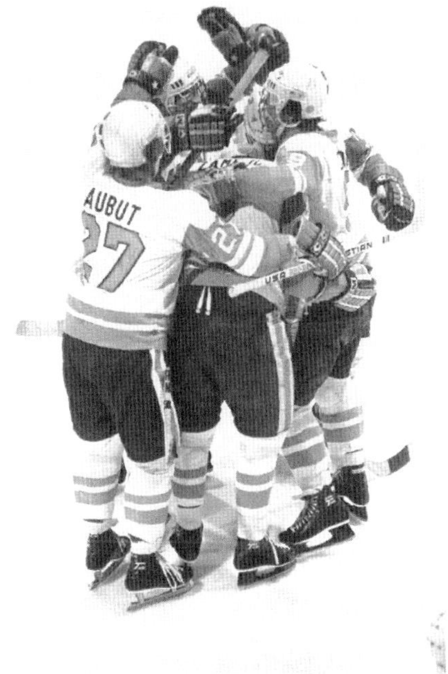

AUBUT AND CONN CONGRATULATING TEAMMATE ROBERT ZAMEJC. The first teams of the modern era of UMaine hockey were dominated by two players, Andre Aubut and Gary Conn. Coach Jack Semler would later say of Conn, "he was the best goal scorer I ever coached. He was also an amazingly tough and gritty player who dug pucks out of corners at both ends of the rink." And of Aubut, "Andre was terrific with the puck, and had great anticipation and hockey sense. . . . He was as famous to all of us as a gentleman as he was a great hockey player." Both players were inducted into the UMaine Sports Hall of Fame.

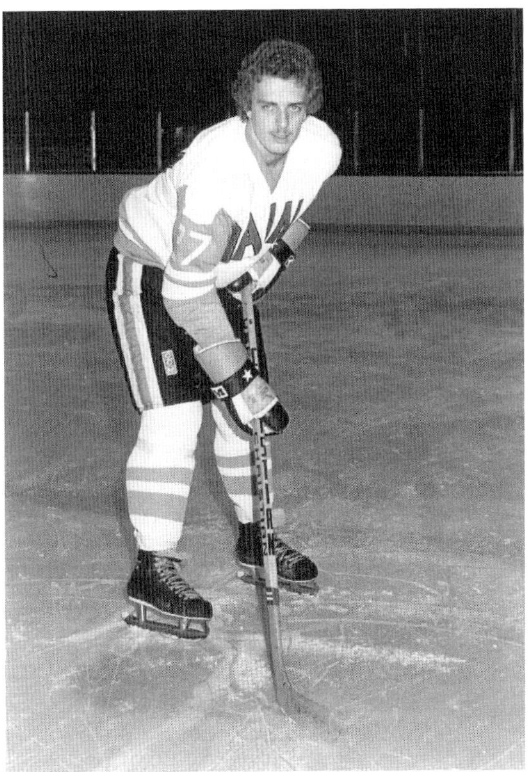

ANDRE AUBUT DURING THE 1978 SEASON. During his career (1978–1982), Aubut established school records for the most points by a defensemen (32), goals in a game (5, versus Salem State in 1981), and shares the record for assists in a game (5 versus St. Thomas in 1979). In 1981, Aubut became the first UMaine hockey player ever to be selected as an All-American, and in 1979, he was named ECAC Division II rookie of the year. Aubut died in a freak hockey accident shortly after graduating from UMaine while playing in a senior hockey league in Montreal.

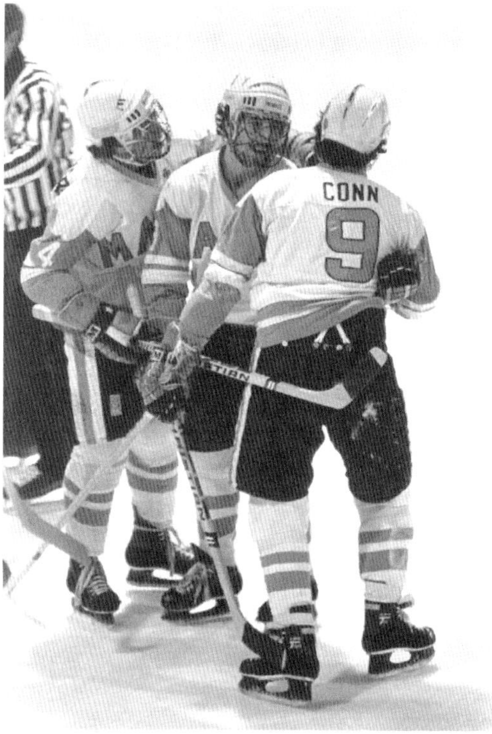

CONN CONGRATULATED AFTER SCORING ANOTHER GOAL. Gary Conn played four seasons at UMaine, 1977–1981. He led the Black Bears to a 78-47-2 record during his tenure and helped the team jump from ECAC Division II to ECAC Division I. Conn finished his career at Maine holding school records for most hat tricks in a season (4), twice scoring school records for points in a game (6), and most goals in a period (4). He is second in career goals with 107.

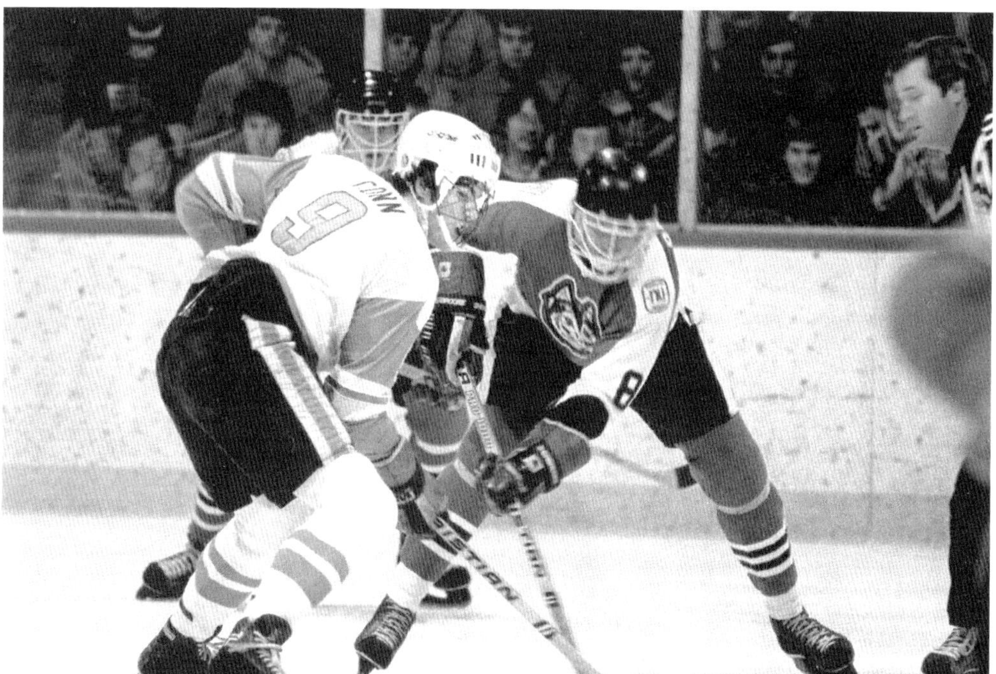

CONN IN ACTION AGAINST HUSKIES. Also noted for his durability, Conn never missed a game in his four-year career at Maine. He was named a first-team All-American in 1981.

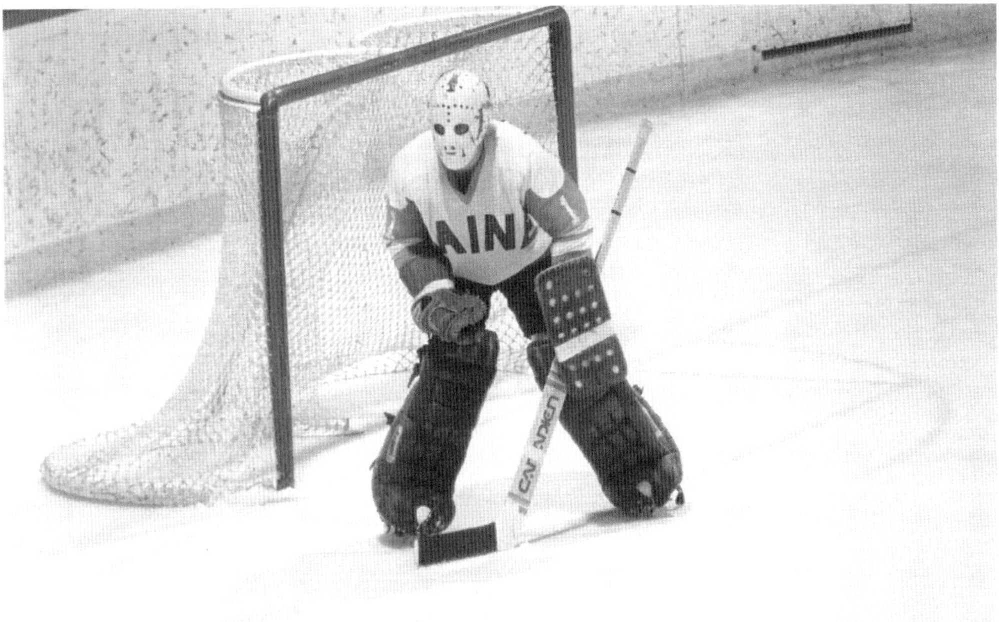

JOHN TORTORELLA. Also starring on teams of the late 1970s and early 1980s were brothers John and Jim Tortorella. They begin a list of brother combinations that played at UMaine that includes Dwight and James Montgomery, David and Jack Capuano, Chris and Peter Ferraro, Eric and Jason Weinrich, Chris and Barrett Heisten, Keenan and John Hopson, and Paul, Steve, and Martin Kariya. Jim Tortorella (No. 1, above) played in the goal the inaugural season of Black Bear hockey and ended a four-year career in 1981. John Tortorella (No. 3, below) played at Maine from 1978 to 1981. They have both extended their hockey careers as coaches.

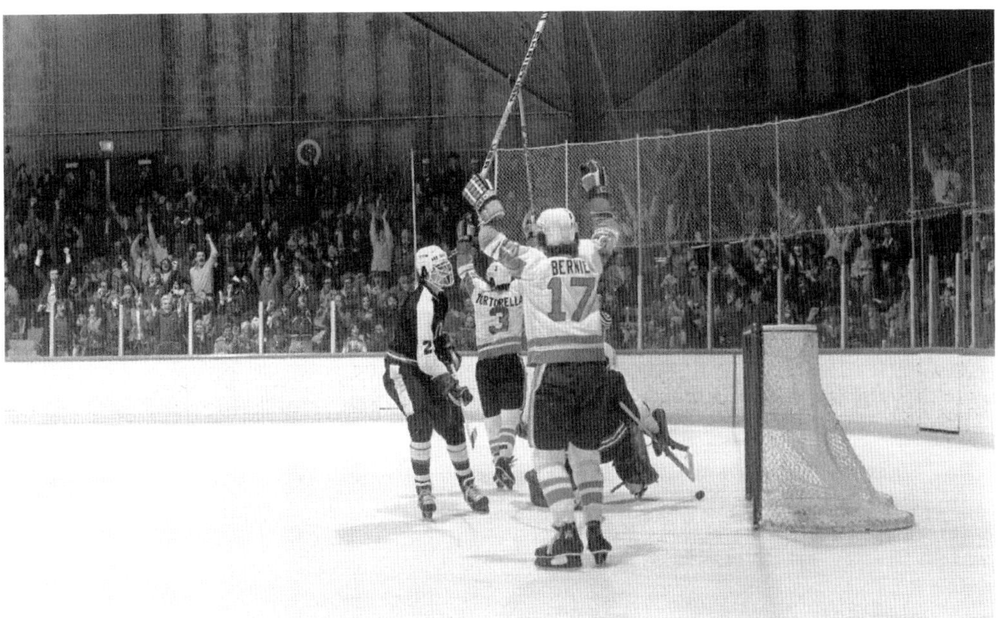

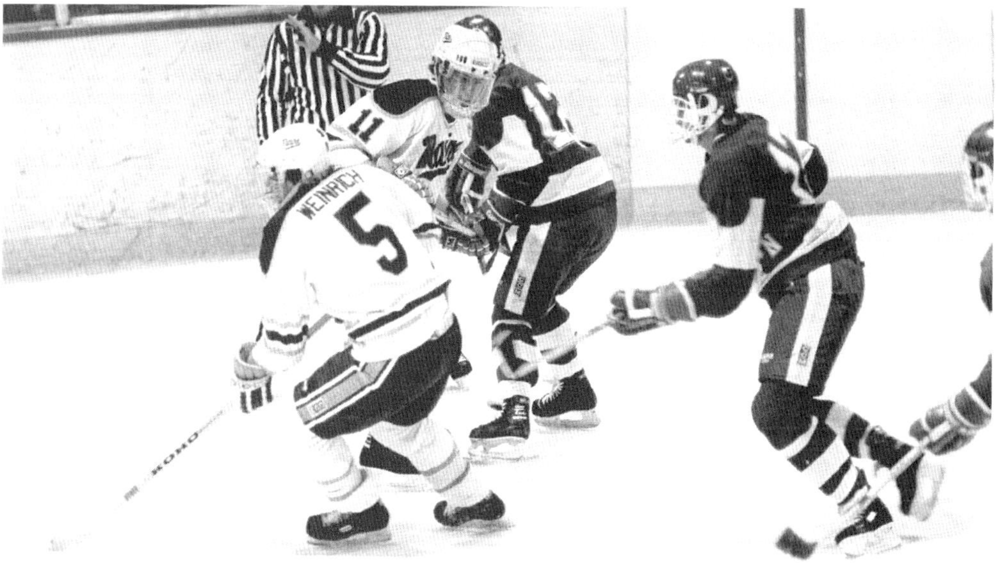

Eric Weinrich, 1985. Eric Weinrich was the state of Maine's early gift to the UMaine hockey program. Weinrich grew up in Gardiner and attended North Yarmouth Academy before entering UMaine in 1985. Early teams were dominated by players from Massachusetts and Canada. The only other Mainers to play on the modern-era teams before Weinrich were Waterville's Mike Vague, Portland's Leon Quiet, and Ray Roy of Lewiston.

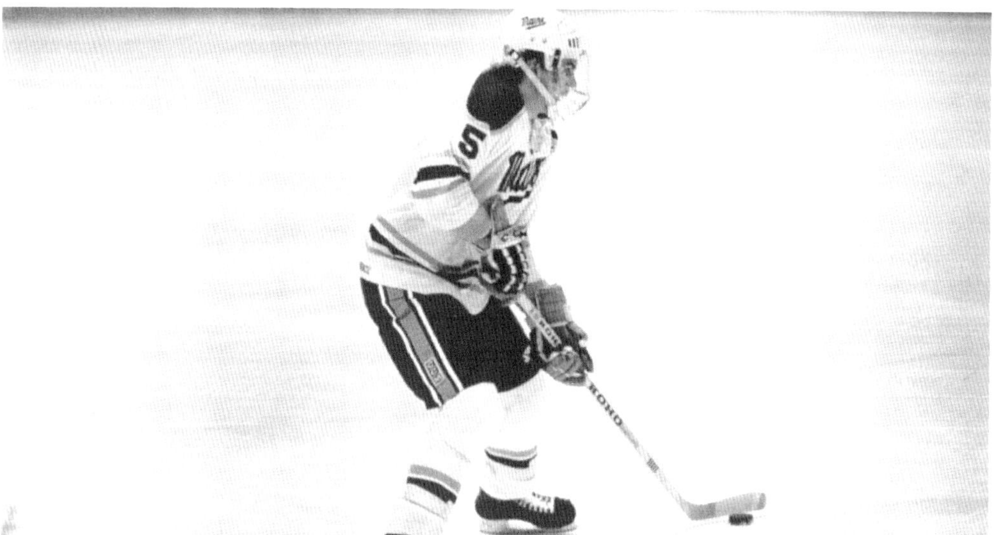

Good with the Puck. Weinrich was drafted by the New Jersey Devils in the second round of the 1985 draft. He would go on to have one of the most productive NHL careers of any UMaine alumnus to date. He spent 18 years in the NHL, compiling 70 goals and 318 assists. He was named to the NHL All-Rookie Team in 1991. In 2007, he skated for the Portland Pirates of the American Hockey League (AHL).

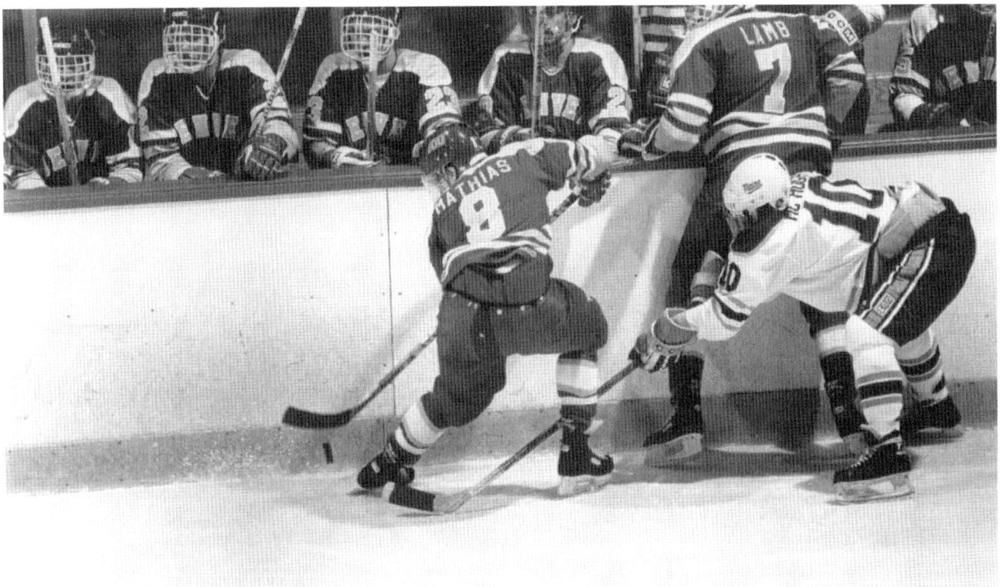

McHugh Digging Out the Puck. An anchor for the great teams in the mid-1980s was Mike McHugh (No. 10, above). He later changed his uniform number to 18. McHugh's accomplishments included making the All-New England Team and All-American squad in 1988. He was also named Hockey East Player of the Year in 1988 and served as team captain. After leaving UMaine in 1988, McHugh played for the Maine Mariners in the AHL before spending time in the NHL with the Minnesota North Stars and San Jose Sharks. He was inducted into the UMaine Sports Hall of Fame in 2006.

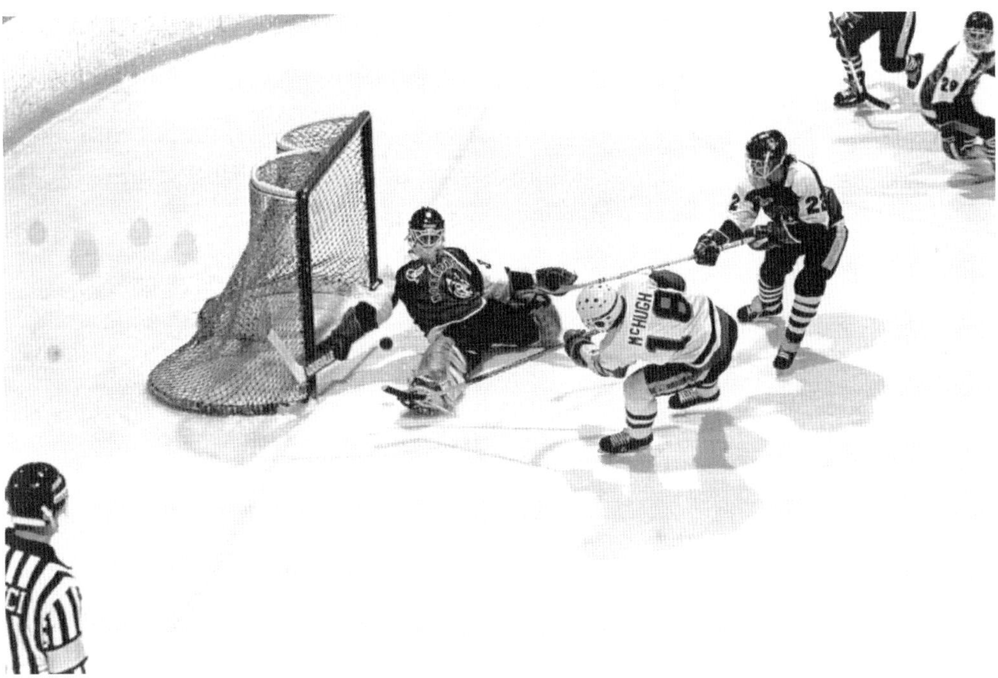

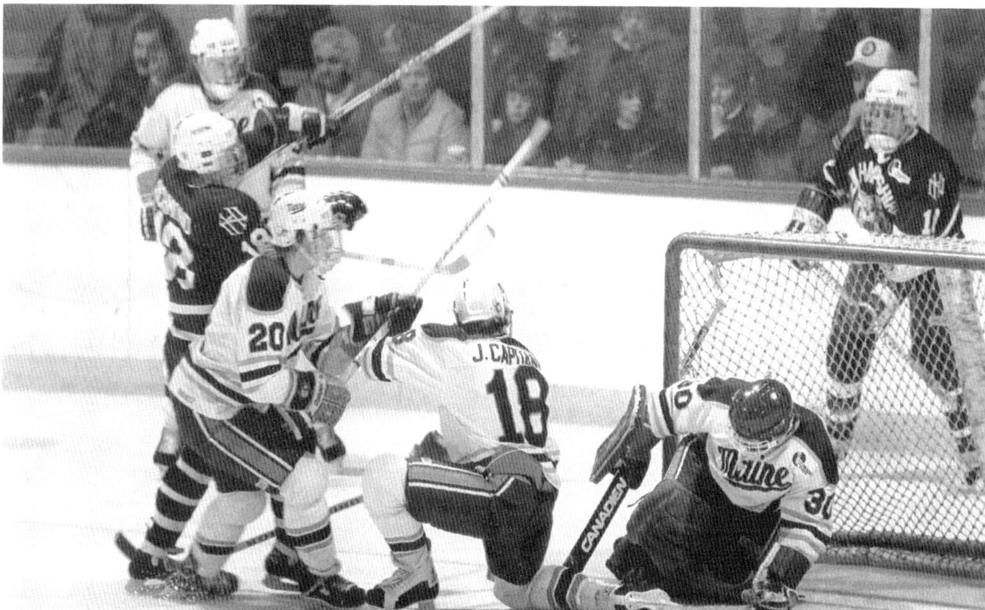

The Capuano Brothers. The Black Bear teams of the mid- to late 1980s were anchored by brothers Jack (No. 18) and David Capuano (No. 11). Jack was a four-year letterman (1985–1988) and twice captained Black Bear teams. In 1988, he was named a first-team All-American. He presently serves as the senior vice president of operations for the Pee Dee Pride in the ECHL. David Capuano (below) played three years at UMaine and was Black Bear captain on the 1998–1999 squad. He was named first-team All-American in 1988 and 1999 and was twice a Hobey Baker Award finalist. He was selected in the second round by the Pittsburgh Penguins in the 1986 draft.

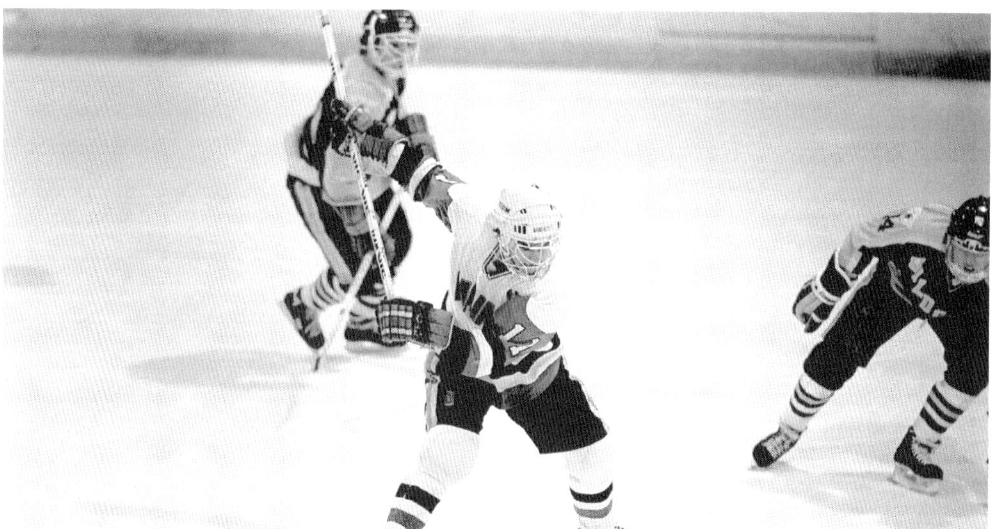

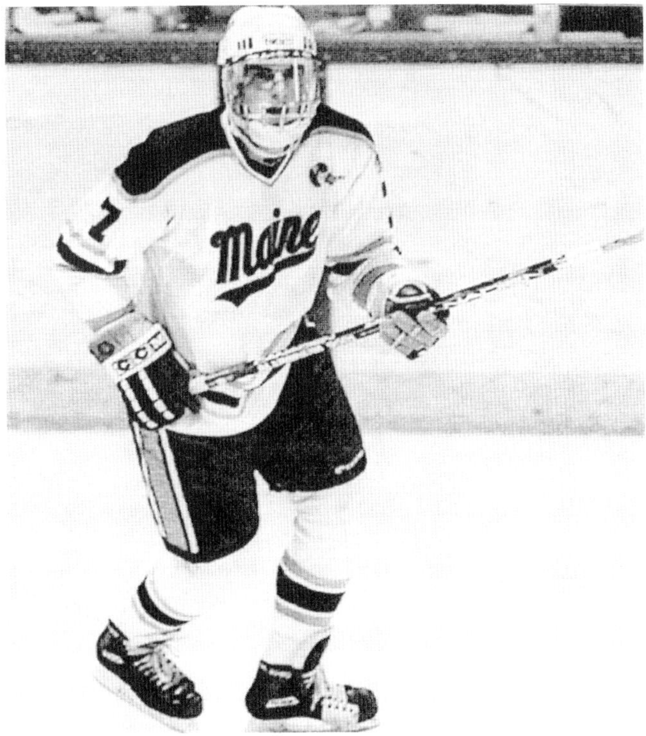

CARNEY SKATES FOR THE BEARS. One of the greatest defensive players to put on a UMaine uniform was Keith Carney (No. 7), who presently holds three Maine defenseman records. Carney played for the Black Bears from 1988 to 1991 and was an All-American in 1990–1991. He was the 1991 Hockey East Defensive Player of the Year and made the All-Rookie Team in 1989.

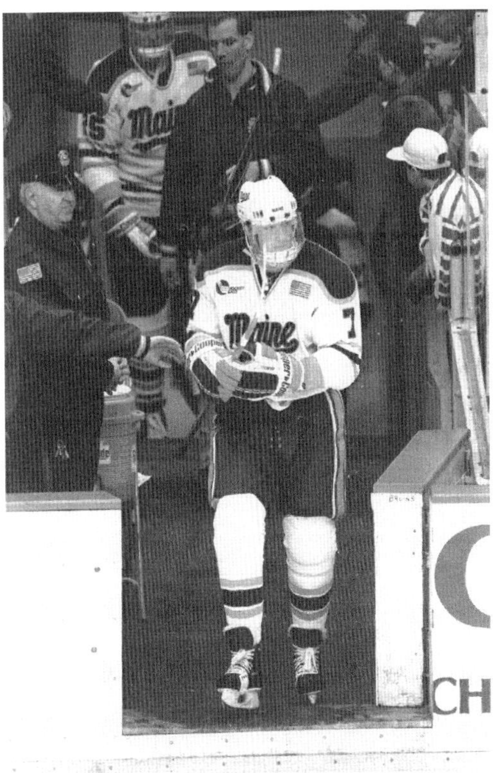

CARNEY RETURNS TO ICE AFTER INTERMISSION. After finishing at UMaine in 1991, Carney played for the Rochester Americans in the AHL. In 1992, Carney moved up to the NHL's Buffalo Sabers before playing for the Chicago Blackhawks, Phoenix Coyotes, and Anaheim Mighty Ducks. In 2006–2007, Carney had a solid year with the Minnesota Wild, appearing in 80 games with 4 goals and 13 assists.

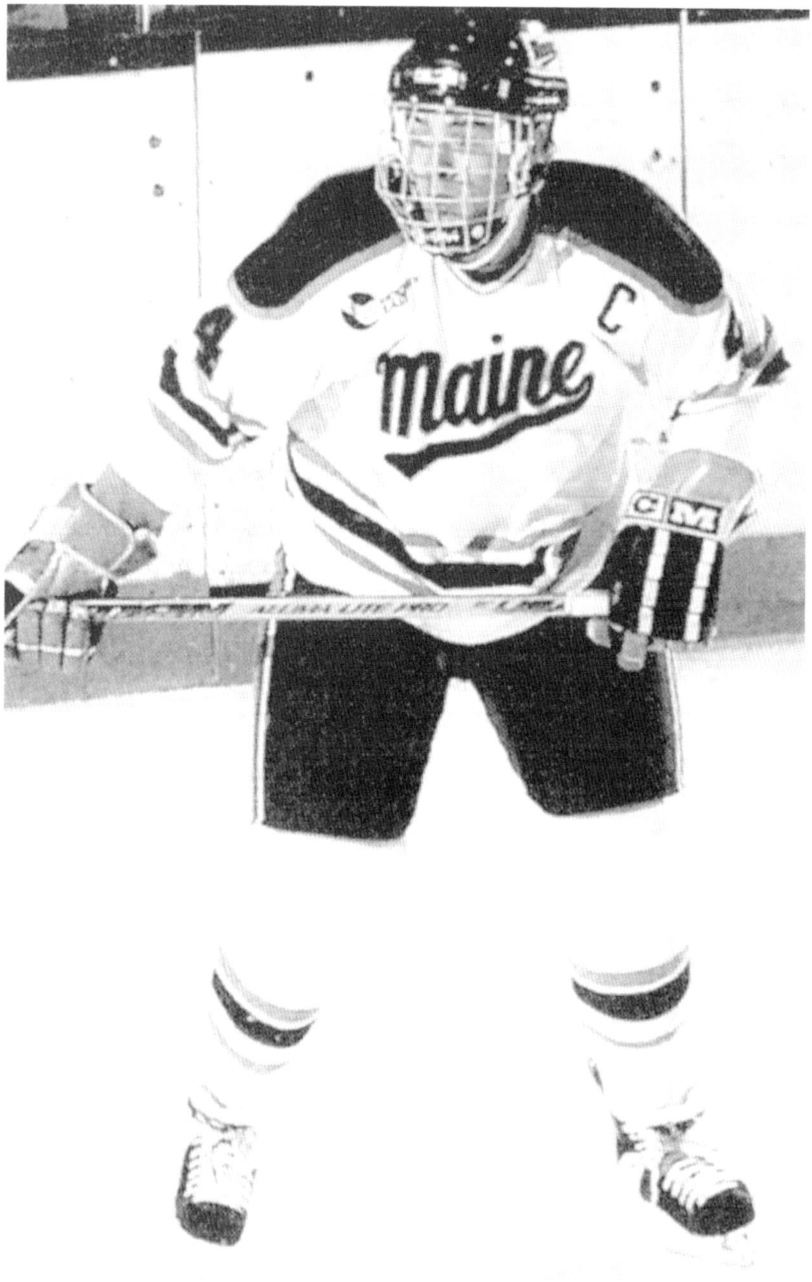

MIKE GOLDEN AND CHRIS IMES. Stalwart players of the late 1980s and early 1990s were Mike Golden (No. 8, not pictured) and Chris Imes (No. 4, pictured). A three-year letterman at UMaine, 1985–1988, Golden was team captain, first-team All-American selection, and Hobey Baker finalist in 1988. Imes lettered at Maine four years, 1991–1995, and was twice named a first-team All-American. In 1995, he was a finalist in the Hobey Baker Award selection. Imes was UMaine captain in 1995. He played on Team USA in the 1994 Olympics.

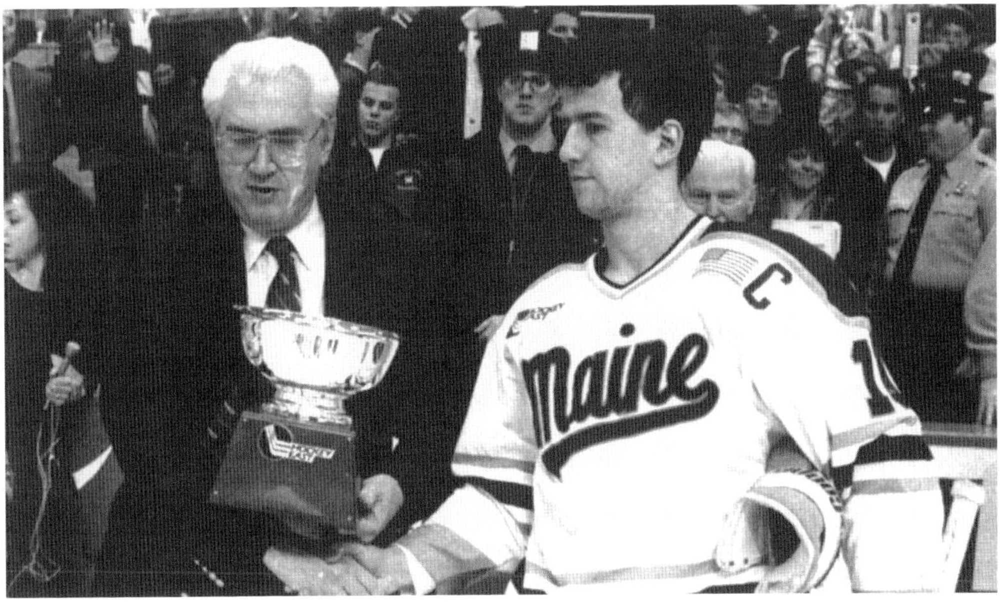

MARTIN ROBITAILLE RECEIVES TROPHY. While he never showed great statistics or earned national accolades, Martin Robitaille (No. 10) proved his worth to the team in abilities not measured by numbers. The gritty player was a four-year letterman (1988–1992) and served as team captain in 1991 and 1992. He won the Richard Britts Coaches Perseverance Award in 1992 and the Jack Semler Award (most improved player) in 1989. He was the Unsung Hero Award winner in 1990.

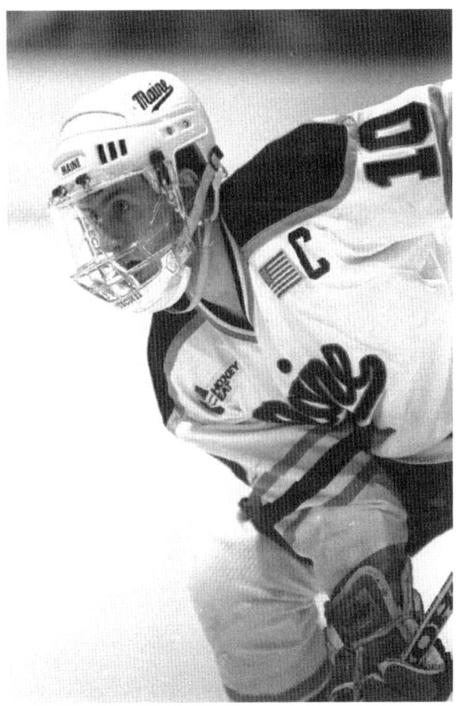

MARTIN ROBITAILLE. Robitaille's career record at Maine was an impressive 114-51-6. He was drafted in the 1990 supplemental draft by the Toronto Maple Leafs.

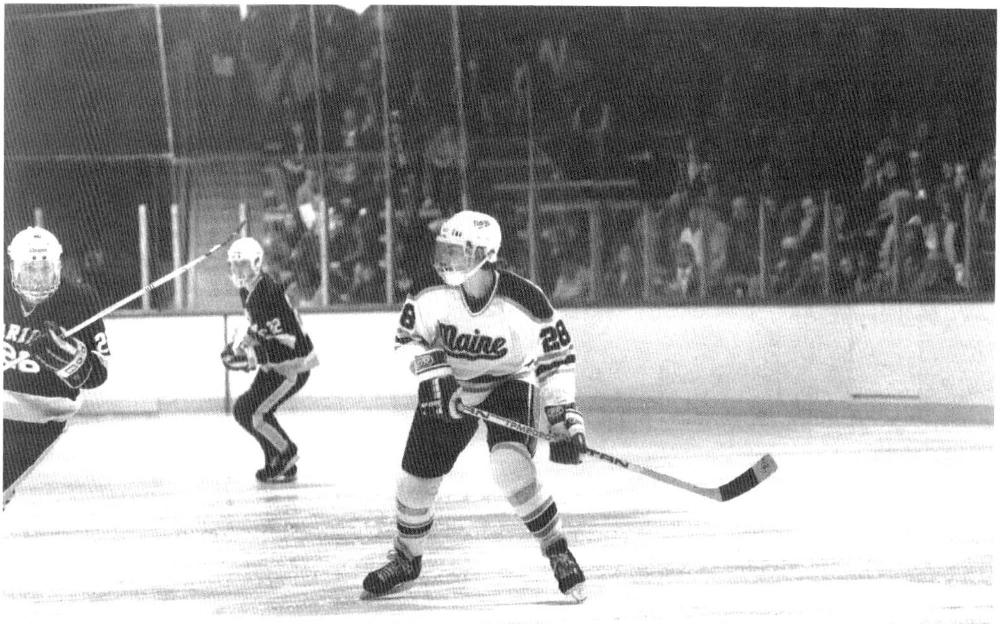

ROY IN ACTION. Jean-Yves Roy is UMaine's all-time leading goal scorer. He scored 108 goals in his four-year career at Maine, 1989–1992 . He made All New England teams in 1991–1992 and was a three-time All-American, being selected in 1990, 1991, and 1992.

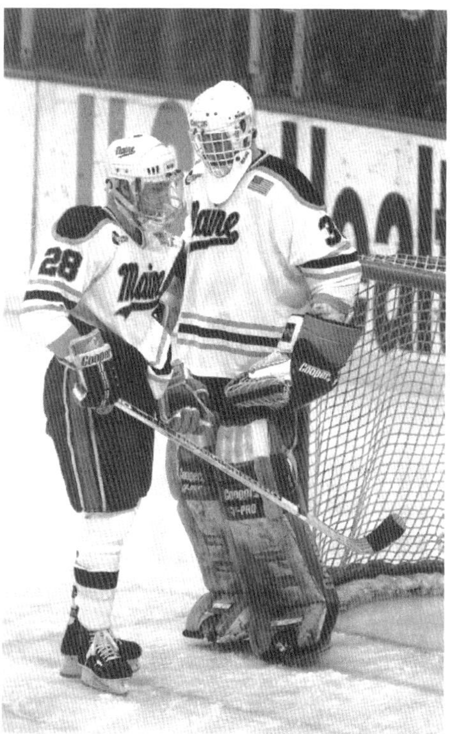

DON'T SCORE AGAINST ME. Roy twice played on the Canadian National Team and played for the Binghamton Rangers in the AHL before jumping to the NHL with the New York Rangers in 1994. He also played on the 1994 Canadian Olympic team that won a silver medal.

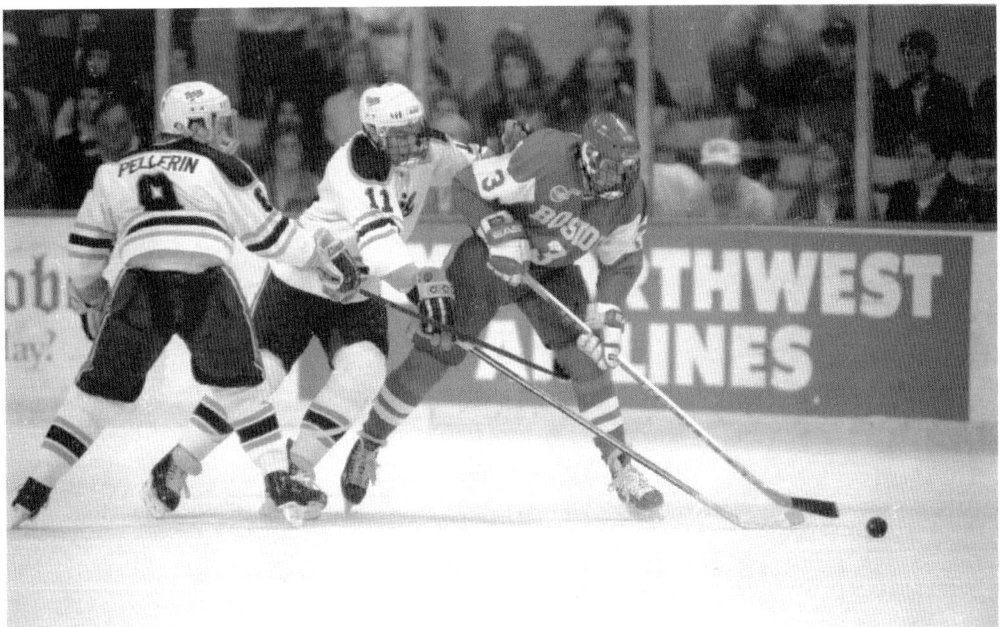

SCOTT PELLERIN IN ACTION AGAINST BOSTON UNIVERSITY. Scott Pellerin holds the Black Bear record for most power-play goals in a career. He was a first-team All-American in 1992, Hockey East Rookie of the Year in 1989, and made the academic honor roll in 1992.

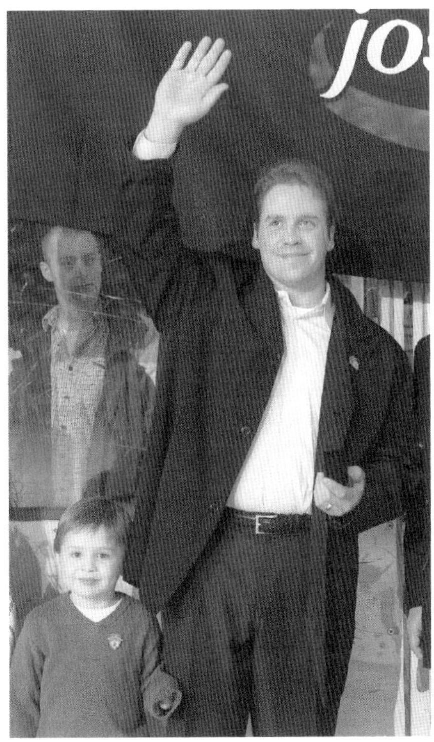

PELLERIN ACKNOWLEDGES FANS AT AWARDS CEREMONY. Pellerin is honored at a ceremony in 1993 when his No. 8 jersey was retired. Pellerin was elected into the UMaine Sports Hall of Fame in 1997. Pellerin continued his hockey career after he left UMaine, playing with the Utica Devils and Portland Pirates in the AHL. His NHL resume includes stints with the New Jersey Devils, St. Louis Blues, and Boston Bruins.

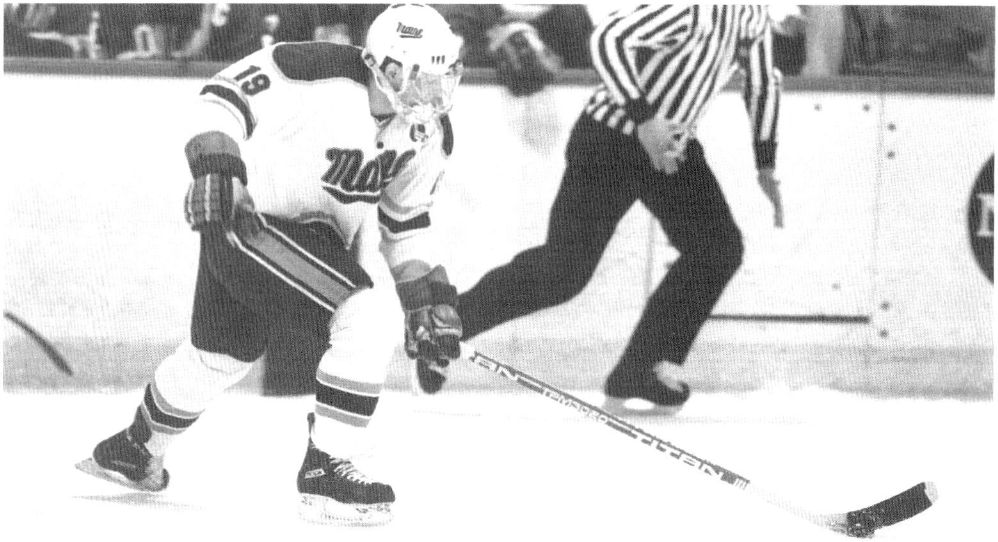

MONTGOMERY CHASES PUCK. The hero of the 1993 national championship team was Jim Montgomery (No. 19). Montgomery was a four-year letterman at UMaine from 1989 to 1993 when the team compiled an incredible 138-25-8 record, two Hockey East championships, and a national championship. He holds career marks for most assists (198), most games played (170), and most shorthanded goals (10). A two-time All-American, Montgomery was named team captain and became a finalist in the Hobey Baker Award voting in 1993.

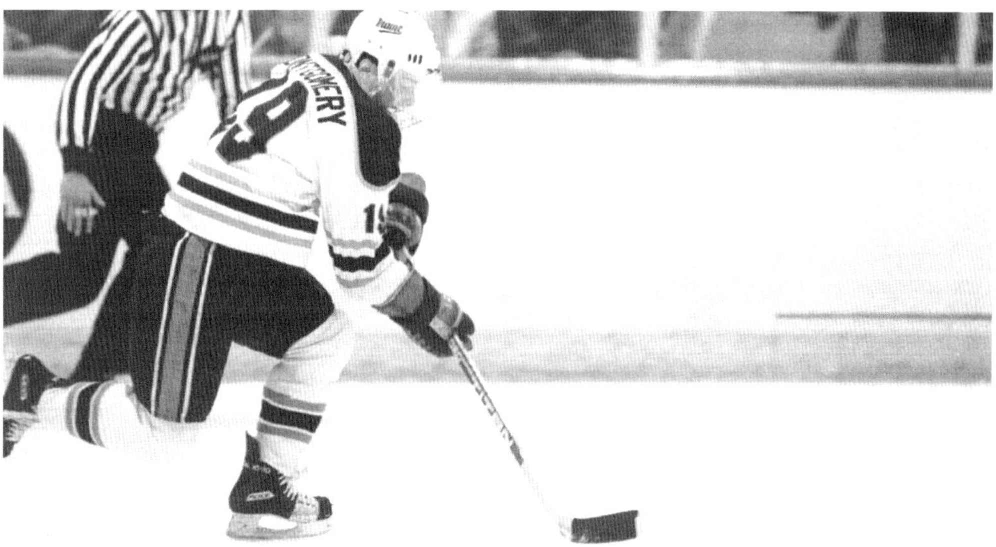

JIM MONTGOMERY. Montgomery was elected to the UMaine Sports Hall of Fame in 1998. His No. 19 jersey was retired in 1994. Montgomery was signed out of college by the St. Louis Blues in 1993. He played a total of 12 years in professional hockey with the Blues, Montreal Canadians, Philadelphia Flyers, San Jose Sharks, and Dallas Stars. He recently joined the coaching ranks as an assistant at Rensselaer.

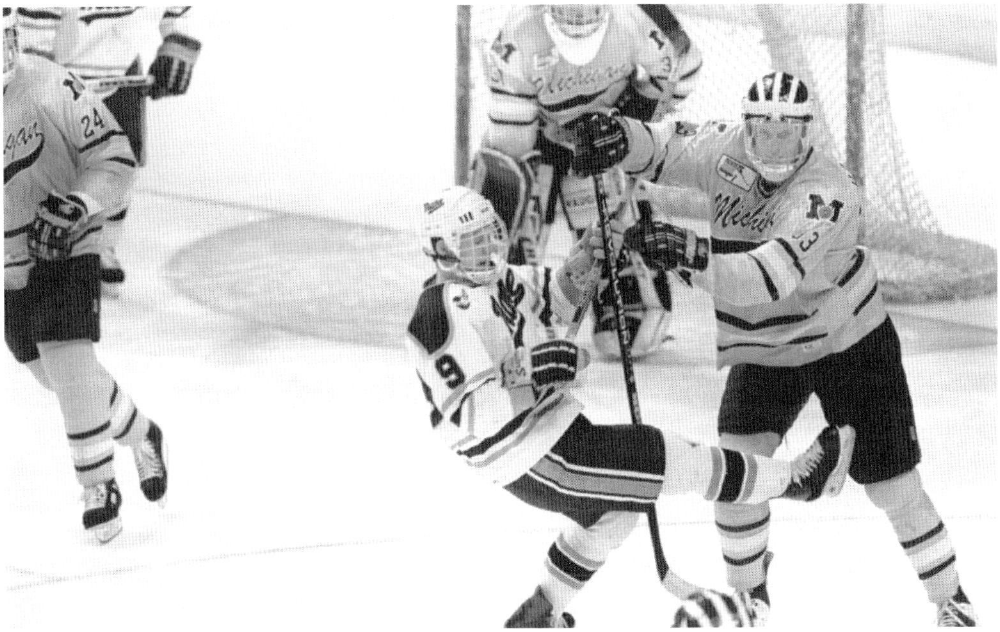

ONE WAY TO STOP HIM. Kariya, just the name struck fear in the hearts of opponents, and it did not matter which one. The first family of UMaine hockey, brothers Paul, Steve, and Martin had careers that spanned the years 1992 to 2003. This tandem of brothers is among the most prolific to ever play collegiate hockey. They were joined at UMaine by sister Noriko, who played field hockey and has tried her hand at professional boxing.

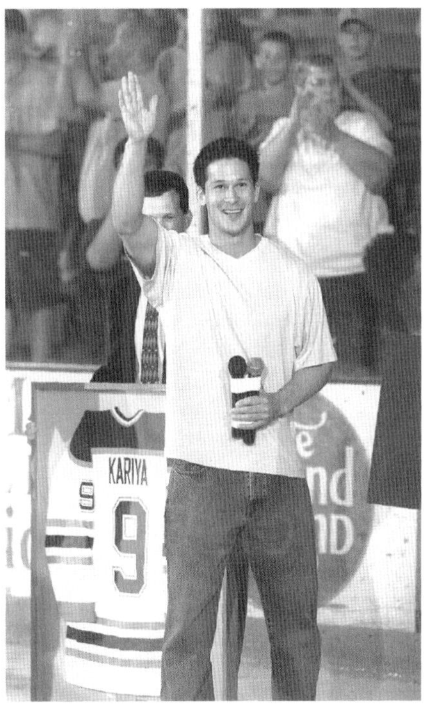

RETIRED JERSEY. Paul Kariya has his uniform (No. 9) retired in a ceremony at Alfond in 2001. He shares that honor with Scott Pellerin and Jim Montgomery. Paul continued his career in the NHL where he has played for the St. Louis Blues, Anaheim Mighty Ducks, Colorado Avalanche, and Nashville Predators. In July 2007, Paul signed a three-year contract with the St. Louis Blues worth $18 million. Is anyone from the alumni association reading?

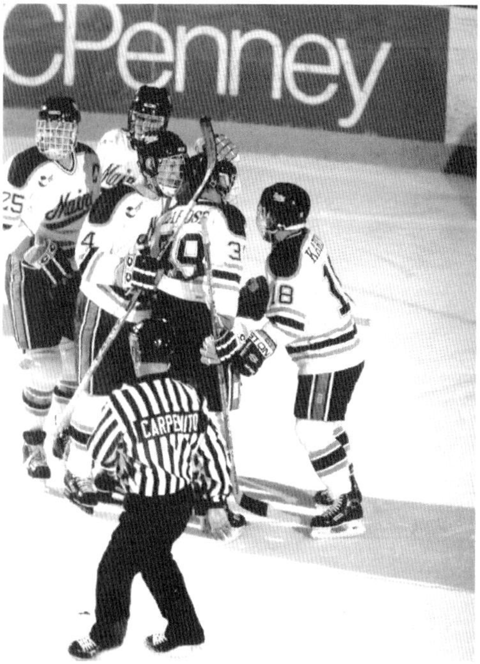

STEVE KARIYA. Like brother Paul, Steve Kariya (No. 18) led Maine to a national championship, where he was a team captain. He was a four-year letterman at Maine and was a Hobey Baker Award finalist in 1999. He earned All-American honors in 1999 and was awarded the Dr. Dale Lick Academic Achievement Award. Three times Steve Kariya was awarded the Hockey East sportsmanship award. Steve Kariya's professional career included a stint with the Vancouver Canuks in the NHL.

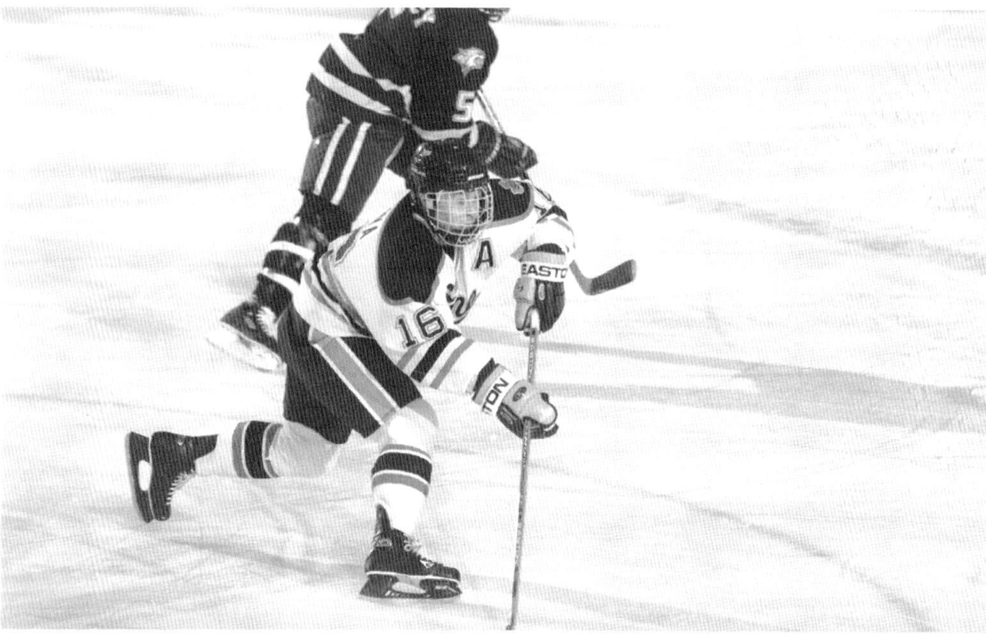

MARTIN KARIYA. The last of the Kariya clan to play at UMaine was No. 16, Martin Kariya. He was a four-year letterman at Maine, 1999–2003, and served as team captain on the 2002 and 2003 squads. He was the winner of the Hockey East sportsmanship award in 2003, Dr. Dale Lick Academic Achievement Award in 2002 and 2003, and the Harold Alfond MVP award in 2003. In 2007, he skated for the Blues of the Finnish National Hockey League (FNL).

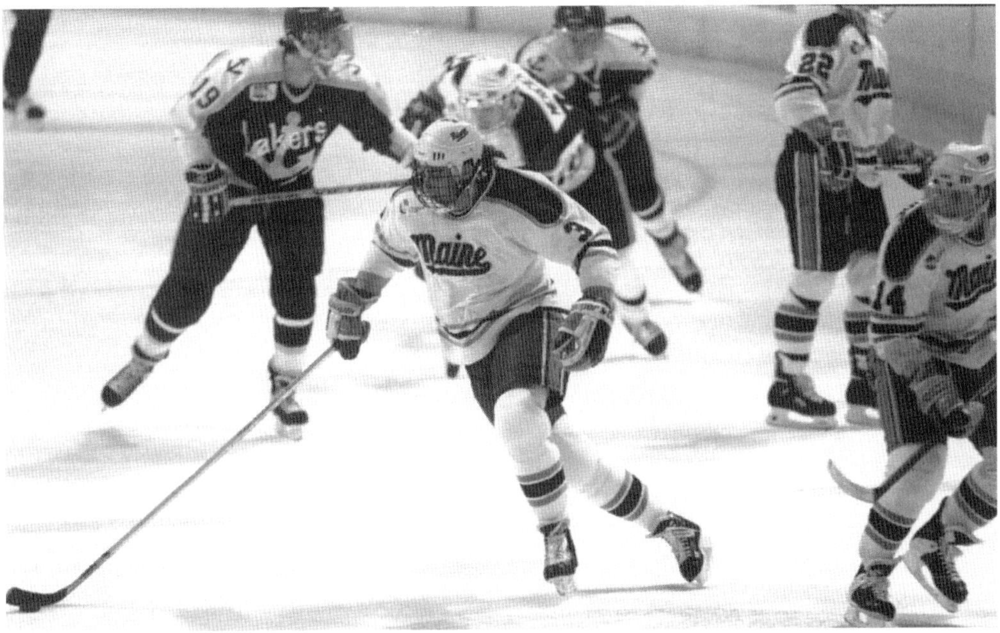

JEFF TORY. Jeff Tory (No. 3) was a three-year letterman at UMaine, 1993–1996. He was named a second-team All-American in 1995 and a first-team All-American in 1996. He was selected to the All-Hockey East squad in 1995 and 1996. In 1977, Tory was a member of the Canadian national team. He has skated professionally for the Kentucky Thoroughbreds and Philadelphia Phantoms of the AHL but has spent the majority of his professional career in the German Professional Hockey League (DEL).

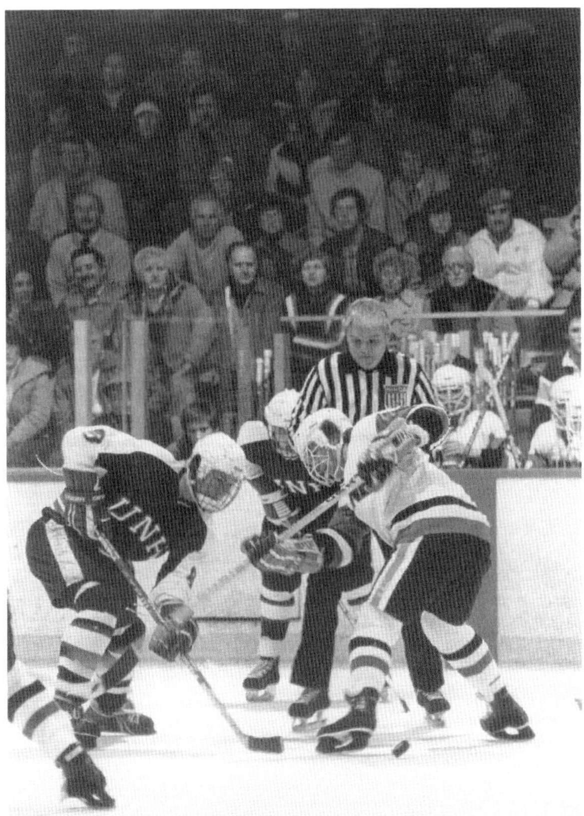

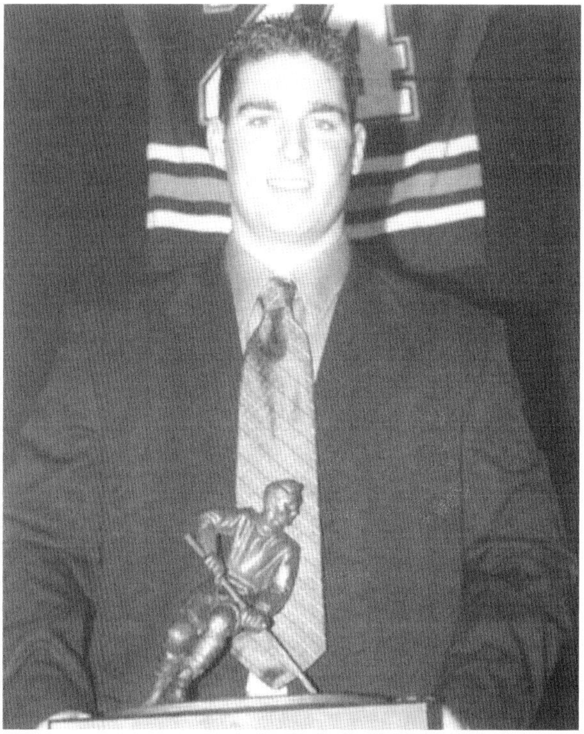

HUMANITARIAN AWARD WINNER JIM LEGER. Greatness by UMaine standards is not only found on the ice but in the classroom and in the community. In 1999–2000, UMaine's Jim Leger was the recipient of the Hockey Humanitarian Award. Leger served as president of the student athletic advisory board, worked for charities such as Toys for Tots, and was active in the local community. He made the academic honor roll in 2000 and is a winner of the Dr. Dale Lick Academic Achievement Award.

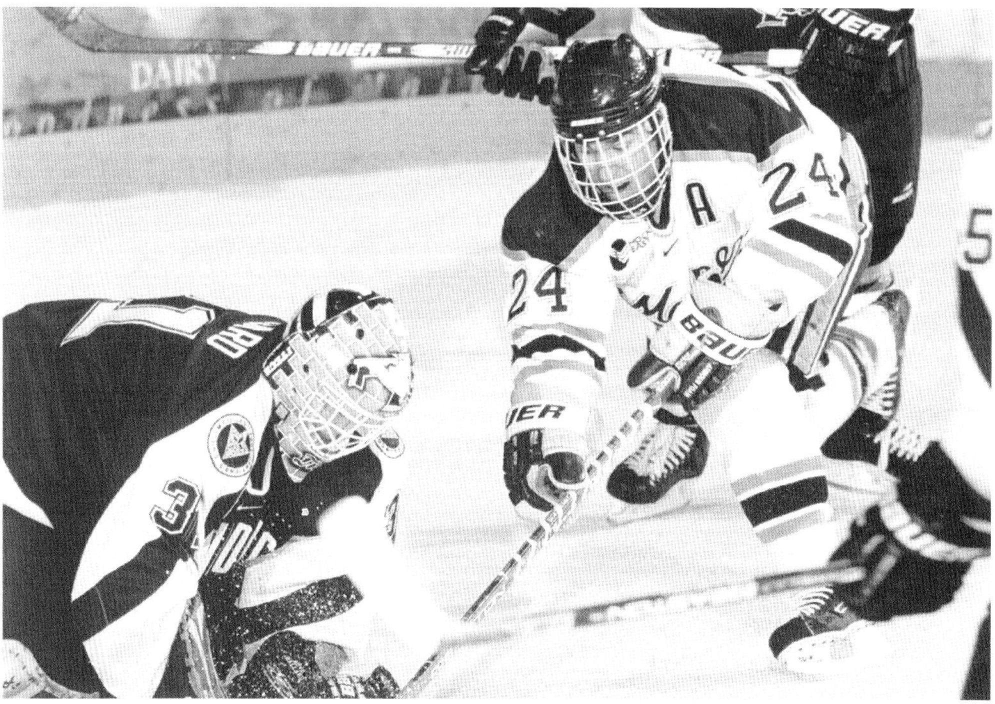

LEGER DIGS OUT PUCK. Leger (No. 24) was a four-year letterman on the Black Bear team and was assistant captain on the 1999–2000 team.

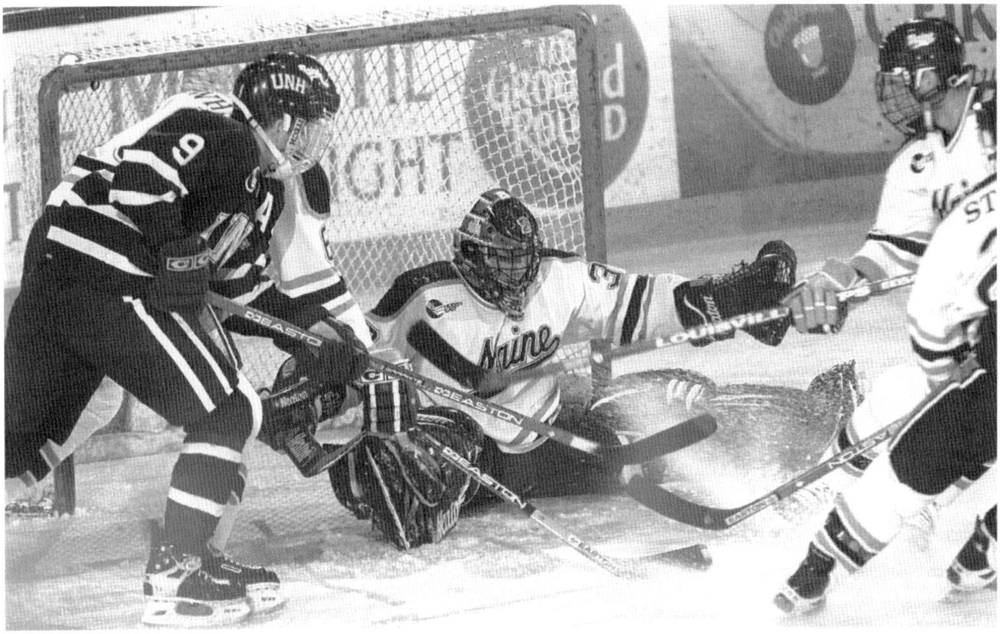

GOALIE JIMMY HOWARD. One of the greatest Black Bear goalies to ever wear the mask was Jimmy Howard (No. 33). Howard holds UMaine records for career goals against average and save percentage. Howard also holds the NCAA record of single-season goals against average 1.19 and save percentage of .956. A second-team All-America selection in 2004, Howard was a three-year lettermen in Maine (2002–2005).

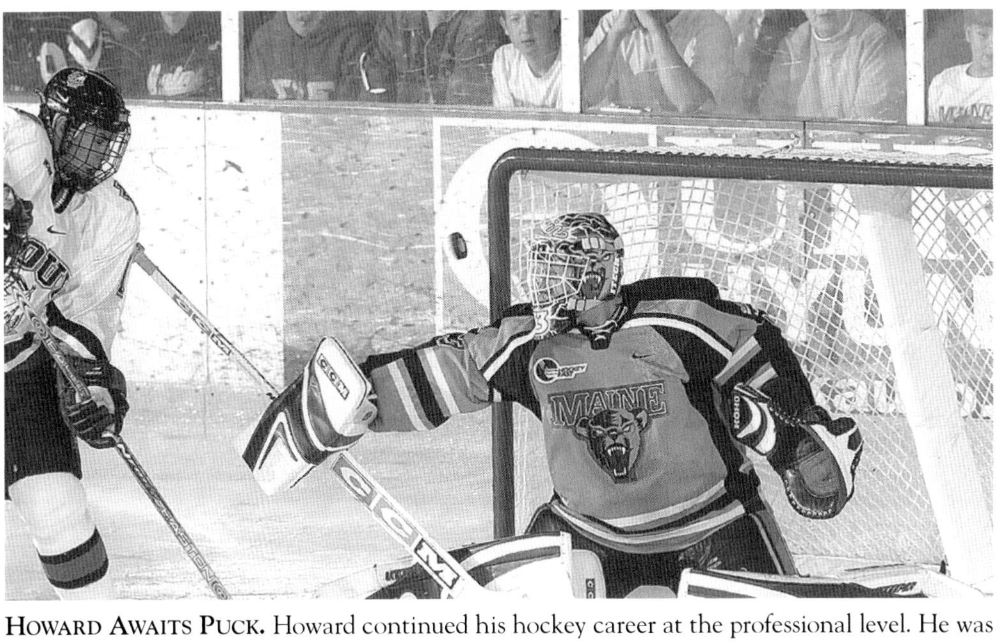

HOWARD AWAITS PUCK. Howard continued his hockey career at the professional level. He was drafted 64th overall by the Detroit Red Wings but was traded to the New York Rangers. He played for the Grand Rapid Griffins of the AHL in 2006–2007.

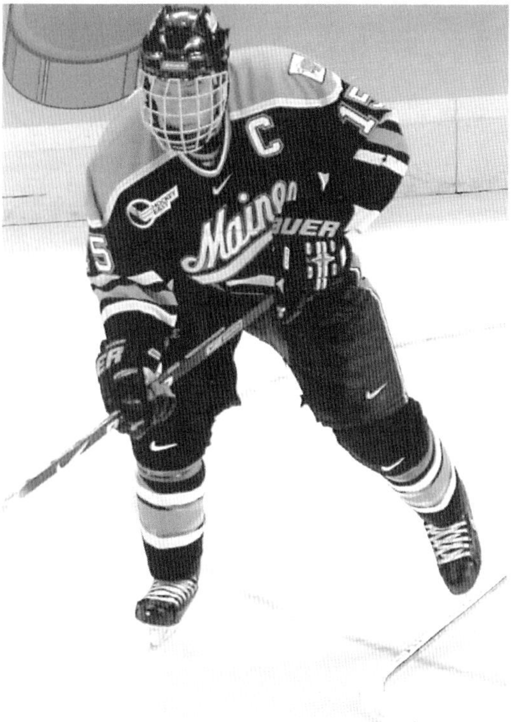

Greg Moore. Greg Moore (No. 15) was a four-year letterman at Maine, 2002–2006. A native of Lisbon, Maine, Moore attended high school at St. Dom's in Lewiston. Moore won the Harold Alfond Award as Maine's most valuable player in 2006. Moore led the team in scoring in 2006 and was voted a first-team All-American.

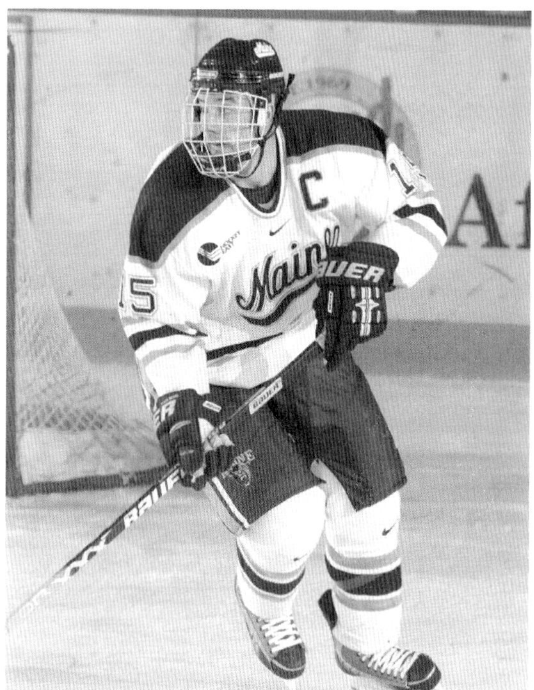

Fan Favorite Greg Moore. Moore was originally drafted by the Calgary Flames of the NHL but was later traded to the New York Rangers. He played in 2006–2007 for the Hartford Wolf Pack in the AHL.

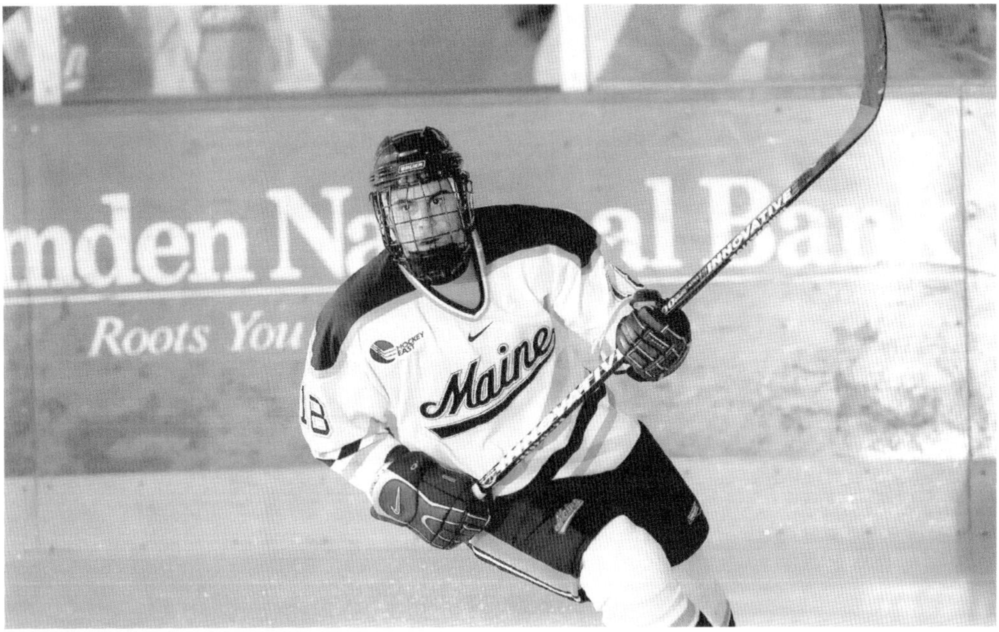

JOSH SOARES. Assistant captain for the 2006–2007 season, Josh Soares (No. 18) provided strong leadership on and off the ice. He joined an elite group of UMaine forwards by leading the team in scoring and registering back-to-back 40-point seasons. A prototype player for the future, Soares combines size and speed and is considered a top professional prospect.

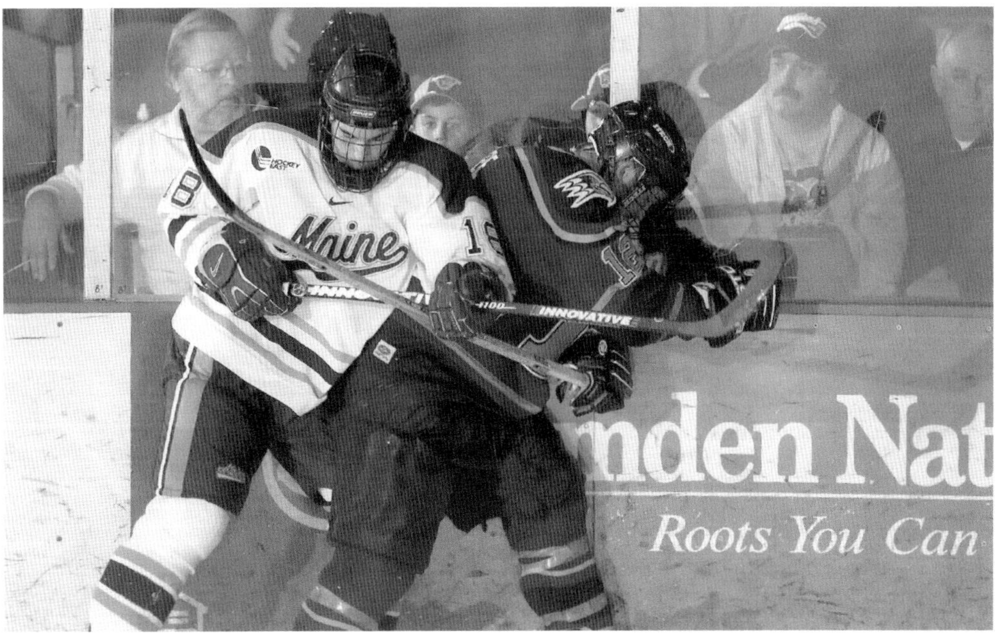

SOARES IN ACTION. Soares signed a tryout contract with the St. Louis Blues organization in 2007. He made his professional debut shortly after leading the Black Bears to another Frozen Four appearance and is now skating for the Peoria Rivermen of the AHL.

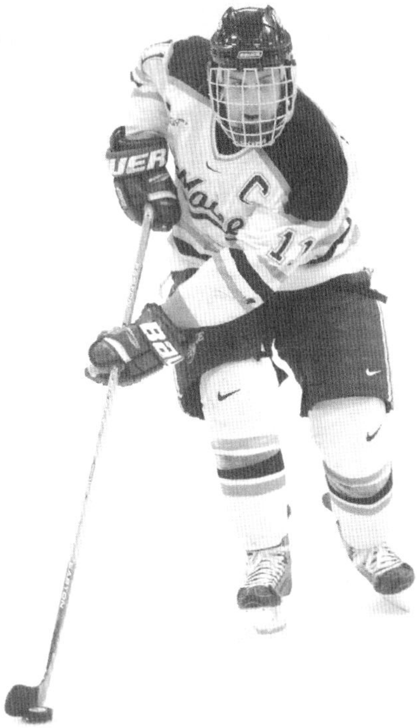

MICHEL LEVEILLE. A three-year letterman at UMaine (2003–2006), Michel Leveille (No. 11) captained UMaine teams in 2004, 2005, and 2006 and was known for his animated leadership. He earned All-America honors in 2006 and 2007, as well as being named to the All-Hockey East Squad. In 2004, Leveille was Hockey East Rookie of the Year. He made the academic honor roll in 2004, 2005, and 2006. In 2007, Leveille began skating with the Toronto Marlies of the AHL.

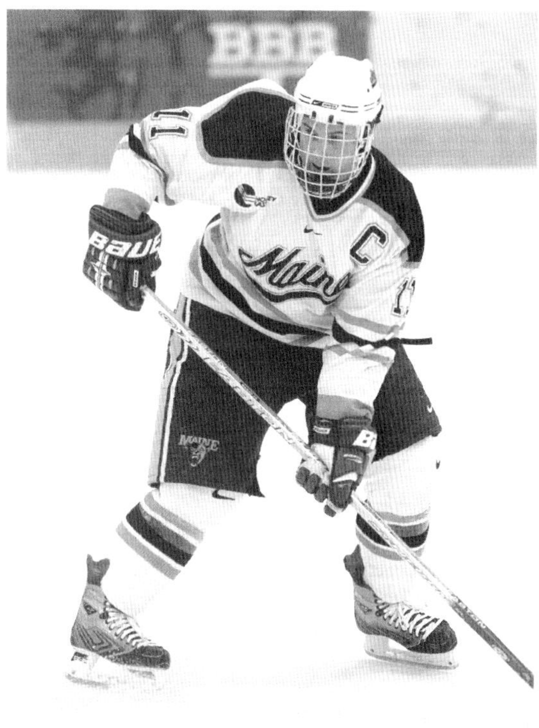

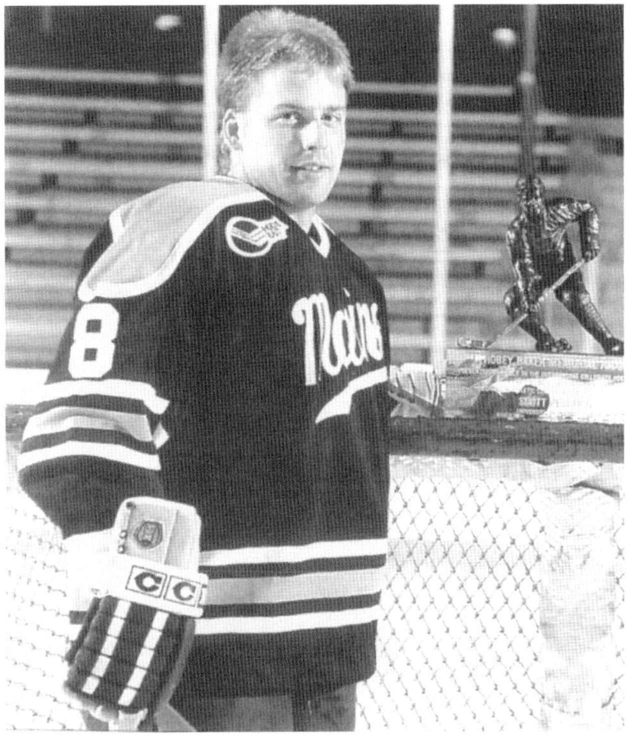

SCOTT PELLERIN, 1992 HOBEY BAKER AWARD WINNER. Scott Pellerin became the first UMaine player to win the most prestigious award given to a college hockey player, the Hobey Baker Award. Pelerin ranks third on the all-time list for goals scored (101) and assists (117) and is second in total points with 223. In 1993, he became the first Black Bear to have his Jersey retired.

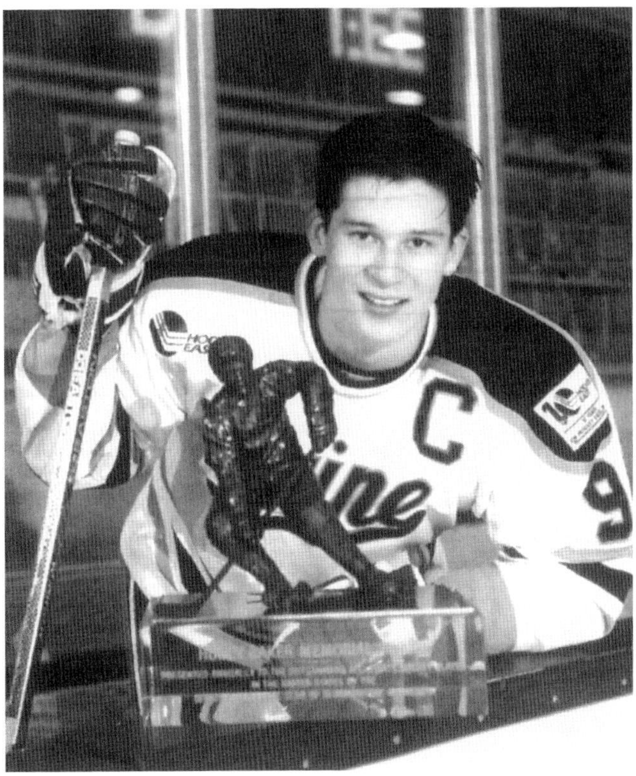

PAUL KARIYA, 1993 HOBEY BAKER AWARD WINNER. Paul Kariya (No. 9) appeared abruptly on the UMaine hockey scene in 1993. He was the first freshman to ever win the Hobey Baker Award, scoring 33 goals and 91 assists in leading the Black Bears to a national championship. He played for Team Canada in 1994 and in the 2002 Winter Olympics.